Rhomobile Beginner's Guide

Step-by-step instructions to build an enterprise mobile web application from scratch

Abhishek Nalwaya

BIRMINGHAM - MUMBAI

Rhomobile Beginner's Guide

First published: July 2011

Production Reference: 1180711

Published by Packt Publishing Ltd.
32 Lincoln Road
Olton
Birmingham, B27 6PA, UK.

ISBN 978-1-849515-16-0

www.packtpub.com

Cover Image by Parag Kadam (paragvkadam@gmail.com)

Credits

Author
Abhishek Nalwaya

Reviewers
Deepak Vohra
Brian Moore

Acquisition Editor
Sarah Cullington

Development Editor
Neha Mallik

Technical Editors
Ajay Shanker
Mohd. Sahil

Project Coordinator
Shubhanjan Chatterjee

Proofreader
Linda Morris

Indexer
Monica Ajmera Mehta

Graphics
Geetanjali Sawant

Production Coordinator
Melwyn D'sa

Cover Work
Melwyn D'sa

About the Author

Abhishek Nalwaya is a Ruby, Rhomobile, and Rails enthusiast. He is a regular participant at Ruby/Rails meetups and has taken technical sessions on Rhodes framework within the company and at Ruby meetups. His blog is listed on the official third-party tutorial section at the Rhomobile site.

He was associated with Tata Consultancy Services and is presently working as an application developer with Column Software Technology. He has worked on many projects providing solutions to Fortune 500 companies using Ruby, Rhodes, and Ruby on Rails.

I would like to express my gratitude to my family and friends especially Akshat Paul, Manu Singhal, and Anuj Bhargava who saw me through this book, who provided support, talked things over, read, wrote, offered comments, without which conceiving this book wouldn't have been possible.

Also, I would like to thank Sarah, Kartikey, Shubhanjan, and the PacktPub team who allowed me to quote their remarks and assisted in the editing, proofreading, and design. Writing a book was not my cup of tea but they made this complicated journey effortless.

About the Reviewers

Deepak Vora is a consultant and a principal member of the NuBean.com Software Company. Deepak is a Sun Certified Java Programmer and Web Component Developer, and has worked in the fields of XML and Java programming and J2EE for over five years. Deepak is the co-author of the Apress book Pro XML Development with Java Technology and was the technical reviewer for the O'Reilly book *WebLogic: The Definitive Guide*. Deepak was also the technical reviewer for the Course Technology PTR book *Ruby Programming for the Absolute Beginner*, and the technical editor for the Manning Publications book *Prototype and Scriptaculous in Action*. Deepak is also the author of the Packt Publishing book *JDBC 4.0* and *Oracle JDeveloper for J2EE Development*, *Processing XML documents with Oracle JDeveloper 11g*, and *EJB 3.0 Database Persistence with Oracle Fusion Middleware 11g*.

Brian Moore is a Senior Engineer at Rhomobile, father of two, and quintessential hacker. Brian began coding at the age of 12. His early love for everything technological led to a job with Apple shortly after high school. Since that time Brian has worked at a series of start-ups and tech companies taking on interesting technical challenges. Brian has become the technical face of Rhomobile as he leads the Rhodes community in the latest Rhomobile innovation during the Friday webinars. When not guiding the next generation of Rhodes developers or hacking on a new debugger, Brian can be found climbing a hill in a remote Southern California desert in his baja bug.

www.PacktPub.com

Support files, eBooks, discount offers and more

You might want to visit www.PacktPub.com for support files and downloads related to your book.

Did you know that Packt offers eBook versions of every book published, with PDF and ePub files available? You can upgrade to the eBook version at www.PacktPub.com and as a print book customer, you are entitled to a discount on the eBook copy. Get in touch with us at service@packtpub.com for more details.

At www.PacktPub.com, you can also read a collection of free technical articles, sign up for a range of free newsletters and receive exclusive discounts and offers on Packt books and eBooks.

http://PacktLib.PacktPub.com

Do you need instant solutions to your IT questions? PacktLib is Packt's online digital book library. Here, you can access, read and search across Packt's entire library of books.

Why Subscribe?

- Fully searchable across every book published by Packt
- Copy & paste, print and bookmark content
- On demand and accessible via web browser

Free Access for Packt account holders

If you have an account with Packt at www.PacktPub.com, you can use this to access PacktLib today and view nine entirely free books. Simply use your login credentials for immediate access.

Table of Contents

Preface 1
What this book covers 1
Who this book is for 2
Conventions 2
Reader feedback 3
Customer support 3
Downloading the example code 3
Errata 4
Piracy 4
Questions 4
Chapter 1: What is Rhomobile? 5
The Rhomobile family 5
Rhodes 6
RhoSync 7
RhoHub 7
RhoGallery 7
Why Rhomobile is cutting edge 8
Which products does Rhomobile support? 9
Rhomobile architecture 10
Rhodes application 10
Rhosync application 11
Backend application 12
FAQ 12
Summary 14
Chapter 2: Installation and Configuration—How to Start off 15
Rhomobile installations 15
Installing Rhomobile 16
Time for action – Installing on Windows 16

Time for action – Installing on Linux 19
Time for action – Installing on a Mac 19
Device SDK installation 20
Blackberry SDK installation 20
Which Operating Systems are supported? 20
Where to get it from: 20
Time for action – Installing Blackberry SDK 21
Android SDK installation 23
Which Operating Systems are supported? 23
Time for action – Installing Android SDK 24
iPhone SDK installation 25
Which Operating Systems are supported? 25
Where to get it from: 25
Time for action – Installing iPhone SDK 26
Time for action – Configuration 28
Time for action – Installing Development Environments—IDE 29
Summary 29
Chapter 3: Instant Gratification—Create Your First Application 31
Let's get started... 31
Time for action – Creating an employee application 32
Building your first Rhodes application 33
Time for action – Build it for different smart phones 33
Navigating the Directory Structure 37
Linking views to the homepage 39
Digging the MVC in our application 52
Model 53
Controller 53
Views 55
Rhodes configuration file—Rhoconfig.txt 57
Building a Configuration file—build.yml 59
Changing the input style 59
Creation of a new page 62
Summary 66
Chapter 4: Rhom—Playing with the Local Database 67
What is ORM? 67
Exploring Rhom 68
Time for action – Creating a company model 68
Association 70
Time for ation – Creating an association between 70
employee and company 70
Exploring methods available for Rhom 72
Time for action – Filtering record by company and gender 73

How Rhodes stores data **78**
Property Bag 79
Fixed Schema model 80
Summary **81**

Chapter 5: RhoSync—Synchronizing Your Data 83

Generating a RhoSync application **84**
Time for action – Creating a RhoSync application **84**
RhoSync source adapters **89**
Time for action – Creating source adapter **89**
Configure the Rhodes application to connect to RhoSync **91**
Time for action – Connecting the Rhodes application to RhoSync **91**
Placing data in the Rhodes application from RhoSync **92**
Time for action – Filling data from RhoSync **93**
Connecting to Backend services **96**
CRUD operation using RhoSync **101**
Create 104
Update 105
Delete 106
Filtering datasets with search **108**
Time for action – Filtering data with search **109**
Authentication **115**
RhoSync REST API **116**
Summary **119**

Chapter 6: Metadata and Push—Creating Agile Views 121

Getting ready for Metadata **121**
Time for action – Installing the Rhodes translator gem **122**
Creating the first view using metadata **122**
Getting all the views for company from Metadata **127**
Understanding the code 130
Digging the code for the new page 130
Digging the code for the show page 132
Digging the code for the edit page 134
Metadata validation **135**
Custom templates **136**
Push data to your phone **136**
Set up the Rhodes application for Push 136
Push for iOS 137
Push for Android 138
Push for Blackberry 138
Testing Push in the Web Console **139**
Summary **141**

Chapter 7: Native User Interface—Cosmetics for Your Smart Phones 143
Device-specific style 143
Time for action – Adding device-specific style 145
Customizing layouts 147
Dynamic loading of custom view files based on the current platform 148
Standard smart phone CSS/HTML architecture 148
pageTitle (<div id="pageTitle">) 149
toolbar (<div id="toolbar">) 149
Toolbar button styles 151
Content (<div id="content">) 152
Application menu 154
Controller action menu 156
Native tab bar 157
Time for action – Creating tabs 157
BlackBerry CSS/HTML architecture 160
Loading screen 160
Time for action – Setting the loading Image 161
Adding transition styles for iPhone/Android 161
Time for action – Adding transaction animation 162
Summary 164
Chapter 8: Unit Testing and Logging—Writing Better Code 165
Unit testing 165
Time for action – Getting ready for testing the Rhodes application 165
Writing your first Rhodes unit test 169
Time for action – Writing the first test 169
Testing the RhoSync application 171
Time for a Action – Running the default test 171
Creating the first unit test for the RhoSync application 174
Time for action – Creating a unit test for the source adapter 174
Query 176
Create 177
Update 177
Delete 178
Logging 178
Time for action – Configure logs for the Rhodes application 178
Where to find logs: 179
iPhone 179
Android 179
Blackberry 180
See the device log on the device 180

RhoError class 181
Summary 181

Chapter 9: RhoHub—Deploying to Cloud 183
Installation and configuration 183
Time for action – Installation and configuration 183
Understanding basic Git 186
Creating a RhoHub project 186
Time for action – Creating a RhoHub project 186
Cloning and committing your Rhodes application 189
Time for action – Pushing Rhodes application 189
Deploying the RhoSync application 191
Time for action – Pushing the RhoSync application 191
RhoHub online editor 193
Creating builds for different phones from RhoHub 194
Time for action – Three steps to build the Rhodes code 195
Deploying the RhoSync application to RhoHub 196
Time for action – Three steps to deploy RhoSync 196
RhoGallery 197
Time for action – Creating a gallery 198
Summary 201

Chapter 10: Rhodes power unleashed 203
System class 203
Time for action – Using the System class 204
Doing more things with System class 207
Exit application 207
Enable\disable phone sleep 207
Managing other applications 207
Time for action – Starting other applications 208
PIM contacts 210
Time for action – CRUD operations on contacts 212
Camera 219
Taking a picture 219
Choosing a picture from an album 219
Time for action – Capturing images 219
Geolocation 223
GeoLocation Ruby class 223
Time for action – Adding Geolocation 224
What just happened? 228

Alerts **228**
Time for action – Creating alerts **230**
Other device capabilities **236**
Barcode 236
Ringtone manager 236
Bluetooth 237
Timer **239**
Summary **240**
Index **241**

Preface

The Rhomobile Beginner's guide will speak to every developer's mind, and especially to the technocrats looking for a reliable cross-platform framework encouraging them to explore and try out these wonderful products by Rhomobile. This book guides you step by step to build an enterprise mobile application from scratch, through to deployment.

What this book covers

Chapter 1, What is Rhomobile?: In this chapter, we will briefly discuss the various products of Rhomobile and their architecture.

Chapter 2, Installation and Configuration—How to Set Off: In this chapter, we will learn to install the necessary softwares that are required before developing our mobile application using Rhomobile.

Chapter 3, Instant Gratification—Create Your First Application: In this chapter, we will create our first application and understand how Rhodes structures the application.

Chapter 4, Rhom—Playing with the Local Database: In this chapter, we'll explore Rhom, which is an Object-Relational Mapping (ORM) provided by Rhodes and take a look at how it manipulates data in our application. We'll find how ORM manages table relationships in this chapter and also dig into the ORM object life cycle.

Chapter 5, RhoSync—Synchronizing your data: In this chapter, we will learn about the synchronization framework RhoSync that keeps application data current and available on user's smart phones. We will create a sample RhoSync application and connect with a Rails application to put the current data on the device.

Chapter 6, Metadata and Push—Creating Agile Views: In this chapter, we will learn about a powerful feature of RhoSync called metadata and also configuring Push messages to the client. We will enhance the application created in the earlier chapter with metadata and Push.

Chapter 7, Native User Interface—Cosmetics for Your Smart Phones: In this chapter, we will learn about Native User Interface for different phones. We will perform device-specific operations to give a more native look to our application.

Chapter 8, Unit Testing and Logging—Writing Better Code: In this chapter, we will learn about testing and logging. We will write unit tests for both Rhodes and RhoSync applications. We will also learn to check logs in different devices.

Chapter 9, RhoHub—Deploying to Cloud: In this chapter, we will host our RhoSync application to RhoHub using Git and learn to create build for our Rhodes application.

Chapter 10, Rhodes Power Unleashed: In this chapter, we will learn about the Rhodes competence to access device-specific capabilities such as GPS, PIM, camera, System attributes, and many more functionalities.

Who this book is for

This book is for developers who are looking to build mobile applications. They may include the ones who are looking for a deep understanding of Rhomobile or they may be completely new to these products.

Familiarity with HTML, CSS, and Ruby will give you an extra edge but you do not need to be an expert on these topics.

Conventions

In this book, you will find a number of styles of text that distinguish between different kinds of information. Here are some examples of these styles, and an explanation of their meaning.

Code words in text are shown as follows: "The `update_attributes` call then takes the rest of the parameters from the request and applies them to this record."

A block of code is set as follows:

```
<div class="toolbar">
   <% if SyncEngine::logged_in > 0 %>
      <div class="leftItem blueButton">
         <a href="<%= url_for :controller => :Settings, :action => :
```

When we wish to draw your attention to a particular part of a code block, the relevant lines or items will be shown in bold:

```
<div class="rightItem regularButton">

<a class="flip" href="<%= url_for :controller => :Settings, :action => :
logout %>">Logout</a>

</div
```

Any command-line input or output is written as follows:

```
sudo apt-get install ruby1.9.1-full
```

New terms and **important words** are shown in bold. Words that you see on the screen, in menus or dialog boxes for example, appear in the text like this: "run the executable file and click **Next**".

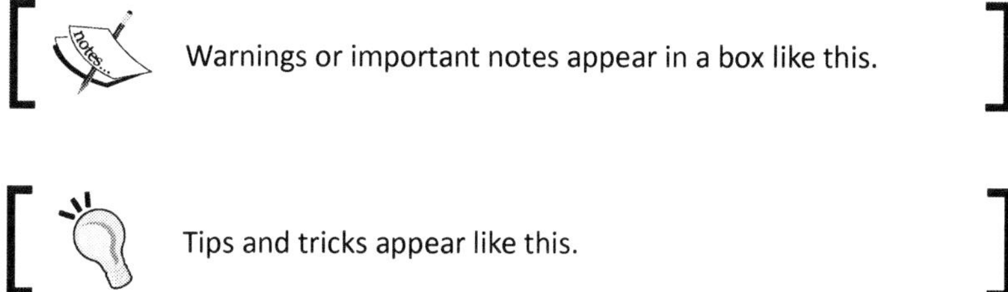

Warnings or important notes appear in a box like this.

Tips and tricks appear like this.

Reader feedback

Feedback from our readers is always welcome. Let us know what you think about this book—what you liked or may have disliked. Reader feedback is important for us to develop titles that you really get the most out of.

To send us general feedback, simply send an e-mail to `feedback@packtpub.com`, and mention the book title via the subject of your message.

If there is a book that you need and would like to see us publish, please send us a note in the **SUGGEST A TITLE** form on `www.packtpub.com` or e-mail `suggest@packtpub.com`.

If there is a topic that you have expertise in and you are interested in either writing or contributing to a book, see our author guide on `www.packtpub.com/authors`.

Customer support

Now that you are the proud owner of a Packt book, we have a number of things to help you to get the most from your purchase.

Downloading the example code

You can download the example code files for all Packt books you have purchased from your account at `http://www.PacktPub.com`. If you purchased this book elsewhere, you can visit `http://www.PacktPub.com/support` and register to have the files e-mailed directly to you.

Errata

Although we have taken every care to ensure the accuracy of our content, mistakes do happen. If you find a mistake in one of our books—maybe a mistake in the text or the code—we would be grateful if you would report this to us. By doing so, you can save other readers from frustration and help us improve subsequent versions of this book. If you find any errata, please report them by visiting `http://www.packtpub.com/support`, selecting your book, clicking on the **errata submission form** link, and entering the details of your errata. Once your errata are verified, your submission will be accepted and the errata will be uploaded on our website, or added to any list of existing errata, under the Errata section of that title. Any existing errata can be viewed by selecting your title from `http://www.packtpub.com/support`.

Piracy

Piracy of copyright material on the Internet is an ongoing problem across all media. At Packt, we take the protection of our copyright and licenses very seriously. If you come across any illegal copies of our works, in any form, on the Internet, please provide us with the location address or website name immediately so that we can pursue a remedy.

Please contact us at `copyright@packtpub.com` with a link to the suspected pirated material.

We appreciate your help in protecting our authors, and our ability to bring you valuable content.

Questions

You can contact us at `questions@packtpub.com` if you are having a problem with any aspect of the book, and we will do our best to address it.

1
What is Rhomobile?

Welcome to the Rhomobile Beginner's Guide. The goal of this book is to teach you how to create your own Mobile application from scratch using Rhomobile. We will learn how to develop a mobile application with Rhomobile by building a sample application from scratch. We will try to have something tangible with running code by the end of every chapter so that you can see a clear progression from chapter to chapter.

Though Rhomobile products are large and part of a fast-moving framework, we'll focus on the smaller, more stable, set of core Rhomobile techniques that have crystallized in the last couple of years. This means that the knowledge you gain here will not become obsolete too quickly. This book is written keeping the Zero to Deployment approach in mind.

The Rhomobile family

Mobile devices are very powerful today and are getting more dominant with time. The success behind the phenomenal growth of smart phones is the mobile application loaded in them, which increases their functionality exponentially. Mobile applications can be developed by using different frameworks and programming languages based on the type of mobile device. Different mobile devices use different hardware components, therefore, mobile software and mobile applications have to be developed using different software architectures. It is a very painful process if we have to develop applications for all of the smart phones in the market. So Rhomobile came up with the idea of developing an application with one code base and building it for all smart phones. Before learning about the Rhomobile architecture we should have an understanding of Rhomobile and its products.

Rhomobile Inc. is a computer software company that provides leading products for building the new generation of mobile applications. It offers an open-source Ruby-based mobile development framework for business mobility solutions through its four major products Rhodes, RhoSync, Rhohub, and RhoGallery.

Rhomobile has revolutionized the process of developing mobile applications. It has enabled developers to become much faster and more efficient, allowing quicker application development. It enables software programmers to build applications for mobile devices using HTML and Ruby instead of proprietary languages such as Objective-C. Currently, the Rhodes framework supports development for the iPhone, Windows Mobile, Google Android, Symbian, and BlackBerry operating systems.

Now we will learn more about the four major products of Rhomobile.

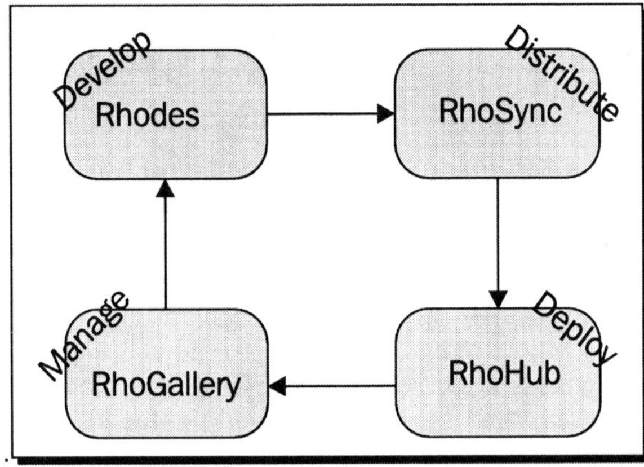

Rhodes

Rhodes is an open source framework by Rhomobile. It develops native applications for almost all smart phones. The applications built through Rhodes are pure native applications and use device capabilities such as GPS, PIM contacts and calendar, camera, native mapping, push, barcode, signature capture, and Bluetooth.

Rhodes accelerates the development of mobile applications without compromising on its portability. This framework is similar to the popular Rails framework. It is based on Model view Controller and has inbuilt Object Relational Manager (ORM) called Rhom that is similar to active Record in Rails. Most user interface customization can be done in HTML templates (ERB, eruby files). A single set of source written with Rhodes can be compiled to run across all of the supported smart phones. This means that we will have the same code base for all your devices.

RhoSync

RhoSync is a standalone mobile sync server that keeps enterprise application data up to date and available on users' smart phones. Enterprise apps require local synchronized data to be used most of the time. The information is stored locally on a users' device and is available to them even in offline mode. It is very easy to write a source adapter as RhoSync generates most of the code while creating the source adapter. The source adapter can also be used to Create, Read, Update, and Delete (CRUD) operations on a model.

Rhosync uses Redis, which is a NoSql Key Value store for data caching. This makes Rhosync more scalable. RhoSync performs its push-based sync using the native smartphone push SDKs. It uses new advanced BlackBerry Enterprise Server and iPhone 3.0 SDKs for Push. It uses BES Push and iPhone Push for synchronization, allowing real-time updates of backend application information. We will explore RhoSync and its features in detail in Chapter 5.

RhoHub

RhoHub is a hosted development environment for Rhodes and Rhosync. The RhoSync application will be deployed on the famous Ruby cloud Heroku with the interface of RhoHub. RhoHub enables git-powered source control and collaboration with your team. It allows us to directly build an application for different smart phones without installing SDKs.

It makes the process of the build very smooth since we don't have to install any development toolkits. It is only a one click process that automatically creates a build for most of the smart phones. We will discuss this in detail in Chapter 9.

Rhohub provides us with the following functionalities:

- Creating a build for a Rhodes application
- Deploying the Rhosync application to the cloud
- Providing version control with git
- Managing collaborators

RhoGallery

RhoGallery provides a hosted mobile app management solution. It allows administrators to manage the set of apps exposed to their users. It also makes it easy for them to get mobile apps onto their devices. It enables users to launch all of their important enterprise apps from a single place. RhoGallery consists of a management console for "app galleries" on RhoHub, as well as a RhoGallery App that users load onto their devices. Even for an individual developer with one or a few apps, RhoGallery makes it easy to expose those apps to their users. RhoGallery handles inviting the users and determining the appropriate downloads to provide to them.

RhoGallery provides the following functionalities:

- Administrator management of exposed apps to end users
- Central user launching of exposed apps
- Automatic provisioning of appropriate apps for end users

Why Rhomobile is cutting edge

The following features give a cutting edge to Rhomobile in mobile application development:

- Model View Controller: Most of the other frameworks available in the market are based on HTML and JavaScript. However, as Rhodes is a Ruby-based framework and its structure is similar to the popular framework Rails, it also supports Model View Controller, so code written with Rhodes is more structured and easy to understand.
- Cross Platform Support for All Devices: Rhodes supports the following devices: Android, Windows Mobile, BlackBerry, and iphone. The best thing is you have a single code base from which you can build applications for different smart phones. It does not work in a traditional way in that we have to write separate code for different types of phones.
- Offline Capabilities using Rhosync: Rhomobile supports local synchronization of data. As we can synchronize the data using Rhosync it provides offline Capabilities. It can work even if you are offline.
- Object Relational Manager: Rhodes provides an inbuilt Object Relational Manager called Rhom. It is similar to Active Record in Rails but with basic functionality only. It helps us to write queries without thinking about which database is being used by phone.
- Rapid Development: One of the most interesting features of Rhodes is that it imposes some fairly serious constraints on how you structure the applications that help us for rapid development. Rhomobile products are properly structured and well organized, which enforce us to do rapid development. Rhodes is very comfortable, familiar, and massively productive.
- Scalable Sync Server: The Sync Server uses a NoSql Database which makes it scalable. Specifically, it is the only sync server that has a built-in "no SQL" Redis key value store, making it more scalable than other sync servers which offer internal relational database servers for caching. RhoSync also performs its push-based sync using the native smart phone push SDKs, which no other sync server does.

- Liberal use of code generation: Rhodes/RhoSync can write a lot of code for you. For example, when you need a class to represent a table in your database, you don't have to write most of the methods. Rhodes even offers an application generator that creates an initial app based on the structure of your models or business objects in your app. It's very similar to the scaffolding offered by most modern web frameworks with basic `list/create/read/update/delete objects` functionality. For each basic CRUD action, views in HTML are also offered. You'll find that you're writing only a fraction of code compared to other frameworks.
- Metadata: Every enterprise application that is used to run a company's core business has a different schema for its business objects. For example, every application has a varying and customized structure that changes with time. It is not possible to install the client application again and again for a small change. The Metadata framework provides a way to handle the view from the Rhosync server. It also provides validation and a custom template. We will discuss this in detail in Chapter 8.
- Hosted Development and Build: Rhomobile also provides a hosted management and Build through Rhohub. We can deploy a Rhosync app and build our Rhodes code for different phones with it.

Which products does Rhomobile support?

Rhomobile supports a variety of smart phone devices and tablets. Currently, Rhodes version 3 supports the following major platforms:

- iPhone and iPad
- Android
- Blackberry
- Windows Mobile including Windows mobile 7

Note: Support for Symbian is no longer available from Rhodes version 2.2.

Rhomobile architecture

One of the interesting features of Rhomobile is that it imposes some fairly serious constraints on how we structure our mobile applications. Surprisingly, these constraints make it easier to create applications—a lot easier than one may think. To understand how these constraints help us, it is essential to understand the architecture first.

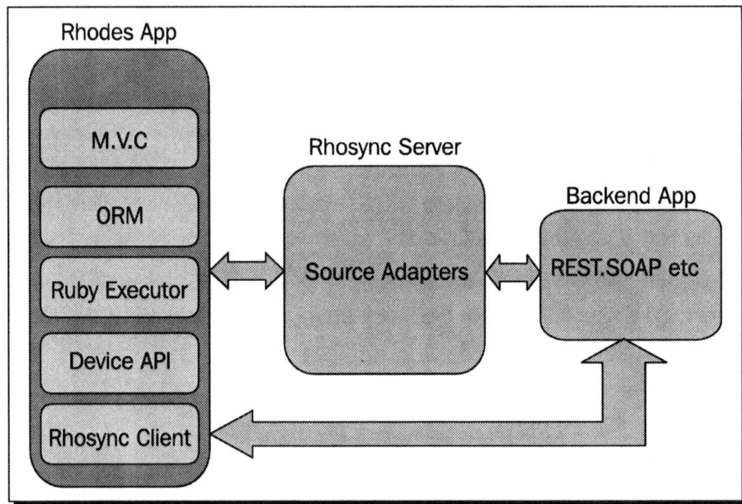

The normal Rhomobile application has a 3-layer architecture:

- Rhodes Application
- Rhosync Server
- Backend Application

Rhodes application

This is the application that will be installed on your smart phone. It can also work independently without using Rhosync. If you don't have any external data, you can only develop your application with Rhodes.

Rhodes applications are developed with MVC. These are true native device applications (NOT mobile web apps) that work with synchronized local data and take advantage of device capabilities such as GPS, PIM contacts and calendar, camera, native mapping, push, barcode, signature capture, and Bluetooth.

The major components of a Rhodes Application are:

- Model View Controller: This is the heart of a Rhodes application that has the major code of your application. The model manages the behavior and data of the application domain, and responds to requests for information about its state (usually from the view), as well as to instructions to change the state. The view manages the display of information. The controller receives input and initiates a response by making calls on model objects. A controller accepts input from the user and instructs the model and viewport to perform actions based on that input.
- Rhom: This is the mini ORM Layer provided by Rhodes that helps us to run a query on Phone Devices. It provides a high level way to make the local database easier to program. That database is SQLite on all platforms except BlackBerry, where it is HSQL. Speeding your time to market continues to be the theme at Rhomobile and including an ORM in the framework saves you time during the development phase by standardizing and simplifying the effort when writing mobile business apps once for all the popular Smartphones.
- Ruby Virtual Machine: This is the inbuilt Executable available for Rhodes that executes the Ruby code.
- Device API: These are APIs that help us to access device capability like GPS, PIM contacts and calendar, camera, native mapping, push, barcode, signature capture, and Bluetooth.
- RhoSync Client: These are the codes to synchronize the data from the Rhosync server. These include code for authentication, Synchronization, Reset Database, etc.

Rhosync application

Rhosync is a Mobile sync Server that keeps enterprise application data up to date and available on users' smart phones. The information is stored locally on a user's device and available when disconnected. The RhoSync server handles the job of connecting the Rhodes application to backend applications, keeping track of multiple devices and what information they need, and sending them just those updates. RhoSync can also be used to register its interest in changing information from the backend. It then efficiently "pushes" the changes to the phones via the native Smartphone push SDKs.

RhoSync consists of the following components:

- Synchronization Framework: The core of RhoSync; this facilitates data synchronization between the Rhodes/RhoSync-Client and a third-party source (SOAP, REST, etc.). Each source is synchronized by implementing a simple "source adapter" class. The client connects with the embedded Sinatra server to interact with the collection of source adapters.

- REST API: The RhoSync API allows you to control, monitor, and debug a running RhoSync application using a simple HTTP API.
- Administration Console: A Sinatra server is used for manipulating and peeking into a running RhoSync app. The console uses the RhoSync API for its functionality.
- Asynchronous Job System: RhoSync uses the Resque library to provide asynchronous execution of various tasks that it needs to perform. These tasks include source adapter execution, sending push messages, preparing bulk data, etc. Resque is dead-simple to use and highly extensible, so it can easily be used for other functionality not described here.

Backend application

This application feeds data using REST, SOAP, or any other API to the RhoSync Server. It can also interact directly with the Rhodes application using Async HTTP calls. This is your basic legacy application that can provide data to the RhoSync Server in JSON, XML, or any other format. These are similar to web services that can be developed in any language. There are plugins that allow the Client application to fetch data directly from a Backend application. It is also possible that RhoSync can interact with multiple Backend Applications.

FAQ

For a first time user many questions must be coming to your mind. Let's make you more familiar with Rhomobile with these FAQ's:

Question:Does Rhomobile create a pure Native Application?

Answer: Yes. Rhomobile creates a pure Native Application. This Application is similar to an Application available in i-store. This application can use device capabilities such as GPS, PIM contacts and calendar, camera, native mapping, push, barcode, signature capture, and Bluetooth. These are much faster than Browser-based applications.

Question: I am new to Ruby should I use Rhomobile?

Answer: Although you need to know Ruby to write Rhodes applications, we realize that many folks reading this book will be learning both Ruby and Rhomobile at the same time. As Rhomobile products require an elementary level of Ruby knowledge, this will not affect your learning curve. But I recommend that you go to any Ruby tutorial online.

Question: Is Rhomobile Free?

Answer: Rhodes is free and open source under MIT Licence. To use RhoSync, you must purchase a commercial license when development commences or you must open source your app under the GPL license. The pricing and details can be found at `www.rhomobile.com`.

Question: Is support available for Rhomobile?

Answer: Yes. However, you have to purchase a Rhodes Enterprise License and the Rhodes Commercial License to get commercial support. Apart from the Rhomobile support, there are various webinars and tutorials available on `www.rhomobile.com`. Another good support resource is the Rhomobile Google group, where Rhomobile experts are there to help you.

Question: What about Rhomobile security?

Answer: Both Rhodes and RhoSync support use of https as a transport. In fact it is easier with Rhodes than with native code. You just list the https URL and Rhodes will connect to the backend appropriately. This is simple in contrast to underlying SDKs where significantly different code is written to connect to an https URL.

Question: Does Rhomobile support HTML5?

Answers: Yes, Rhomobile supports HTML5 tags provided the device you are targeting also supports them.

Question: Can we write unit test case for the code?

Answers: Yes, we can write unit test case in Rhodes, which will be shown in Chapter 7.

Question: Can we use Ruby gems with Rhodes?

Answers: Yes, we can use Ruby gems with Rhodes. We have to include them in the Rhodes configuration file. We will discuss this in later chapters.

Question: Do we need to have knowledge of different device databases?

Answer: No, we don't need to have prior knowledge of those databases, Rhodes will take care of this. We write our query using Object-relational mapping (ORM) called Rhom and it is the work of ORM to shape the query.

Summary

Now we have understood Rhomobile and its architecture. Following are the topics we have covered:

- What is a mobile app
- What is Rhomobile Inc. and its products
- What is the difference between Rhomobile and other products in the market
- What is the architecture of Rhomobile

In the next chapter, we will learn to install and configure various Rhomobile products on different platforms such as Windows, Mac, and Linux.

2

Installation and Configuration—How to Start off

We learnt about Rhomobile and its products in the last chapter. Now it's time to install all the necessary software and get ready for the development of our mobile application. We will begin with the installation of Rhomobile products on the following Operating Systems:

- Microsoft Windows
- Apple Mac
- Linux

After installing Rhomobile and its dependencies on different Operating Systems, we will install the software development kit (SDK) and simulator for the following devices:

- iPhone
- Android
- Blackberry

It is not necessary to install all the SDKs. You can choose your target device for which you want to develop applications and install the SDK for only that device.

Rhomobile installations

We need to install the following software to set up Rhomobile:

- Ruby 1.8.6 or above
- Rubygems v1.8.7 and above
- GNU make 3.80 or higher (required by gem)
- JDK version 1.6.0_2 or higher

- Rhodes
- Redis
- RhoSync

Now run these setups according to your operating systems.

Installing Rhomobile

In this section, you will learn how to install Rhomobile on three different environments, Windows, Linux, and Mac.

Time for action – Installing on Windows

There are two ways to install Rhomobile products on Windows. We can either install all the products and dependencies individually or the efficient way would be to use the Windows installer provided by Rhomobile. You can download the installer from `www.rhomobile.com`

After downloading the executable file, follow these steps:

1. Run the executable file and click **Next**:

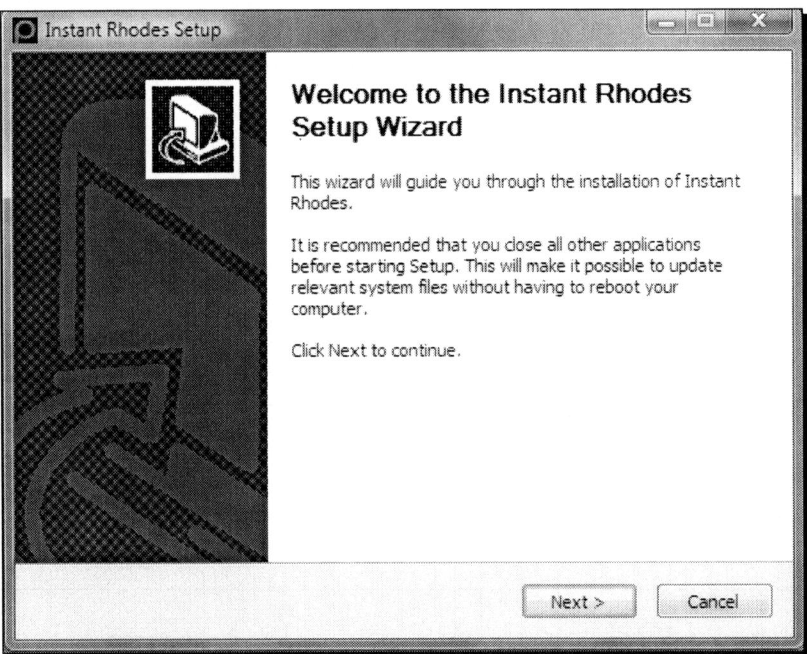

2. Accept the agreement after reading it:

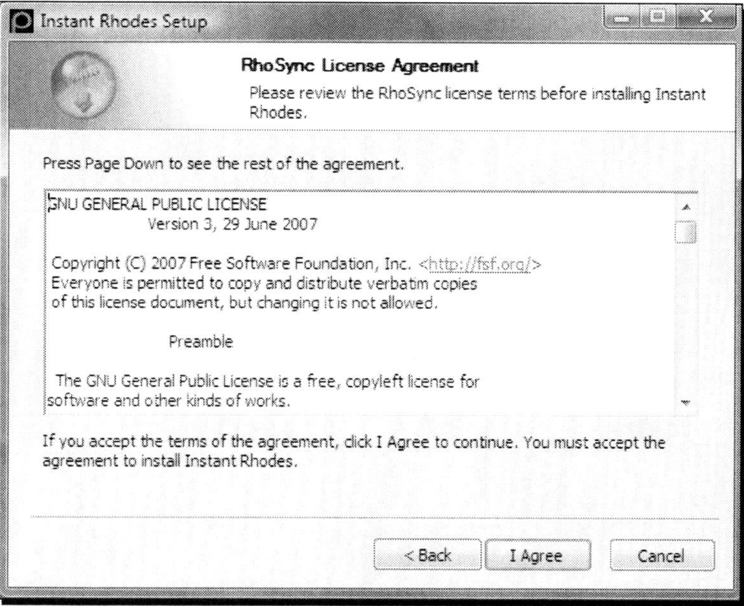

3. Now check the required components that you want to install. If you are new, I would suggest checking all the components:

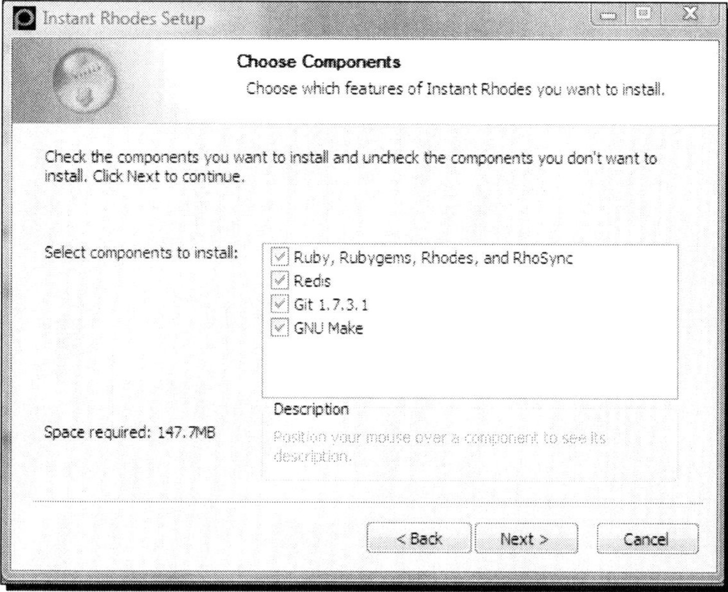

4. Select the location where you want to keep all the Rhomobile package files:

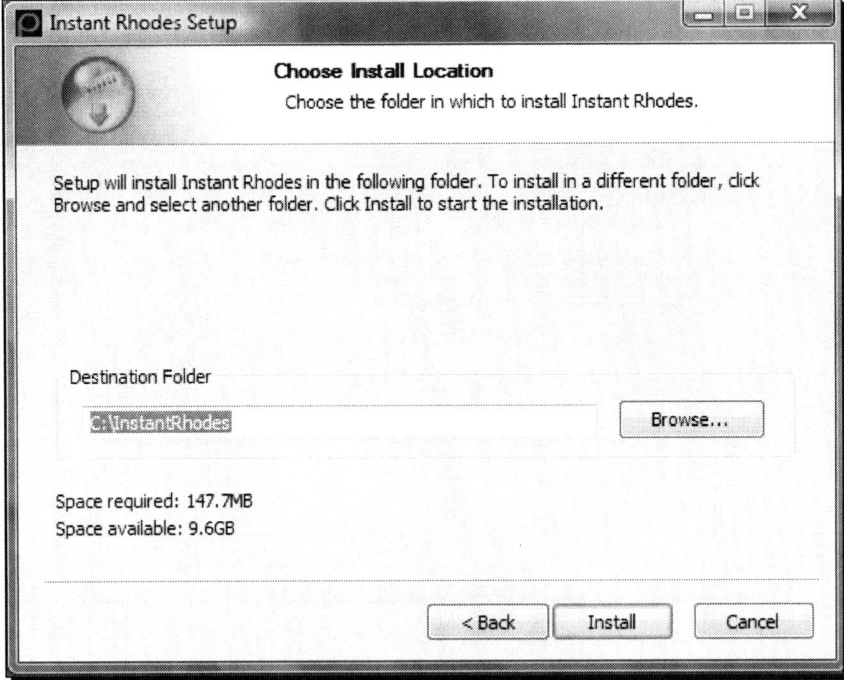

5. Rhomobile setup is complete now.

6. Download JDK version 1.6.0_2 or higher from `http://www.oracle.com/technetwork/java/javase/downloads/index.html` and then install it on 32bit Windows machine.

7. Add `JAVA_HOME` and `JAVA_HOME/bin` in your environment variable, `PATH`. To add this in PATH click on **Environment Variables** in **Advanced Tab** of **System Property**. Select Path in System variables and add `JAVA_HOME` and `JAVA_HOME/bin` to textbox and click **Ok.**

You can also download all the components separately and then install them.

> Windows does not come with the necessary UNIX tools to install gems ('make', for example). There are various sources to get these tools. GnuWin32 project has developed a few of these tools, which can be conveniently installed using the GetGnuWin32 installer. These tools are not required if you have used the Windows installer.

Time for action – Installing on Linux

To setup Rhodes/Rhosync on Linux, follow these steps:

1. Ruby – There are several ways to install Ruby depending on the distribution that you are using. One way is to simply download the source code above and then compile. The better way is to type the following command prompt in a terminal:

   ```
   sudo apt-get install ruby1.9.1-full
   ```

2. Ruby gems – You can download `RubyGems .zip` or `.gem file` and then type the following line in the terminal:

   ```
   ruby setup.rb
   ```

3. Rhodes gem – You can install Rhodes as a gem. Go to a terminal and type:

   ```
   sudo gem install Rhodes
   ```

4. Gems is a package manager that provides a standard format for distributing Ruby programs and libraries; it is designed to easily manage and install the Ruby program.

5. RhoSync – You can install it as a gem. Go to the terminal and type:

   ```
   sudo gem install Rhosync
   ```

Rhodes and RhoSync are installed and ready to use on Linux.

Time for action – Installing on a Mac

To setup Rhomobile on a Mac, follow these steps:

1. Ruby: Ruby might be pre installed on a Mac. You can check it by typing `ruby -v` on the terminal. If it is there you can skip this step. If it is not there, then you can install it by using Locomative, Macport, or Fink.

2. Install rubygems: Download one of three files available at RubyGems: `.tgz`, `.zip`, or `.gem`.

3. Rhodes: You can install Rhodes as a gem. Go to the terminal and type:

   ```
   sudo gem install Rhodes
   ```

4. Rhosync: You can install it as a gem. Go to the terminal and type:

   ```
   sudo gem install Rhosync
   ```

Rhodes and RhoSync are installed and ready to use on a Mac.

What just happened?

We just installed the Rhomobile products: Rhodes, Rhosync and their dependencies on Microsoft Windows, Linux, and Apple Mac. Now, we are ready to create a Rhodes and Rhosync Application. However, to build and test applications we have to install a device simulator.

Device SDK installation

We installed Rhodes and Rhosync in our previous section. Now, it's the turn for a device SDK. The device SDK is necessary to test and build your application. It is not mandatory to install SDK for all the devices. Choose the specific installation section as per your target device.

Blackberry SDK installation

If you want to develop and build applications for Blackberry, then just install the Blackberry SDK. This will also include the Blackberry simulator, which would help in testing the code.

Which Operating Systems are supported?

Blackberry development is only supported on Windows.

Where to get it from:

We have to install the following software for Blackberry:

- Blackberry JDE
- BlackBerry MDS Simulator

These can be downloaded from here: http://na.blackberry.com/eng/developers/

You need to register on the Blackberry Developer form before downloading JDE. For using different Blackberry versions you have to install the corresponding JDE versions. For example if you want to build for Blackberry 6 then you have to install Blackberry JDE 6. The preferred version is the basic 4.6.0. Since Blackberry doesn't support very much JavaScript and CSS tags, the basic 4.6.0 version will be a good litmus test for all Blackberries.

The documentation describing the limitations of the Blackberry Browser on CSS, HTML, and JavaScript is available at the following location:

`http://na.blackberry.com/eng/support/docs/subcategories/?userType=21&category=BlackBerry+Browser`
Choose Blackberry version and download the documents.

Time for action – Installing Blackberry SDK

This section describes the steps to install the Blackberry SDK and set up your development environment for the first time:

1. Click on the Blackberry Windows installer and then press **Next**:

2. Accept the agreement after reading it:

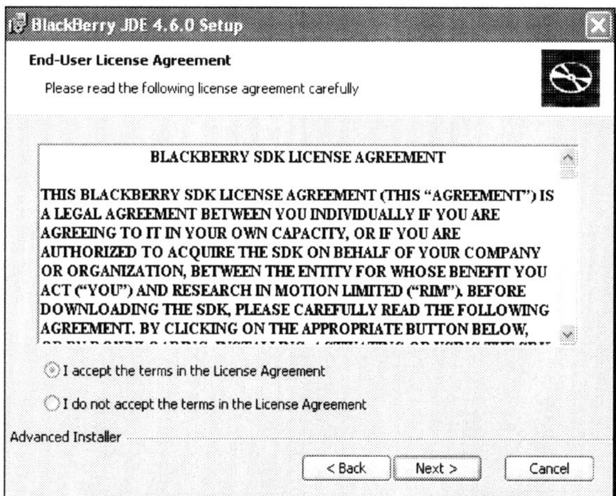

3. Enter your **User Name** and **Organization**:

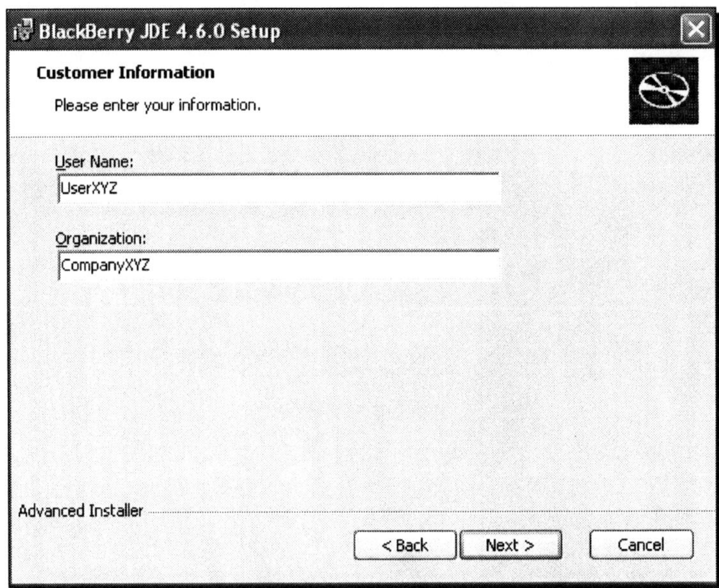

4. Select the location where you want to install the Blackberry SDK. You can select the default location to install the SDK:

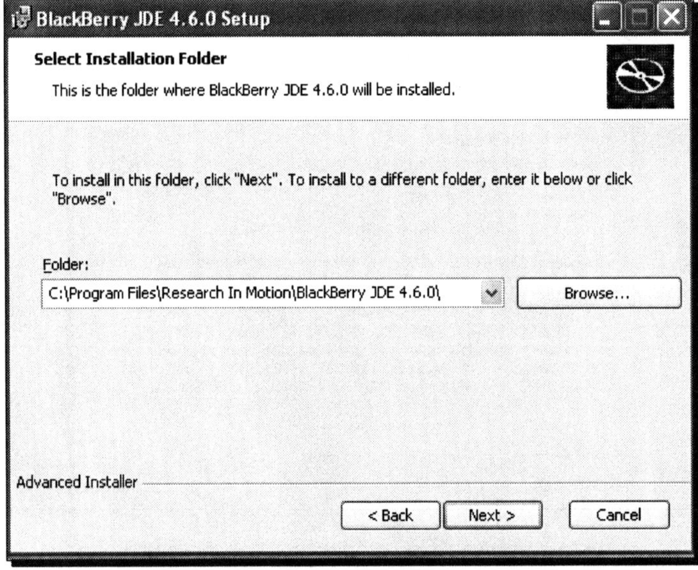

5. Click on **Install**:

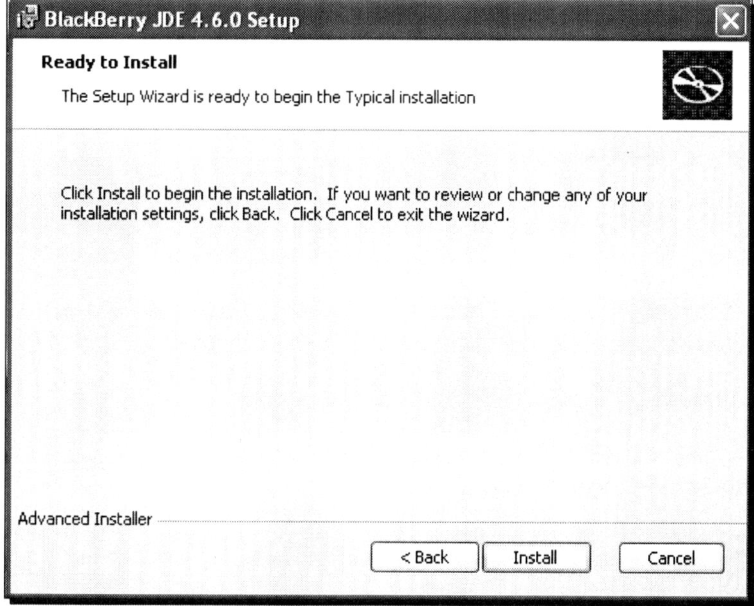

Your Blackberry SDK setup is complete and is ready to use.

Android SDK installation

If you want to develop and build applications for Android then we need to install the Android SDK and NDK. This will also include the Android simulator, which would help in testing the code.

Which Operating Systems are supported?

The following operating systems are supported by Android SDK:

- Windows XP (32-bit), Vista (32- or 64-bit), or Windows 7 (32- or 64-bit)
- Mac OS X 10.5.8 or later (x86 only)
- Linux (tested on Ubuntu Linux, Lucid Lynx)

Where to get it from:

We need to install the following packages:

- Android SDK Starter Package
- Android NDK

You can download SDK from http://developer.android.com/sdk/index.html and NDK from http://developer.android.com/sdk/ndk/index.html

Time for action – Installing Android SDK

This section describes step by step ways to install the Android SDK and set up your development environment for the first time:

1. Run <sdk>/tools/android on OS X or Linux (<sdk>/SDK Setup.exe on Windows).
2. Go to **Settings** | check **Force https://... sources to be fetched using http://** and press **Save&Apply**. Skip this step if you are using the latest version of SDK.
3. Go to **Available** | Expand **https://dl-ssl.google.com**.
4. Download the latest SDK version, latest platform (SDK Platform 2.2, for example), and the latest **Google APIs** available.

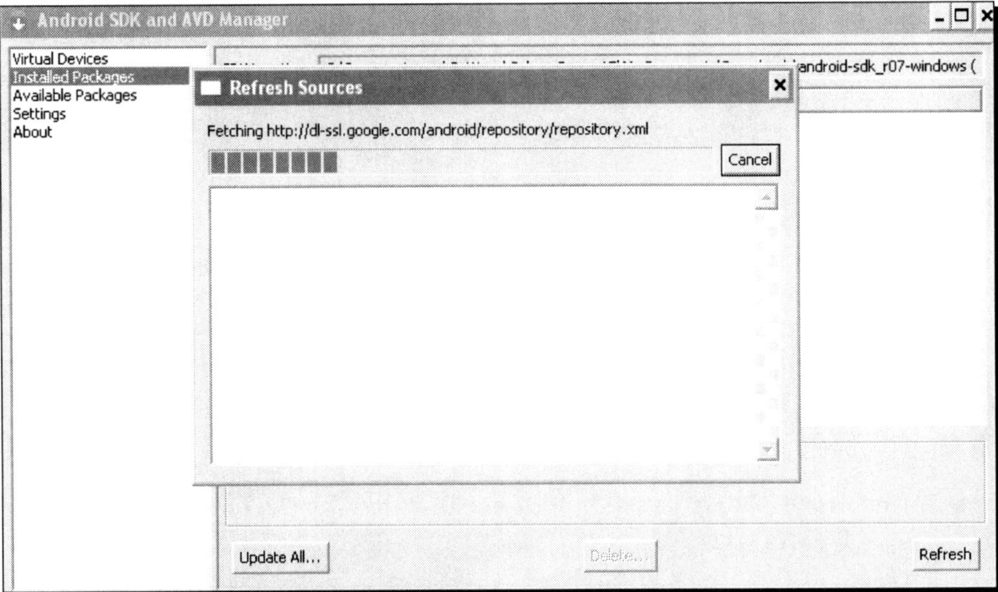

5. Click on **Install**:

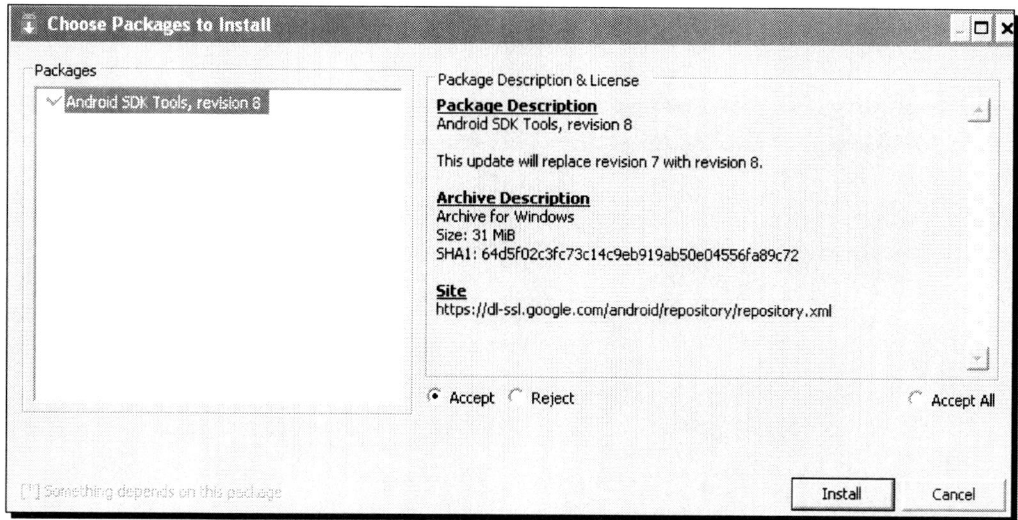

6. Set the environment variables `ANDROID_HOME` to the [directory] where you installed the SDK, and add `<sdk path>/tools` to `PATH`.

7. Download and install the Android NDK.

iPhone SDK installation

If you want to develop and build an application for iPhone then you just need to install the SDK for iPhone. This will also include the iPhone simulator, which will help in testing the code.

Which Operating Systems are supported?

The iPhone SDK installation is supported by iPhone SDK Mac OS X 10.5.8 or later (x86 only).

Where to get it from:

You need to install the following dependencies:

- Xcode
- iPhone SDK

These packages come together for Apple, so you don't need to install them separately.

You can download them from `http://developer.apple.com/devcenter/ios/index.action`.

You need to register with Apple to be able to download them.

Time for action – Installing iPhone SDK

Follow these steps to install iPhone Xcode and SDK:

1. Execute the Xcode executable and click **Continue**:

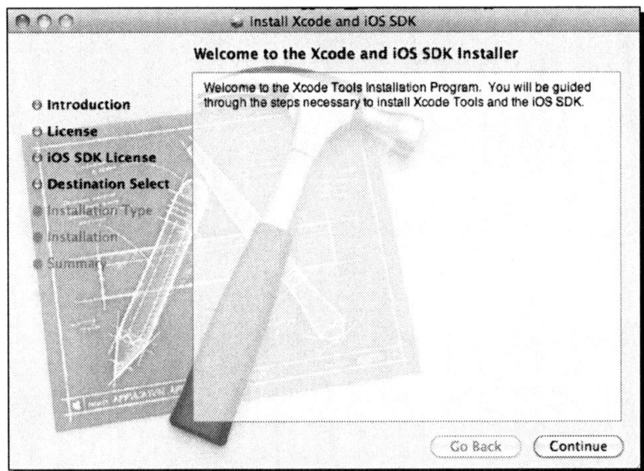

2. Agree to the Software Licence Agreement as this is what is shown in the screen shot.:

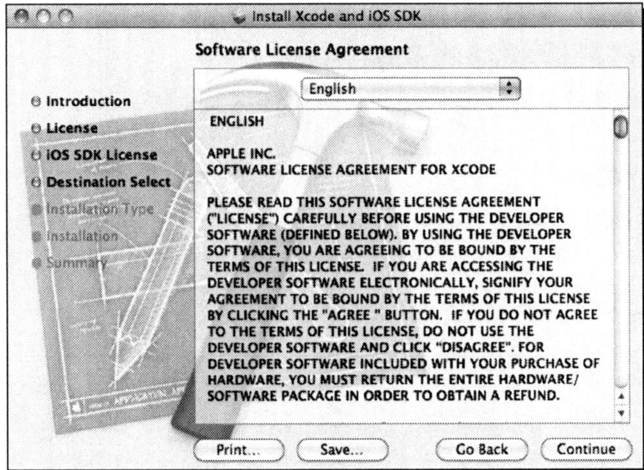

3. Select the default location where you want to keep all the Xcode files. Currently, only the default location is supported by Rhodes:

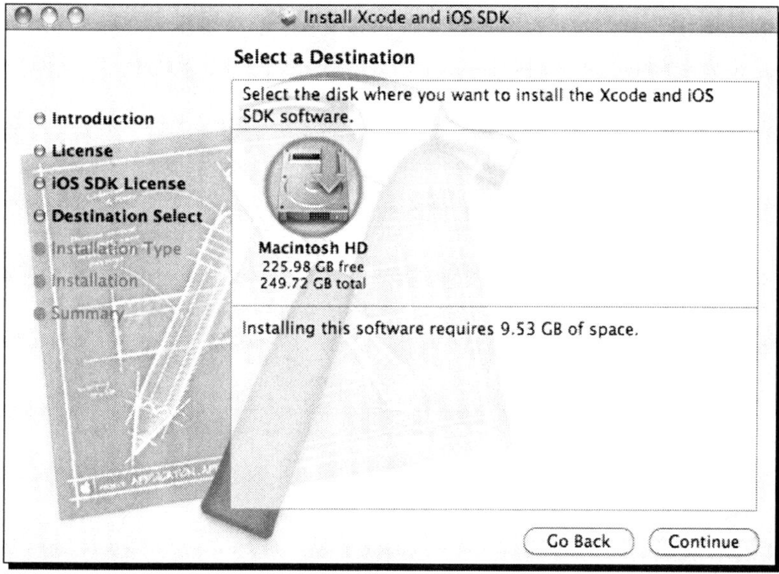

4. Check all the options in the next box and then click **Continue**:

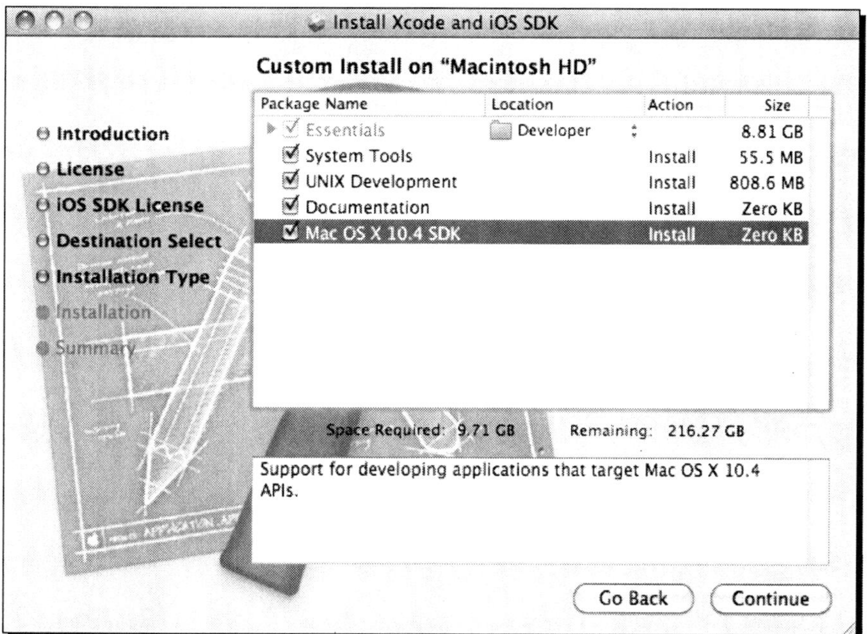

5. Click on **Install**:

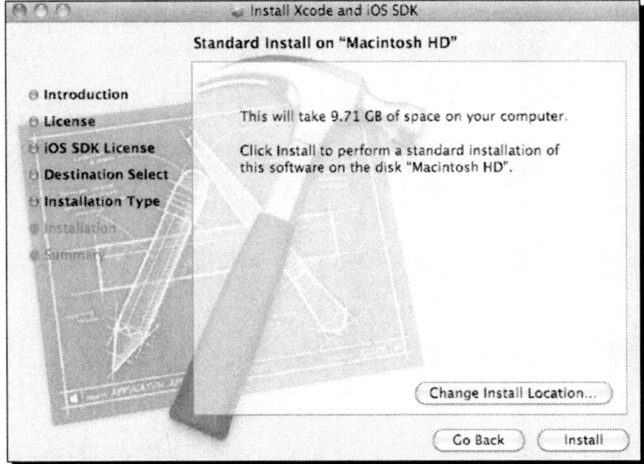

Xcode and IPhone SKD is installed.

Time for action – Configuration

After installing the required software, we will configure Rhodes.

First, we need to configure the environment by running the `rhodes-setup` script. This will attempt to auto-detect the installed SDKs and will prompt you to verify them or enter ones that cannot be detected. If you are not building for a specific platform (for example, you can't build for the iPhone on Windows), you can leave that SDK location blank.

```
Start Command Prompt with Ruby

C:\>rhodes-setup
We will ask you a few questions below about your dev environment.

JDK path (required) (C:/Program Files/Java/jdk1.6.0_21): C:\Program Files\Java\j
dk1.6.0_21
Android SDK path (blank to skip) (C:\Documents and Settings\ColumnSupport5\My Do
cuments\Downloads\android-sdk_r07-windows\android-sdk-windows): D:\android\andro
id-sdk-windows
Android NDK path (blank to skip) (D:/android/android-ndk-r4b-windows): D:\androi
d\android-ndk-r4b
Windows Mobile 6 SDK CabWiz (blank to skip) ():
BlackBerry JDE 4.6 (blank to skip) (C:/Program Files/Research In Motion/BlackBer
ry JDE 4.6.0): C:\Program Files\Research In Motion\BlackBerry JDE 4.6.0
BlackBerry JDE 4.6 MDS (blank to skip) (C:/Program Files/Research In Motion/Blac
kBerry JDE 4.6.0/MDS): C:\Program Files\Research In Motion\BlackBerry JDE 4.6.0/
MDS
BlackBerry JDE 4.2 (blank to skip) ():
BlackBerry JDE 4.2 MDS (blank to skip) ():

If you want to build with other BlackBerry SDK versions edit: C:/Ruby187/lib/rub
y/gems/1.8/gems/rhodes-2.2.5/rhobuild.yml
```

What just happened?

We just configured Java JDK path and our device simulator SDK's path on Rhodes. Now every Rhodes application will take the default path that are set during this configuration.

Time for action – Installing Development Environments—IDE

There is no shortage of Ruby-supported IDEs. You can use any IDE of your choice that supports Ruby. All are cross-platform, and have plenty of nice features. I encourage you to try them and see if they work for you. The following IDEs are my personal choices that I would recommend:

- Macintosh OS X: textmate
- Linux: gedit
- Windows Netbeans, Redrails, Ruby-mine, Scite

You can choose any one of the above IDEs. Also, Rhomobile recently launched RhoStudio Beta, the IDE for Rhomobile. It is a local Eclipse IDE that performs app generation, editing, and build of all Rhodes projects. You can download Rhostudio from `https://github.com/rhomobile/rhostudio/`.

What just happened?

We have just installed your favourite IDE on the platform that you are using. Now we are ready to create our first application.

Summary

After reading this chapter, we learned to install Rhodes, Rhosync, and its dependencies on different operating systems: Microsoft Windows, Mac, and Linux. We also installed various device SDKs (Software development kit) and simulators for the iPhone, Blackberry, and Android. These installations are sufficient to begin coding on Rhomobile and creating your first application.

In the next chapter, we will create our first Rhodes application and will run it for different smart phones.

3

Instant Gratification—Create Your First Application

In the last chapter we learnt to install Rhodes, Rhosync, and our desired SDK on our workstations. Now, it's time to create our first application and understand how Rhodes structures the application.

Let's get started...

When you install the Rhodes framework, you get a new command-line tool. The Rhogen command simply creates this directory structure for us and populates it with some standard Rhodes code. Why do we need a tool to do this—why can't we just hack away in our favourite editor, creating the source for our application from scratch? Well, we could just hack. After all, a Rhodes application is just Ruby source code. But Rhogen also does a lot of magic behind the curtain to get our applications to work with a minimum of explicit configuration. To get this magic to work, Rhodes needs to find all the various components of your application. As we'll see later in this chapter, this means that we need to create a specific directory structure, and slot our written code into the appropriate places.

We will create a sample application for employee management to understand Rhodes. The employee application will help us to manage employee details by creating, deleting, and modifying an employee. We can filter this according to our needs. Does the world need an employee application? Nope, but that hasn't stopped hundreds of developers from writing one. Why should we be different?

More seriously, it will help us to explore many features of Rhodes development. We'll see how to create a simple page, link database tables, handle sessions, work offline, connect to other servers, push, create forms, and many more features.

Time for action – Creating an employee application

To create a Rhodes Application, we can either use Rhogen or its alias; Rhodes commands. Virtually all Rhodes applications start the same way; with the Rhogen command. This handy program creates a skeleton of a Rhodes application in a directory of your choice. To get started, make a directory for your Rhodes projects and then run the command `rhogen app <application_name>` to make the initial sample application.

For our employee application, we'll run the following commands:

```
$ mkdir Rhodes_app
$ cd Rhodes_app
$ rhogen app employee_application
```

Generating with app generator:

```
[ADDED]   employee_application/rhoconfig.txt
[ADDED]   employee_application/build.yml
[ADDED]   employee_application/app/application.rb
[ADDED]   employee_application/app/index.erb
[ADDED]   employee_application/app/index.bb.erb
[ADDED]   employee_application/app/layout.erb
[ADDED]   employee_application/app/loading.html
[ADDED]   employee_application/Rakefile
[ADDED]   employee_application/app/helpers
[ADDED]   employee_application/icon
[ADDED]   employee_application/app/Settings
[ADDED]   employee_application/public
[ADDED]   employee_application/app/loading.png
```

Notice the output, how many files and directories the Rhogen command creates. This automatic generation of standard directories and file structure is one of the many advantages of Rhodes. It immediately gets you from zero to a basic functional application. Moreover, since the structure is common to all the Rhodes apps, you can immediately get your bearings when looking at someone else's code. We'll learn about most of these files and the directories in the rest of this book.

What just happened?

We just created an employee application using the Rhogen command. This command automatically generates a basic skeleton for your application, which can be enhanced easily according to your needs.

Have a go hero – Exploring the Rhogen command

Now, we will explore the capabilities of the Rhogen command. To get a list of all the options available for this command, type the following in the command prompt:

```
$ rhogen
```

The following output should be generated:

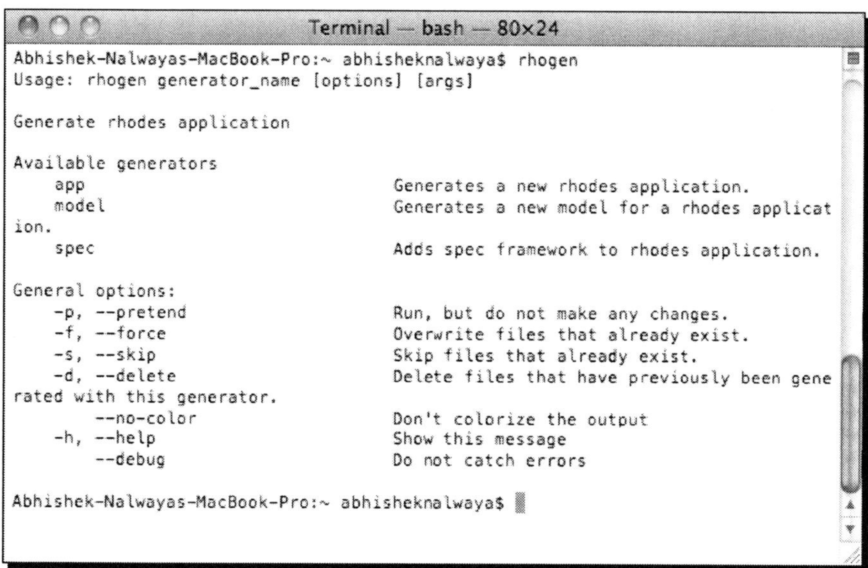

Building your first Rhodes application

We saw the magic of the Rhogen command in the last section and how it does most of the work for you. But now the question is how will we run our application and see the output. So, in this section we will build and test our employee application for various smart phones.

Time for action – Build it for different smart phones

It's time to make the first build for our application and see the magic that the Rhogen command has done. We will build our employee application for iPhone, Android, and Blackberry.

Let's go to the application directory and build it for iPhone, Blackberry, Android, and Windows phone:

```
$ cd employee_application
```

We will now learn about the rake command, which will help us when building our application. To get all the options available with the rake command, go to your application directory and type:

```
rake -T
```

You will get a list of all the options available with rake command:

```
rake clean:android                  # Clean Android

rake clean:bb                       # Clean bb

rake clean:iphone                   # Clean iphone

rake clean:win32                    # Clean win32

rake clean:wm                       # Clean wm

rake clobber_rdoc                   # Remove rdoc products

rake config:checkbb                 # Check local blackberry configuration

rake device:android:debug           # Build debug self signed for device

rake device:android:production      # Build production signed for device

rake device:bb:debug                # Build debug for device

rake device:bb:production           # Build production for device

rake device:iphone:production       # Builds and signs iphone for
production

rake device:wm:production           # Build production for device or
emulator

rake package:bb:production_sim      # Package all production (all parts in
one ...

rake run:android                    # build and launch emulator

rake run:android:device             # build and install on device

rake run:bb                         # Builds everything, loads and starts
bb si...

rake run:bb:startsim                # Start Blackberry simulator

rake run:bbapp                      # Builds everything and loads
application o...

rake run:bbdev                      # Same as run:bb, but only supports
```

```
one app...

rake run:iphone                  # Builds everything, launches iphone
simulator

rake run:win32                   # Run win32

rake run:wm                      # Build and run on WM6 emulator

rake run:wm:cab                  # Build, install .cab and run on WM6
emulator

rake run:wm:device               # Build and run on the Windows Phone

rake run:wm:device:cab           # Build, install .cab  and run on the
Windo...

rake uninstall:android           # uninstall from emulator

rake uninstall:android:device    # uninstall from device
```

Now, we will use the following commands for building the application for different phones:

1. For building it for iPhone, we will use the following command and then our employee application will start in an iPhone simulator:

   `$ rake run:iphone`

2. For building it for Blackberry, we will use the following command and then our employee application will start in the Blackberry simulator:

```
$rake run:bb
```

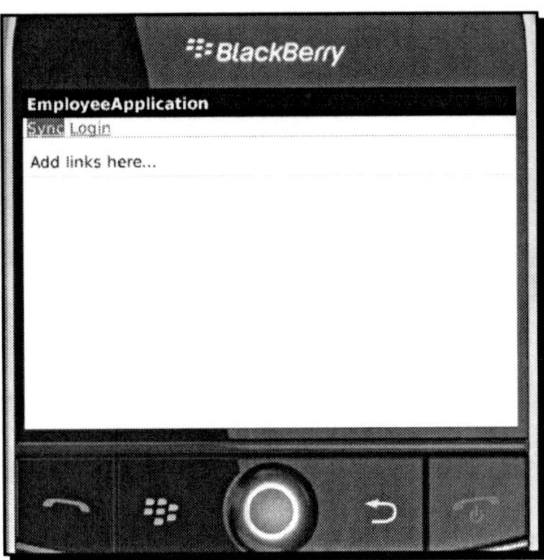

3. For building it for Android we will use the following command and then our employee application will start in the Android simulator:

```
$rake run:android
```

4. To build it for other phones we can use the following commands:
   - Windows Mobile
     ```
     rake run:wm
     ```
   - Windows 7
     ```
     rake run:wp
     ```

What just happened?

We have just run our cross-platform employee application on various smart phones and tested it on device simulators. We have also seen how they will appear on the iPhone, Blackberry, and Android.

Navigating the Directory Structure

As we have seen, Rhodes is smart enough to create the elementary folders and files for you. We will now understand the basic directory structure of a Rhodes application.

A Rhodes application has the following directories and files:

- `app` – This is the heart of your application, which contains the controllers, models, and views for your application.
- `public` – This folder contains all the static files like stylesheet, JavaScript, and images for your application.
- `rhoconfig.txt` – This file is used for configuring your application. We will discuss this in detail later in the book.
- `build.yml` – This is a very important file for configuration as this contains all the configuration that is needed for building an application. It also contains your application name, version, vendor, etc. It has device SDKs, Rhodes location, and also the extensions that you are using in your application. We will discuss this in detail later in the book.
- `Rakefile` – This file is used by Rhodes to execute the inbuilt rake commands.

- `icon` – This folder will contain our application icon.

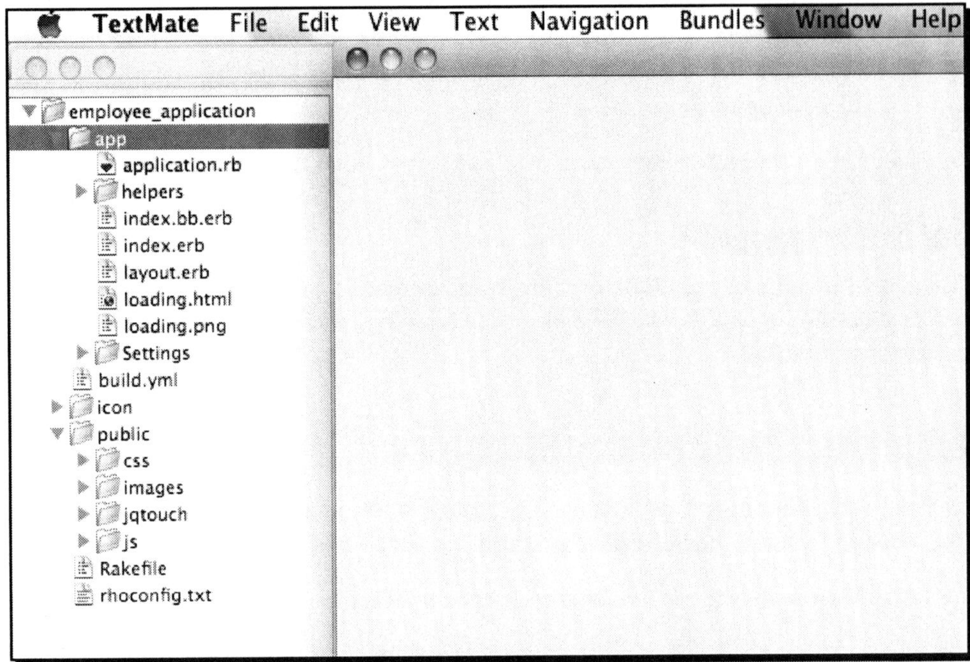

Now that your app is compiled and runs, you can start adding models and controllers. When the model is generated, Rhodes will also create files for a standard User Interface for displaying and editing the model. This follows the standard model-view-controller paradigm.

Time for action – Creating the model

Now, it's time to create the Model, View, and Controller for our employee application. We will create a model employee with attributes such as name, company, address, age, gender, and salary.

```
$ rhogen model employee name,company,address,age,gender,salary
```

The model generator will provide us with the following:

```
[ADDED]  app/Employee/index.erb
[ADDED]  app/Employee/edit.erb
[ADDED]  app/Employee/new.erb
[ADDED]  app/Employee/show.erb
[ADDED]  app/Employee/index.bb.erb
[ADDED]  app/Employee/edit.bb.erb
[ADDED]  app/Employee/new.bb.erb
```

```
[ADDED]  app/Employee/show.bb.erb
[ADDED]  app/Employee/employee_controller.rb
[ADDED]  app/Employee/employee.rb
[ADDED]  app/test/employee_spec.rb
```

You will see that RhoGen creates a controller (`employee_controller.rb`) and several HTML templates (`.erb files`) for reading and editing objects for the specified model and we have seen the magic of the Rhogen model command. It has generated a lot of code for us. We can divide the generated code into four parts:

- Model: A model represents the information (data) of the application and the rules to manipulate that data. The file `employee.rb` is the model for employee application. It contains all the logic.
- Controller: The controller provides the bond between the model and view. In Rhodes, the controller is responsible for processing incoming requests, interrogating the models for data, and passing that data on to the views for presentation. The file `employee_controller.rb` is the controller for employee application.
- View: Views represent the user interface of your application. In Rhodes, views are often HTML files with embedded Ruby code that perform tasks related solely to the presentation of the data. These are `index.erb`, `edit.erb`, etc.
- Spec file: These are the files where we write unit test cases for our code. The file `employee_spec.rb` is the spec file for employee application.

If you look closely with a single `rhogen` command, Rhodes has generated piles of files. You must be wondering what the uses for these files and folders are. Well, these files and folders are responsible for basic CRUD operations for your employee model. CRUD operations are CREATE, READ, UPDATE, and DELETE. If you have worked with Ruby on Rails, it is similar to the scaffold command.

What just happened?

We have created an employee model using the Rhogen command. Also, now we are familiar with CRUD operations and the logic behind them.

Linking views to the homepage

Now we will add a link to the default homepage of our Rhodes application that redirects us to the index action of the employee controller.

Time for action – Linking the employee view to the homepage

We will first link employee views on an iPhone. This index page in an app directory is the default homepage, which will be loaded in our application.

You can edit the generated ERB files to customize the HTML as desired. Typically, you will provide links to the employee index page from the home screen. Below is the generated top level `index.erb` file for our application:

```
<div class="pageTitle">
  <h1>EmployeeApplication</h1>
</div>

<div class="toolbar">
  <% if SyncEngine::logged_in > 0 %>
      <div class="leftItem blueButton">
        <a href="<%= url_for :controller => :Settings, :action => :
do_sync %>">Sync</a>
      </div>
      <div class="rightItem regularButton">
        <a href="<%= url_for :controller => :Settings, :action => :
logout %>">Logout</a>
      </div>
  <% else %>
      <div class="rightItem regularButton">
        <a href="<%= url_for :controller => :Settings, :action => :
login %>">Login</a>
      </div>
  <% end %>
</div>

<div class="content">
  <ul>
    <li>
      <a href="#"><span class="title"> Add Links Here...</span><span
class="disclosure_indicator"/></a>
    </li>
  </ul>
</div>
```

To provide a link to the Employee index page and templates, you can replace the list item with the title **Add links here** with:

```
<a href="<%= url_for :controller => :Employee %>">Employee</a>
```

Let's stop for a moment to consider how we generated this link. `url_for` is a helper method of Rhodes that generates a link. We have to pass the controller name and action name as a parameter to create the desired link. We will discuss this in detail as we proceed.

If you look at `url_for` carefully, there are no parentheses and if you come from the school of Java style of coding, you might be surprised that Ruby doesn't insist on parentheses around method parameters. However, you can always add them if you like.

Now, we will build our code using `rake run:iphone` and as you navigate you can see the following screens :

- **Default Index page in app folder**: This is the homepage of our application that will be loaded once the application is started:

- **Listing all employees**: The easiest place to start looking at functionality is with the code that lists all the employees. Open the file `app/employee/employee_controller.rb` and look at the index action:

```
def index
    @employees = Employee.find(:all)
    render
  end
```

This code sets the `@employees` instance variable to an array of all employees in the database. `Employee.find(:all)` calls the Employee model to return all of the employees that are currently in the database, with no limiting conditions. Rhodes makes all of the instance variables from the action available to the view. Here's `app/employee/index.erb`:

```
<div class="pageTitle">
  <h1>Employees</h1>
</div>

<div class="toolbar">
  <div class="leftItem regularButton">
    <a href="<%= Rho::RhoConfig.start_path %>">Home</a>
  </div>
  <div class="rightItem regularButton">
    <a class="button" href="<%= url_for :action => :new %>">New</a>
  </div>
</div>

<div class="content">
  <ul>
    <% @employees.each do |employee| %>

        <li>
          <a href="<%= url_for :action => :show, :id => employee.
object %>">
            <span class="title"><%= employee.name %></span><span
class="disclosure_indicator"></span>
          </a>
        </li>

    <% end %>
  </ul>
</div>
```

This view iterates over the contents of the `@employees` array to display content and links. A few things to note in the view:

- The page is divided into three part with page title, toolbar, and content
- `Rho::RhoConfig.start_path` redirects to the default page mentioned in `rhoconfig.txt`
- `url_for` helper is an inbuilt method to create a link

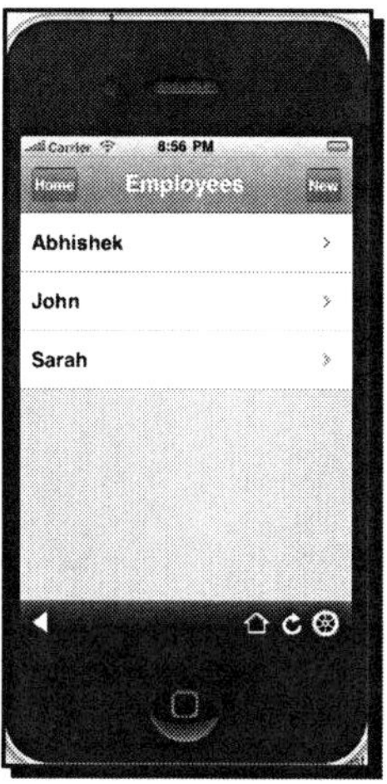

◆ **Creating a new employee**: Creating a new employee involves two actions. The first is the new action, which instantiates an empty employee object:

```
def new
    @employee = Employee.new
    render :action => :new
  end
```

The new.html.erb view displays this empty employee to the user:

```
<div class="pageTitle">
  <h1>New <%= @employee.title %></h1>
</div>

<div class="toolbar">
  <div class="leftItem backButton">
    <a class="cancel" href="<%= url_for :action => :index
%>">Cancel</a>
  </div>
</div>

<div class="content">
  <form method="POST" action="<%= url_for :action => :create %>">
    <input type="hidden" name="id" value="<%= @employee.object
%>"/>
    <ul>

          <li>
            <label for="employee[name]" class="fieldLabel">Name</
label>
            <input type="text" name="employee[name]" <%=
            placeholder("Name") %> />
```

```
          </li>

    <li>
            <label for="employee[company]" class="fieldLabel">Comp
any</label>
            <input type="text" name="employee[company]" <%=
            placeholder("Comapany") %> />
          </li>

                <li>
            <label for="employee[address]" class="fieldLabel">Addr
ess</label>
            <input type="text" name="employee[address]" <%=
            placeholder("Address") %> />
          </li>

          <li>
            <label for="employee[age]" class="fieldLabel">Age</
label>
            <input type="text" name="employee[age]" <%=
            placeholder("Age") %> />
          </li>

              <li>
            <label for="employee[gender]" class="fieldLabel">Gende
r</label>
            <input type="text" name="employee[gender]" <%=
            placeholder("Gender") %> />
          </li>

               <li>
            <label for="employee[salary]" class="fieldLabel">Salar
y</label>
            <input type="text" name="employee[salary]" <%=
            placeholder("Salary") %> />
          </li>

    </ul>
    <input type="submit" class="standardButton" value="Create"/>
  </form>
</div>
```

We have just created an HTML form. When the user clicks the **Create** button on this form, the application will send information back to the create method of the controller.

```
def create
    @employee = Employee.create(@params['employee'])
    redirect :action => :index
  end
```

The create action instantiates a new employee object from the data supplied by the user on the form, which Rhodes makes available in the `params` hash. After saving this hash the controller will redirect to index action.

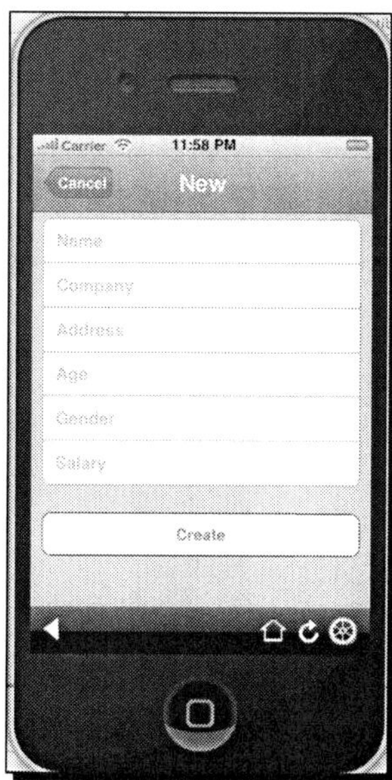

- **Showing an Individual employee**: When we click any employee name on the index page, Rhodes interprets this as a call to the show action for the resource, and passes `:id` as parameter. Here's the show action:

```
def show
  @employee = Employee.find(@params['id'])
  if @employee
    render :action => :show
  else
    redirect :action => :index
  end
end
```

The show action uses `Employee.find` to search for a single record in the database by its ID value. After finding the record, Rhodes displays it by using `show.erb`:

```
<div class="pageTitle">
  <h1><%= @employee.name %></h1>
</div>

<div class="toolbar">
  <div class="leftItem backButton">
    <a href="<%= url_for :action => :index %>">Back</a>
  </div>
  <div class="rightItem regularButton">
    <a href="<%= url_for :action => :edit, :id => @employee.object
%>">Edit</a>
  </div>
</div>

<div class="content">
  <ul>

        <li>
          <div class="itemLabel">Name</div>
          <div class="itemValue"><%= @employee.name %></div>
        </li>

        <li>
          <div class="itemLabel">Company</div>
          <div class="itemValue"><%= @employee.company %></div>
        </li>

        <li>
          <div class="itemLabel">Address</div>
          <div class="itemValue"><%= @employee.address %></div>
        </li>

        <li>
          <div class="itemLabel">Age</div>
          <div class="itemValue"><%= @employee.age %></div>
        </li>

        <li>
          <div class="itemLabel">Gender</div>
          <div class="itemValue"><%= @employee.gender %></div>
        </li>
```

```
        <li>
          <div class="itemLabel">Salary</div>
          <div class="itemValue"><%= @employee.salary %></div>
        </li>

  </ul>
</div>
```

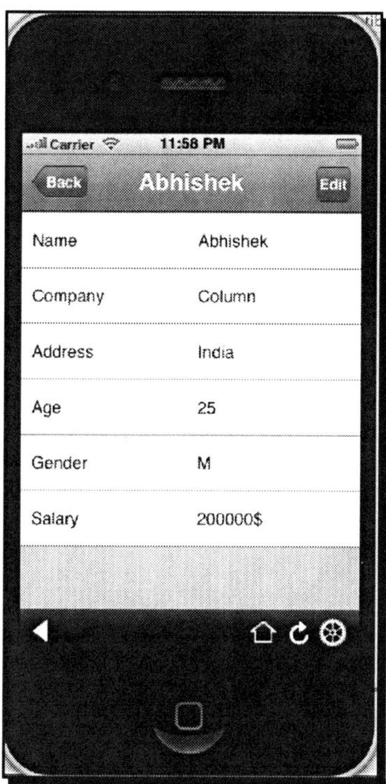

- **Editing the page to modify the employee details**: Like creating a new employee, editing an employee is a two-part process. The first step is a request to a particular employee. This calls the edit action in the controller:

```
def edit
    @employee = Employee.find(@params['id'])
    if @employee
      render :action => :edit
    else
      redirect :action => :index
    end
  end
```

After calling the edit action it will render the `edit.erb` file:

```
<div class="pageTitle">
  <h1>Edit <%= @employee.name %></h1>
</div>

<div class="toolbar">
  <div class="leftItem backButton">
    <a href="<%= url_for :action => :show, :id => @employee.object
%>">Cancel</a>
  </div>
  <div class="rightItem regularButton">
    <a class="button" href="<%= url_for :action => :delete, :id =>
@employee.object %>">Delete</a>
  </div>
</div>

<div class="content">
  <form method="POST" action="<%= url_for :action => :update %>">
    <input type="hidden" name="id" value="<%= @employee.object
%>"/>
    <ul>

          <li>
            <label for="employee[name]" class="fieldLabel">Name</
label>
            <input type="text" name="employee[name]" value="<%= @
employee.name %>" <%= placeholder( "Name" ) %> />
          </li>

          <li>
            <label for="employee[company]" class="fieldLabel">Comp
any</label>
            <input type="text" name="employee[company]" value="<%=
@employee.company %>" <%= placeholder( "Company" ) %> />
          </li>

          <li>
            <label for="employee[address]" class="fieldLabel">Addr
ess</label>
```

```
            <input type="text" name="employee[address]" value="<%=
@employee.address %>" <%= placeholder( "Address" ) %> />
          </li>

          <li>
            <label for="employee[age]" class="fieldLabel">Age</
label>
            <input type="text" name="employee[age]" value="<%= @
employee.age %>" <%= placeholder( "Age" ) %> />
          </li>

          <li>
            <label for="employee[gender]" class="fieldLabel">Gende
r</label>
            <input type="text" name="employee[gender]" value="<%=
@employee.gender %>" <%= placeholder( "Gender" ) %> />
          </li>

          <li>
            <label for="employee[salary]" class="fieldLabel">Salar
y</label>
            <input type="text" name="employee[salary]" value="<%=
@employee.salary %>" <%= placeholder( "Salary" ) %> />
          </li>

    </ul>
    <input type="submit" class="standardButton" value="Update"/>
  </form>
</div>
```

This is a normal HTML form. Submitting the form created by this view will invoke the update action within the controller:

```
def update
    @employee = Employee.find(@params['id'])
    @employee.update_attributes(@params['employee']) if @employee
    redirect :action => :index
  end
```

In the update action, Rhodes first uses the `:id` parameter passed back from the edit view to locate the database record that's being edited. The `update_attributes` call then takes the rest of the parameters from the request and applies them to this record.

- **Deleting an employee**: Finally, clicking on **Delete** links sends the associated ID to the delete action:

```
def delete
  @employee = Employee.find(@params['id'])
  @employee.destroy if @employee
  redirect :action => :index
end
```

Rhode's philosophy is to make a developer's life easy, as you have learned with a single command an elementary CRUD application is ready in minutes. Similarly, we can build and test the same code for other smart phones. However, a few minor changes will be required for BlackBerry in `.bb.erb` files. This is because lower versions of Blackberry support very less CSS and JavaScript. So, to overcome this limitation we have separate views for Blackberry.

Until now we have seen and tested our application on iPhone. For other smart phones, you can run it in the same way. But for Blackberry we have to edit `.bb.erb` files.

For Blackberry, add this line to `index.bb.erb`:

```
<%= link_to "Employee", :controller => :Employee%>
```

`link_to` is a helper provided by Rhodes to create a link similar to `url_for`.

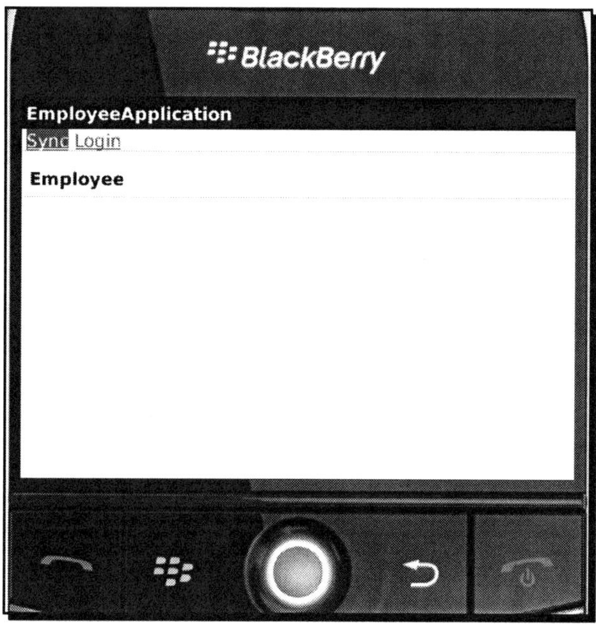

Now you can navigate the employee model on Blackberry in a similar way as we did on iPhone.

Have a go hero – Exploring url_for

We will explore the inbuilt helper of Rhodes to create a link with the following examples:

Example 1

```
url_for :action => :index
```

It will link to the index action of current controller `/app/controller`.

Example 2

```
url_for :action => :create
```

It will link to create action of current controller `/app/controller`.

Example 3

```
url_for :action => :new
```

It will redirect to new action of current controller `/app/model/new`.

Example 4

```
url_for :action => :show, :id => '{12}'
```

It will redirect to show the action of current controller with parameter ID value as 12 `/app/model/{12}/show`

Example 5

```
url_for :model => :another_model, :action => :show, :id => '{12}'
```

It will link to `another_model` action of current controller `/app/another_model/{12}/show`

Example 6

```
url_for :controller => :another_controller, :action => :show, :id =>
'{12}'
```

It will create a link to show action of `another_controller` controller `/app/another_controller/{12}/show`

Example 7

```
url_for :action => :create, :query => {:name => 'John Smith',
'address' => "http://john.smith.com"}
```

It will link to create action of current controller with parameter name and address:

`/app/model?name=John%20Smith&address=http%3A%2F%2Fjohn.smith.com`

Example 8

```
url_for :action => :show, :id => '{12}', :fragment => "an-anchor"
```

It will link to create action of current controller with a fragment an-anchor `/app/model/{12}/show#an-anchor`

Digging the MVC in our application

We have seen the output but now the question that arises is how does it work? Well to know that, first we have to understand all the code generated by the Rhogen model command:

Model

The `employee.rb` file in the employee folder is the model. We will write model-specific code in this file.

By default there is a class Employee generated by Rhodes generator. We can also configure a few properties of Model from this file such as:

- Type of schema—we can choose either of the two type of schema PropertyBag or Fixed schema. We will discuss this in detail in next chapter.
- Enabling Sync—this will enable the sync for the model. We will discuss this in Chapter 5.

This is the model code generated by Rhodes generator:

```
class Employee
  include Rhom::PropertyBag

  # Uncomment the following line to enable sync with Employee.
  # enable :sync

  #add model specifc code here
end
```

Controller

The `employee_controller.rb` file in employee folder is the controller. It has all the basic CRUD operations. The file looks like this:

```
require 'rho/rhocontroller'
require 'helpers/browser_helper'

class EmployeeController < Rho::RhoController
  include BrowserHelper

  #GET /Employee
  def index
    @employees = Employee.find(:all)
    render
  end

  # GET /Employee/{1}
  def show
    @employee = Employee.find(@params['id'])
    if @employee
      render :action => :show
```

```
    else
      redirect :action => :index
    end
  end

  # GET /Employee/new
  def new
    @employee = Employee.new
    render :action => :new
  end

  # GET /Employee/{1}/edit
  def edit
    @employee = Employee.find(@params['id'])
    if @employee
      render :action => :edit
    else
      redirect :action => :index
    end
  end

  # POST /Employee/create
  def create
    @employee = Employee.create(@params['employee'])
    redirect :action => :index
  end

  # POST /Employee/{1}/update
  def update
    @employee = Employee.find(@params['id'])
    @employee.update_attributes(@params['employee']) if @employee
    redirect :action => :index
  end

  # POST /Employee/{1}/delete
  def delete
    @employee = Employee.find(@params['id'])
    @employee.destroy if @employee
    redirect :action => :index
  end
end
```

From the above code we understand the following points:

- Every controller in Rhodes is a sub class of RhoController
- All the CRUD operations for employee controller
- Rhodes has a unique way of interacting with database using Rhom, which we will discuss in Chapter 4
- If you are familiar with Ruby on Rails, the syntax of Rhodes controller is similar to that of Rails controller

Views

These are the .erb files that will have basic UI stuff. You may notice that there are two types of view files .bb.erb and .erb files (Example: index.bb.erb and index.erb). The .bb.erb files are for Blackberry and .erb are for other phones. This is because Blackberry has limited support for HTML and CSS tags, so it uses more of the table-based user interface.

Now, we will explore the index.erb file:

```
<div class="pageTitle">
  <h1>Employees</h1>
</div>

<div class="toolbar">
  <div class="leftItem regularButton">
    <a href="<%= Rho::RhoConfig.start_path %>">Home</a>
  </div>
  <div class="rightItem regularButton">
    <a class="button" href="<%= url_for :action => :new %>">New</a>
  </div>
</div>

<div class="content">
  <ul>
    <% @employees.each do |employee| %>

        <li>
          <a href="<%= url_for :action => :show, :id => employee.
object %>">
            <span class="title"><%= employee.name %></span><span
class="disclosure_indicator"></span>
          </a>
        </li>

    <% end %>
  </ul>
</div>
```

If we see any page in view, it is divided into three parts:

1. pageTitle – This code is for selecting the title of the page:

   ```
   <div class="pageTitle">
     <h1>Employees</h1>
   </div>
   ```

2. toolbar – This code will generate right and left links, which will be shown on the toolbar:

   ```
   <div class="toolbar">
     <div class="leftItem regularButton">
       <a href="<%= Rho::RhoConfig.start_path %>">Home</a>
     </div>
     <div class="rightItem regularButton">
       <a class="button" href="<%= url_for :action => :new %>">New</
   a>
     </div>
   </div>
   ```

3. content – This contains the page content that will be displayed on screen:

   ```
   <div class="content">
     <ul>
       <% @employees.each do |employee| %>

           <li>
             <a href="<%= url_for :action => :show, :id => employee.
   object %>">
               <span class="title"><%= employee.name %></span><span
   class="disclosure_indicator"></span>
             </a>
           </li>

       <% end %>
     </ul>
   </div>
   ```

There is no strict rule that we have to divide the view in three sections. However, if we follow this it will give a native look to your application. We can design our own CSS accordingly if we want to design in some other way. But if you are using the default styling, which is generated by the Rhogen command, then we have to use this type of styling.

Rhodes configuration file—Rhoconfig.txt

Each Rhodes application contains a configuration file called `rhoconfig.txt`. This file takes care of all the configurations for your application.

I am listing a few of its configurations:

- We can set up a startup page for our application by:

  ```
  start_path = '/app'
  ```

- We can set the path to the options page by:

  ```
  options_path = '/app/Settings'
  ```

- We can set location of bundle URL (i.e. from rhohub.com); used by desktop win32 simulator by:

  ```
  rhobundle_zip_url = ''"
  ```

- We can set an optional password to access bundle (usually not required); used by desktop win32 simulator by:

  ```
  rhobundle_zip_pwd = nil
  ```

- We can set Rhodes log property by MinSeverity. It decides the level of logging. 0-trace, 1-info(app level), 3-warnings, 4-errors. Make sure that for production set it to 3; otherwise it will affect your application performance.

  ```
  MinSeverity  = 1
  ```

- We can enable copy log messages to standard output, useful for debugging:

  ```
  LogToOutput = 1
  ```

- We can set max log file size in KB, set 0 to unlimited size; when limit is reached, log wraps to beginning of file:

  ```
  MaxLogFileSize=50
  ```

- We can set turn on local http server traces, off by default:

  ```
  net_trace = 0
  ```

- We can set timeout of network requests in seconds (30 by default):

  ```
  net_timeout = 60
  ```

- We can set where log will be posted by RhoConf.send_log:

  ```
  logserver = 'http://rhologs.heroku.com'
  ```

- We can set log file prefix—contain human-readable text:

  ```
  logname='helloworld'
  ```

- We can keep track of the last visited page:

```
KeepTrackOfLastVisitedPage = 0
LastVisitedPage = ''
```

- We set sync server url URL by:

```
syncserver = 'http://localhost:9292/application'
```

- We can open the Rhodes app in full screen mode:

```
full_screen = 1
```

- We can set the port of the local (embedded) HTTP server. This parameter is mainly for debug purposes. If not specified, the application will use a dynamically selected one. WARNING!!! Remove this parameter before putting the application to production:

```
local_server_port = 8080
```

- We can show the status bar on Windows mobile. Its default value is 1:

```
wm_show_statusbar = 1
```

- We can disable screen rotation (enabled by default)—disable possible for ANDROID and iPhone ONLY:

```
disable_screen_rotation = 1
```

- We can disable close app when pressing back on the home screen on the Blackberry:

```
bb_disable_closebyback = 0
```

- We can load images in the background, this improves reaction speed on user actions, 0 by default:

```
bb_loadimages_async = 0
```

- We can hide the forward button and animate back button transition:

```
jqtouch_mode=1
splash_screen='zoom'
```

We can do our custom configuration also in this file. To access `rhoconfig.txt` from application code, use the `Rho::RhoConfig` class:

```
Rho::RhoConfig.full_screen
Rho::RhoConfig.app_property='some value'
if Rho::RhoConfig.exists?('some_property')
  #do something
end
```

Building a Configuration file—build.yml

Rhodes applications contains a configuration file called `build.yml`. This file takes care of the entire configuration for your application, which we need when building an application.

- We can set up the application name by:

  ```
  name: <application_name>
  ```

- We can set the version number by:

  ```
  version: <version_number>
  ```

- We can add the vendor name by:

  ```
  vendor: <vender_name>
  ```

- We can set the location of Rhodes path from:

  ```
  sdk: <sdk_location>
  ```

- We can add more Ruby libraries as an extension by:

  ```
  extensions: ["extenstion_name"]
  ```

- We can specify the device SDK to be used and the also the simulator for debugging.

Changing the input style

Previously, we created our model and basic CRUD operations using the Rhogen command. Now, we will modify the HTML input form, by adding textarea, radiobuttons, etc.

Time for action – Editing view

We will customize the `new.erb` and `new.bb.erb`, which is responsible for creating a new employee. By default if we generate code using Rhogen all the fields in the form are textboxes. We will change these textboxes to textarea, radiobutton, and selectbox.

Follow these steps to create them:

1. Replace the code for address by the following lines, which changes it to textarea:

```
      <h4 class="groupTitle">Address</h4>
      <ul>
          <li class="textarea">
              <textarea rows="5" cols="30" name=
"employee[address]" > </textarea>
          </li>
      </ul>
```

This code will create a textarea input type as shown in this image:

2. Replace the code for company with the following lines, which changes it to a select box:

```
<h4 class="groupTitle">Company</h4>
      <ul>
          <li>
              <select name="employee[company]">
                  <option value="Facebook" selected>Facebook</
option>
                  <option value="Twitter">Twitter</option>
                  <option value="Google">Google</option>
              </select>
          </li>
      </ul>
```

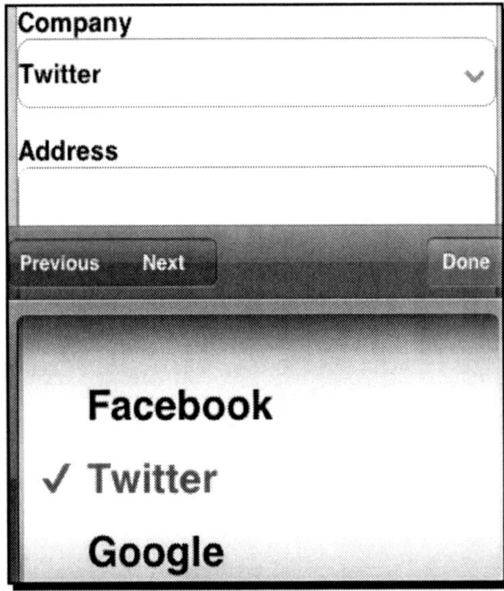

3. Replace the code for gender with the following lines, which changes it to radio buttons:

```
<h4 class="groupTitle">Gender</h4>
       <ul>
            <li><label for="employee[gender]">Male</label>
                <input type="radio" name="employee[gender]"
value="male"/>
            </li>
            <li><label for="task[status]">Female</label>
                <input type="radio" name="employee[gender]"
value="female"/>
            </li>

       </ul>
```

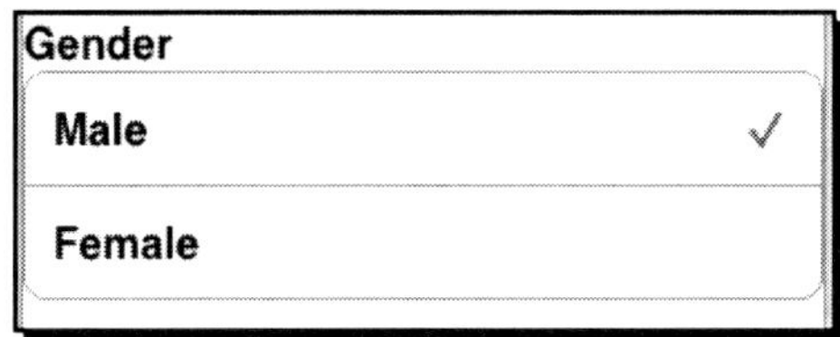

Now, we will work for blackberry and edit `new.bb.erb`.

4. Modifying the field Company to a select box:

```
<tr>
               <td class="itemLabel">Company: </td>
               <td class="itemValue">
            <select name="employee[company]">
                  <option value="Facebook" selected>Facebook</
option>
                  <option value="Twitter">Twitter</option>
                  <option value="Google">Google</option>
                 </select>
           </td>
   </tr>
```

5. Modifying the field Address to text area:

```
     <tr>
               <td class="itemLabel">Address: </td>
               <td class="itemValue"><textarea rows="3" cols="10"
name= "employee[address]" ></textarea></td>
            </tr>
Modifying the field Gender to a radio button
```

```
    <tr>
                <td class="itemLabel">Gender: </td>
                <td class="itemValue">
             Male      <input type="radio" name="employee[gender]"
value="male"/>
             Female  <input type="radio" name="employee[gender]"
value="female"/>
             </td>
             </tr>
```

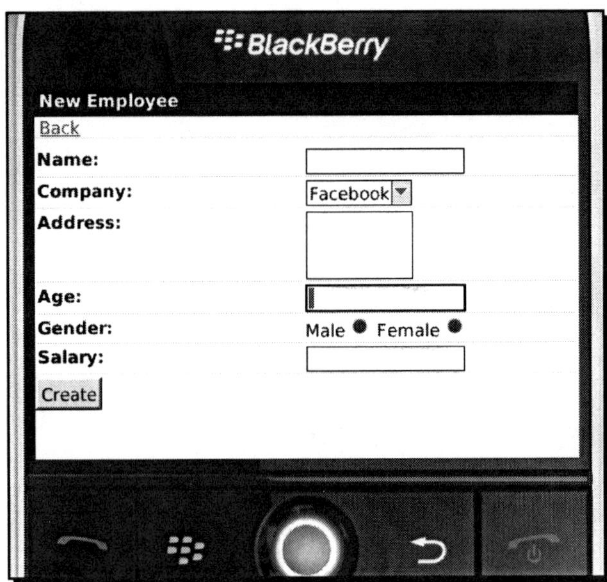

What just happened?

We just edited the employee page that we created earlier in this chapter and modified the fields to textarea, select box, and radiobutton.

Creation of a new page

We will now add a new page manually in our employee application, which will list all the employee names and their respective designations.

Let us include following use-cases to make our application more interesting:

- If age < 30 then, designation – Developer
- If age >= 30 && age <40 then, designation – Senior Developer
- If age >= 40 then, designation – Architect

Time for action – Creation of the new page

We will now create a new page (`employee_details.erb`) that will display the employee name and designation.

Follow these steps to create the page:

1. Create an action `employee_details` in `employee_controller`. We write all the database queries using Rhom, which is an ORM of Rhodes:

```
def employee_details
    @employee = Employee.find(:all)
end
```

By adding `Employee.find(:all)` we will return an array of an object from the Employee Model.

2. Create a page `employee_details.erb` and `employee_details.bb.erb` in the `Employee` directory and add the following lines to `employee_details.erb`:

```
<div class="pageTitle">
  <h1>Employees Details</h1>
</div>

<div class="toolbar">
  <div class="leftItem regularButton">
    <a href="<%= Rho::RhoConfig.start_path %>">Home</a>
  </div>
  <div class="rightItem regularButton">
    <a class="button" href="<%= url_for :action => :new %>">New</
a>
  </div>
</div>

<div class="content">
  <ul>
    <% @employees.each do |employee| %>

        <li>
          <a href="<%= url_for :action => :show, :id => employee.
object %>">
            <span class="title"><%= employee.name %> is <%= find_
desigation(employee.age.to_i)%></span><span class="disclosure_
indicator"></span>
          </a>
        </li>
```

```
    <% end %>
  </ul>
</div>
```

3. And, add these lines to `employee_details.bb.erb`:

```
<div id="pageTitle">
   <h1>Employees Details</h1>
</div>


<div id="toolbar">
    <%= link_to "New", :action => :new %>
    <%= link_to "Home", RhoConfig::start_path %>
</div>

<div id="content">
  <table>
    <tr>
    <% @employees.each do |obj| %>

          <td class="recordLabel"><%= link_to "#{obj.name} is 
#{find_desigation(obj.age.to_i)}  ", :action => :show, :id => obj.
object %></td>

    <% end %>
    </tr>
  </table>
</div>
```

We have used a helper method find_designation, which returns the designation of that employee. This helper is created in the next step.

4. Create a file `employee_helper.rb` in the helpers folder.

5. Include the `employee_helper` in controller so that it can be accessed in our view:

```
require 'helpers/employee_helper'
include EmployeeHelper
Add the logic in employee_helper.rb which we created in the last 
section
module EmployeeHelper
  def find_desigation age
    if age < 30=
      return "Developer"
    elsif age >= 30 and age < 40
      return "Senior Developer"
```

```
    else
      return " Architect"
    end
  end
end
```

6. Edit `index.erb` file in app folder to add a link:

```
        <li>
      <a href="<%= url_for :controller => :Employee, :action =>
:employee_details %>"><span class="title"> Employee Details</
span><span class="disclosure_indicator"/></a>
    </li>
```

7. Edit `index.bb.erb` in the app folder and add a link to our page for Blackberry:

```
<tr>
        <td class="recordLabel">  <%= link_to "Employee Details",
:controller => :Employee, :action => :employee_details%>
</td>
```

Now, build this code for iPhone as explained in this chapter earlier:

```
$rake run:iphone
```

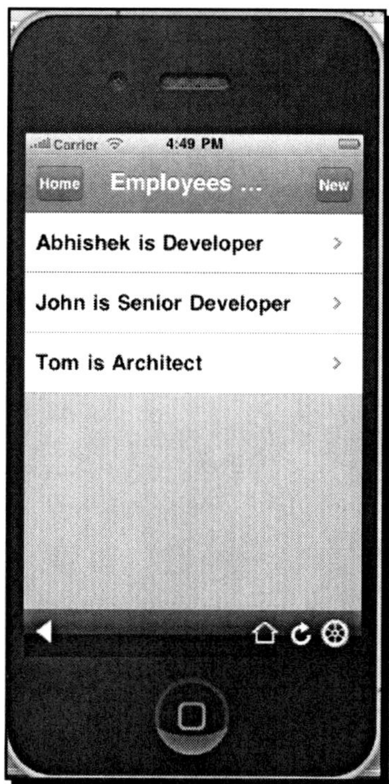

8. And similarly for Blackberry by:

```
$rake run:bb
```

We just created a new page in which the designation of employees are calculated on the basis of their age. We have also learnt how to write a helper method in our application.

Summary

In this chapter we have covered the following points:

- Creating a Rhodes application, using and understanding Model view controller architecture
- Exploring the directory structure of a Rhodes application
- Investigating CRUD operations generated using the Rhogen command
- Created and inserted a new page in our application

In the next chapter we will learn how to interact with a database using Rhom, which is Rhomobile Object-relational mapping(ORM).

4
Rhom—Playing with the Local Database

In the last chapter, with the help of the Rhogen command, we created an employee application for various smartphones. We have also created an employee model and linked this to our homepage.

In this chapter, we'll explore Rhom, which is Object-Relational Mapping (ORM) provided by Rhodes and look at how it manipulates data in our application. We'll find how ORM manages table relationships in this chapter and dig into the ORM object life cycle.

What is ORM?

ORM stands for Object-Relational Mapping. ORM libraries map database tables to classes, rows of those tables to objects of the class, and columns to object attributes. Object wraps a row of a database table or view, encapsulates the database access, and adds domain logic on that data.

ORM connects business objects and database tables to create a domain model where logic and data are presented in one wrapping.

In addition, the ORM classes wrap our database tables to provide a set of class-level methods that perform table-level operations. For example, we might need to find the Employee with a particular ID. This is implemented as a class method that returns the corresponding Employee object. In Ruby code, this will look like:

```
employee= Employee.find(1)
```

This code will return an employee object whose ID is 1.

Exploring Rhom

Rhom is a mini Object Relational Mapper (ORM) for Rhodes. It is similar to another ORM, Active Record in Rails but with limited features. Interaction with the database is simplified, as we don't need to worry about which database is being used by the phone. iPhone uses SQLite and Blackberry uses HSQL and SQLite depending on the device.

Now we will create a new model and see how Rhom interacts with the database.

Time for action – Creating a company model

We will create one more model company, which is similar to the employee model that we created in the last chapter. In addition to a default attribute ID that is created by Rhodes, we will have one attribute name that will store the name of the company.

Now, we will go to the application directory and run the following command:

```
$ rhogen model company name
```

which will generate the following:

```
[ADDED]  app/Company/index.erb
[ADDED]  app/Company/edit.erb
[ADDED]  app/Company/new.erb
[ADDED]  app/Company/show.erb
[ADDED]  app/Company/index.bb.erb
[ADDED]  app/Company/edit.bb.erb
[ADDED]  app/Company/new.bb.erb
[ADDED]  app/Company/show.bb.erb
[ADDED]  app/Company/company_controller.rb
[ADDED]  app/Company/company.rb
[ADDED]  app/test/company_spec.rb
```

We can notice the number of files generated by the Rhogen command, which was explained in the last chapter.

Now, we will add a link on the index page so that we can browse it from our homepage.

Add a link in the `index.erb` file for all the phones except Blackberry. If the target phone is a Blackberry, add this link to the `index.bb.erb` file inside the app folder. As I've explained previously, we will have different views for Blackberry.

```
<li>
    <a href="<%= url_for :controller => :Company %>"><span
class="title"> Company</span><span class="disclosure_indicator"/></a>
  </li>
```

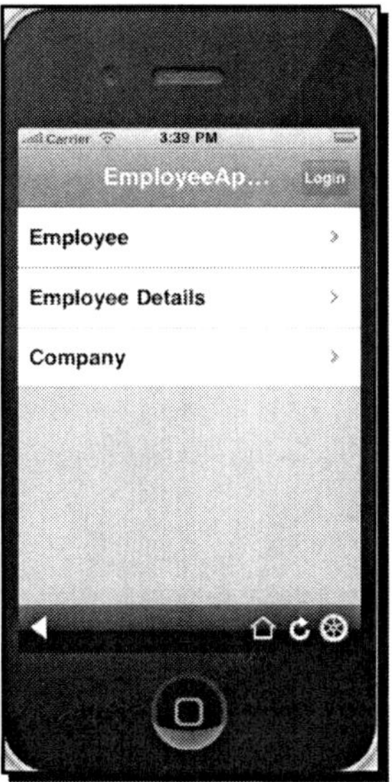

We can see from the image that **a Company** link is created on the homepage of our application. Now, we can build our application to add some dummy data.

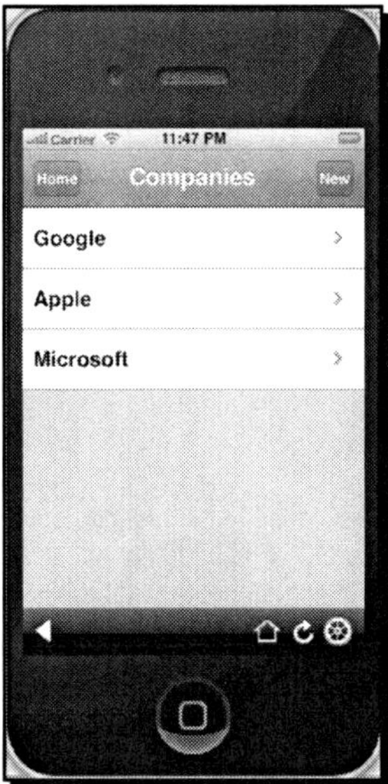

You can see that we have added three companies **Google**, **Apple**, and **Microsoft**.

What just happened?

We just created a model company with an attribute name, made a link to access it from our homepage, and added some dummy data to it. We will add a few companies' names because it will help us in the next section.

Association

Associations are connections between two models, which make common operations simpler and easier for your code. So we will create an association between the Employee model and the Company model.

Time for ation – Creating an association between employee and company

The relationship between an employee and a company can be defined as "An employee can be in only one company but one company may have many employees". So now we will be adding an association between an employee and the company model. After we make entries for the company in the company model, we would be able to see the company select box populated in the employee form.

The relationship between the two models is defined in the `employee.rb` file as:

```
belongs_to :company_id, 'Company'
```

Here, `Company` corresponds to the model name and `company_id` corresponds to the foreign key.

Since at present we have the `company` field instead of `company_id` in the employee model, we will rename `company` to `company_id`.

To retrieve all the companies, which are stored in the Company model, we need to add this line in the new action of the `employee_controller`:

```
@companies =  Company.find(:all)
```

The `find` command is provided by Rhom, which is used to form a query and retrieve results from the database. `Company.find(:all)` will return all the values stored in the Company model in the form of an array of objects.

Now, we will edit the `new.erb` and `edit.erb` files present inside the Employee folder.

```
<h4 class="groupTitle">Company</h4>
<ul>
    <li>
```

```
<select name="employee[company_id]">
    <% @companies.each do |company|%>
        <option value="<%= company.object%>"
     <%= "selected"  if company.object == @employee.company_id%>
    >
    <%=company.name %></option>
        <%end%>
        </select>
     </li>
</ul>
```

If you observe in the code, we have created a select box for selecting a company. Here we have defined a variable `@companies` that is an array of objects. And in each object we have two fields named company name and its ID. We have created a loop and shown all the companies that are there in the `@companies` object.

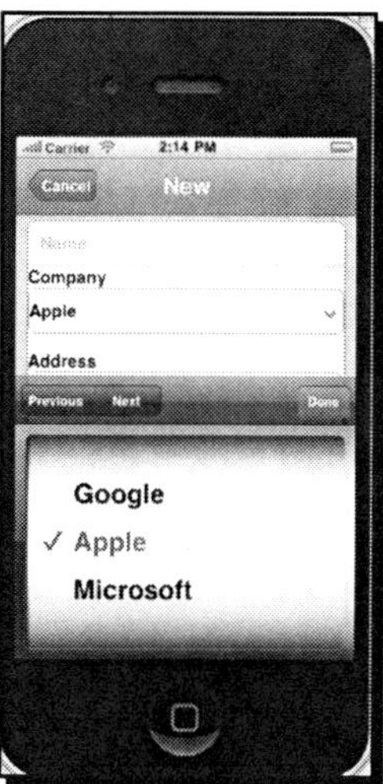

In the above image the companies are populated in the select box, which we added before and it is displayed in the employee form.

What just happened?

We just created an association between the employee and company model and used this association to populate the company select box present in the employee form.

> As of now, Rhom has fewer features then other ORMs like Active Record. As of now there is very little support for database associations.

Exploring methods available for Rhom

Now, we will learn various methods available in Rhom for CRUD operation. Generally, we need to Create, Read, Update, and Delete an object of a model. Rhom provides various helper methods to carry out these operations:

- `delete_all`: deletes all the rows that satisfy the given conditions.

  ```
  Employee.delete_all(:conditions => {gender=>'Male'})
  ```

  The above command will delete all the male employees.

- `destroy`: this destroys the Rhom object that is selected.

  ```
  @employee = Employee.find(:all).first
  @employee.destroy
  ```

  This will delete the first object of employees, which is stored in `@employee` variable.

- `find`: this returns Rhom object(s) based on arguments.
- We can pass the following arguments:
- `:all`: returns all objects from the model
- `:first`: returns the first object
- `:conditions`: this is optional and is a hash of attribute/values to match with (i.e. `{'name' => 'John'}`)
- `:order`: it is an optional attribute that is used to order the list
- `:orderdir`: it is an optional attribute that is used to order the list in the desired manner ('ASC' - default, 'DESC')
- `:select`: it is an optional value which is an array of strings that are needed to be returned with the object
- `:per_page`: it is an optional value that specifies the maximum number of items that can be returned
- `:offset`: it is an optional attribute that specifies the offset from the beginning of the list
- Example:

  ```
  @employees = Employee.find(:all, :order => 'name', :orderdir =>
  'DESC')
  ```

  This will return an array of employee objects that are ordered by name in the descending order:

  ```
  Employee. find( :all,:conditions =>["age > 40"],  :select =>
  [name,company] )
  ```

It will return the name and company of all the employees whose age is greater then 40.

- `new` : Creates a new Rhom object based on the provided attributes, or initializes an empty Rhom object.

  ```
  @company = Company.new({'name'=>'ABC Inc.')
  ```

  It will only create an object of Company class and will save to the database only on explicitly saving it.

- `save` : Saves the current Rhom object to the database.

  ```
  @company.save
  ```

  It will save company object to the database and returns true or false depending on the success of the operation.

- `Create` : Creates a new Rhom object and saves it to the database. This is the fastest way to insert an item to a database.

  ```
  @company = Company.create({'name' => 'Google'})
  ```

  It will insert a row with the name "Google" in the database.

- `Paginate`: It is used to display a fixed number of records on each page.

  ```
  paginate(:page => 1, :per_page => 20)
  ```

  It will return records numbered from 21 to 40.

- `update_attributes(attributes)`: Updates the specified attributes of the current Rhom object and saves it to the database.

  ```
  @employee = Employee.find(:all).first
  @employee. update_attributes({'age' => 23})
  ```

  The age of the first employee stored in the database is updated to 23.

We have now understood all the basic helper methods available in Rhom that will help us to perform all the basic operations on the database. Now we will create a page in our application and then use the find method to show the filtered result.

Time for action – Filtering record by company and gender

We will create a page that will allow us to filter all the records based on company and gender, and then use the find command to show the filtered results on the next page.

We will follow these steps to create the page:

1. Create a link for filter page on the home page i.e. `index.erb` in the app folder:

```
<li>
      <a href="<%= url_for :controller => :Employee, :action => :
filter_employee_form %>"><span class="title"> Filter Employee </
span><span class="disclosure_indicator"/></a>
    </li>
```

We can see in the screenshot that a **Filter Employee** link is created on the home page.

2. Create an action `filter_employee_form` in `employee_controller.rb`:

```
def filter_employee_form
  @companies =  Company.find(:all)
  end
```

We have used the find helper provided by Rhom that will retrieve all the companies and store them in `@companies`.

3. Create a page `filter_employee_form.erb` in the `app/Employee` folder and write the following code:

```
<div class="pageTitle">
    <h1>Filter Page</h1>
</div>

<div class="toolbar">
  <div class="leftItem backButton">
    <a class="cancel" href="<%= url_for :action => :index
```

```
>">Cancel</a>
  </div>
</div>

<div class="content">
    <form method="POST" action="<%= url_for :controller => :
Employee, :action => :filter_employee_result %>">

          <h4 class="groupTitle">Gender</h4>
          <ul>
               <li><label for="gender">Male</label>
                   <input type="radio" name="gender"
value="Male"/>
               </li>
               <li><label for="gender">Female</label>
                   <input type="radio" name="gender"
value="Female"/>
               </li>
          </ul>
         <h4 class="groupTitle">Company</h4>
         <ul>
             <li>
                 <select name="company_id">
            <% @companies.each do |company|%>
                     <option value="<%= company.object%>"
            >
            <%=company.name %></option>
                 <%end%>
                 </select>
             </li>
         </ul>


        <input type="submit" class="standardButton" value="Filter"
/>
    </form>
</div>
```

As we can see, this page is divided into three sections: toolbar, title, and content. If we see the content section, we have created radio buttons for Gender and a select box to list all the companies. We can select either Male or Female from the radio button and one company from the list of dynamically populated companies.

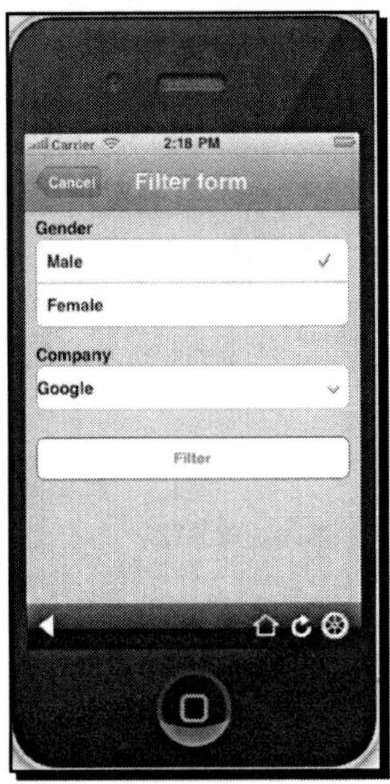

4. Create an action `filter_employee_result` in `employee_controller.rb`:

```
def filter_employee_result
    @employees = Employee.find(:all, :conditions =>{'gender' => @
params['gender'],'company_id'=> @params['company_id']})
  end
```

The `conditions` symbol in the find statement is used to specify the condition for the database query and `@params` is a hash that contains the selections made by the user in the filter form. `@params['gender']` and `@params['company']` contains the gender and `company_id` is selected on the filter page.

5. Create a file called `filter_employee_result.erb` and place it in the `app/Employee` folder.

```
<div class="pageTitle">
  <h1>Filter by Company and Gender</h1>
</div>

<div class="toolbar">
  <div class="leftItem regularButton">
```

```
      <a href="<%= Rho::RhoConfig.start_path %>">Home</a>
    </div>
    <div class="rightItem regularButton">
      <a class="button" href="<%= url_for :action => :new %>">New</
a>
    </div>
</div>

<div class="content">
    <ul>
      <% @employees.each do |employee| %>
          <li>
            <a href="<%= url_for :action => :show, :id => employee.
object %>">
              <span class="title"><%= employee.name %></span><span
class="disclosure_indicator"></span>
            </a>
          </li>
      <% end %>
    </ul>
</div>
```

This result page is again divided into three sections: toolbar, title, and content. All the employees filtered on the basis of specified selections made on the filter page are stored in `@employees` and displayed inside the content section of this page.

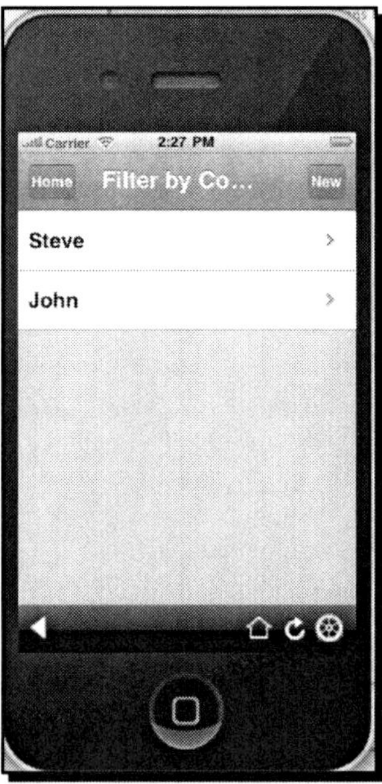

What just happened?

We created a filter page to filter all the employees on the basis of their gender and company. Then, by using the find method of Rhom, we filtered employees for the specified gender and company and displayed the results on a new page.

Have a go hero – find (*args) Advanced proposal

We have learnt in this section to use find helper to write only simple queries. To write advanced queries, Rhom provides find (*args) Advanced.

A normal query would look like this:

```
@employees = Employee.find(:all, :conditions =>{'gender' => @params['g
ender'],'company_id'=> @params['company_id']})
```

This can also be written as:

```
   @employees = Employee.find(:all, :conditions =>{
      {:name =>'gender' ,:op =>"like"} => @params['gender'],
      {:name =>'company_id', :op => 'like'}=> @params['company_id']},
:op => 'AND'
      )
```

The advantage of using the latter form is that we can write advanced options with our query.

Let's say we want to create a hash condition for the following SQL:

```
find( :all,
      :conditions =>["LOWER(description) like ? or LOWER(title) like
?", query, query],
      :select => ['title','description'] )
```

It can be written in this way:

```
find( :all,
      :conditions => { {:func=>'LOWER', :name=>'description', :
op=>'LIKE'}=>query,
       {:func=>'LOWER', :name=>'title', :op=>'LIKE'}=>query}, :op =>
'OR',
      :select => ['title','description'])
```

How Rhodes stores data

As we have already discussed, iPhone and Android use SQLite. And for Blackberry it uses SQLite on a device it supports, otherwise it will use HSQL database. But the question is how does Rhom store data and how can we handle migration?

Rhodes provides two ways to store data in a phone:

1. Property Bag
2. Fixed Schema

Property Bag

Property Bag is the default option available for our models. In Property Bag, the entire data is stored in a single table with a fixed number of columns.

The table contains the following columns:

- Source_id
- attribute
- object
- value
- update_type

When you use the Property Bag model, you don't have to track schema changes (adding or removing attributes). However, Rhodes uses the Property Bag schema to store app data in a SQL database. If the internal Property Bag schema changes after an application is updated or reloaded, the database will be (re)created and all existing data would be erased. See `rhodes\lib\rhodes.rb` and `rhodes\lib\framework\rhodes.rb` for the internal database schema version:

```
DBVERSION = '2.0.3'
```

On the first launch of the application after it is installed/updated/reloaded, a database will be (re)created if `app_db_version` in the `rhoconfig.txt` is different from what it was before. If the database version is changed and the database is recreated, then all data in the database will be erased.

Since Rhodes 2.2.4, the Rhosync session is kept in the database, so `SyncEngine.logged_in` will return true. At the start of the application we can check if the database is empty and the user is still logged in and then run sync without interactive login.

Application db version in `rhoconfig.txt`:

```
app_db_version = '1.0'
```

We can list a few advantages and disadvantages of the fixed schema:

Advantages

1. It is simple to use, attributes are not required to be specified before use
2. We don't need to migrate data if we add/remove attributes

Disadvantages

1. Size is three times bigger than the fixed schema
2. Slow while synchronizing

Fixed Schema model

While using the Fixed Schema model, the developer is entirely responsible for the structure of the SQL schema. So when you add or delete some properties, or just change app logic you may need to perform data migration or database reset. To track schema changes, use the `schema_version` parameter in the model:

```
class Employee
    include Rhom::FixedSchema
     set :schema_version, '1.1'
end
```

We can see that we have set the schema version to 1.1. Now, if we change the schema then we have to change the version in the model.

We can list a few advantages and disadvantages of the fixed schema:

Advantages

- Smaller size, you can specify index for only required attributes.
- Faster sync time than Property bag.

Disadvantage

- You have to support all schema changes.

This is how the model looks in a Fixed Schema:

```
class Employee
  include Rhom::FixedSchema
  # Uncomment the following line to enable sync with Employee.
  # enable :sync
  set :schema_version, '1.1'
  property :name, :string
```

```
    property :age, :string
    property :company, :string
    property :address, :string
    property :gender, :string
    property :salary, :string
    #add model specifc code here
  end
```

To add a column in the table we have to add a property and then reset the Device. It is important to note that we have to reset the database to reflect the changes.

To create an index in fixed schema we will write following line in model:

```
index :by_name_tag, [:name, :tag] #will create index for name and tag
columns
```

To create a primary key in the fixed schema we will write following line in model:

```
unique_index :by_phone, [:phone]
```

Choosing between Property Bag or Fixed Schema depends on your requirement. If your schema is not fixed and keeps changing then use Property Bag and if we have huge data and non-changing schema then we use Fixed Schema.

Summary

We have the covered following topics in this chapter:

- What is ORM
- What is Rhom
- What is an Association
- We have explored various commands provided by Rhom
- Difference between Property Bag and Fixed Schema.

Now that we've learned about using Rhom with Rhodes, we will learn about RhoSync in the next chapter.

5

RhoSync—Synchronizing Your Data

In the previous chapter, we learnt Rhom in our employee application. I think we are very much clearer how a normal Rhodes application works along with Rhom.

In this chapter, we will learn about the synchronization framework RhoSync that keeps application data current and available on user's smart phones. The information is stored locally on a user's device and is available even when the user is disconnected or offline. The RhoSync server handles the job of connecting the Rhodes client to a backend application, keeping track of multiple devices and what information they request, and sending them just those updates. RhoSync can also be used to keep track of the changes in data and then efficiently "push" those changes to the connected users via the native smart phone push SDKs.

Synchronization servers for mobile apps have existed for a long time. RhoSync is different from other sync servers as it has very high scalability via NoSQL caching. It can also easily synchronize using source adapter, and also supports native smart phone push APIs.

RhoSync consists of the following components:

- Synchronization Framework – This is the core of RhoSync. It facilitates data synchronization between the Rhodes/RhoSync-Client and a third-party source (SOAP, REST, etc.). Each source is synchronized by creating a simple "source adapter" class, which will be discussed later in the chapter.
- REST API – RhoSync exposes a simple REST API for interacting with an application.
- Administration Console – It is a Sinatra server that is used for manipulating and peeking into a running RhoSync app. The console uses the RhoSync API for everything it does.
- Asynchronous Job System – RhoSync uses the `resque` library to provide asynchronous execution of various tasks it needs to perform. These tasks include source adapter execution, sending push messages, preparing bulk data, etc. Resque is dead-simple to use and highly extensible, which makes it easy to use for other functionalities not described here.

Generating a RhoSync application

We will now create a simple RhoSync application using the `rhosync` command. Thereafter, we will understand the folder structure of RhoSync. We will also look into the options available with the administration console.

Time for action – Creating a RhoSync application

Using the `rhosync` command, let us now create our employee-server RhoSync application.

The `rhosync` utility is a command line tool for generating RhoSync applications and sources. For creating our employee-server application, we will run the following command on command prompt:

```
rhosync app employee-server
    Generating with app generator:
        [ADDED]  employee-server/config.ru
        [ADDED]  employee-server/settings/settings.yml
        [ADDED]  employee-server/settings/license.key
        [ADDED]  employee-server/application.rb
        [ADDED]  employee-server/Rakefile
        [ADDED]  employee-server/spec/spec_helper.rb
```

The app name is passed as a parameter. Now what `rhosync` utility does is to generate a directory for your application with all the necessary files to get started.

You can check what options are available with RhoSync by running the following commands on the command prompt.

$ rhosync

Usage: `rhosync generator_name [options] [args]`

RhoSync generator:

The available generators are:

`app`	Generates a new rhosync application
`source`	Generates a new source adapter

General options:

`-p, --pretend`	Run, but do not make any changes
`-f, --force`	Overwrite files that already exist
`-s, --skip`	Skip files that already exist
`-d, --delete`	Delete files that have previously been generated with this generator
`--no-color`	Don't colorize the output
`-h, --help`	Show this message
`--debug`	Do not catch errors

Here's a basic rundown of each of the files that were just generated:

- `config.ru` – This is a rackup file that will load your application. RhoSync uses the excellent Sinatra web framework to run the application.
- `settings/settings.yml` – This contains settings for your application such as redis connection details, source adapters present and their parameters. You can also put your custom settings here.
- `settings/license.key` – This contains the RhoSync license associated with your application. The default license allows up to ten devices to synchronize with the application.
- `application.rb` – The RhoSync application class where you can implement authentication. You can also add other custom methods here to use in your application. This class is a singleton, so all methods should be added to the class << self block.
- `Rakefile` – This contains tasks that can be run from the terminal.

- `spec/spec_helper.rb` – A helper file that loads the environment for running specs.

After understanding the directory structure, now we will understand how to run our application.

Each RhoSync application uses rake to manage development tasks such as starting/stopping the app, starting resque task, and running specs.

To run a RhoSync rake task, simply type rake the-task-to-run in your RhoSync application's root directory. Before starting the RhoSync server, we need to make sure that the `redis` server is already running.

Starting the Redis server:

```
cd employee-server/
rake redis:start
```

```
[7681] 06 Feb 23:25:06 # Warning: no config file specified, using the default co
nfig. In order to specify a config file use 'redis-server /path/to/redis.conf'
[7681] 06 Feb 23:25:06 * Server started, Redis version 2.0.4
[7681] 06 Feb 23:25:06 * DB loaded from disk: 0 seconds
[7681] 06 Feb 23:25:06 * The server is now ready to accept connections on port 6
379
[7681] 06 Feb 23:25:07 - DB 0: 23 keys (0 volatile) in 48 slots HT.
[7681] 06 Feb 23:25:07 - 0 clients connected (0 slaves), 1079056 bytes in use
[7681] 06 Feb 23:25:12 - DB 0: 23 keys (0 volatile) in 32 slots HT.
[7681] 06 Feb 23:25:12 - 0 clients connected (0 slaves), 1079056 bytes in use
[7681] 06 Feb 23:25:17 - DB 0: 23 keys (0 volatile) in 32 slots HT.
[7681] 06 Feb 23:25:17 - 0 clients connected (0 slaves), 1079056 bytes in use
[7681] 06 Feb 23:25:22 - DB 0: 23 keys (0 volatile) in 32 slots HT.
[7681] 06 Feb 23:25:22 - 0 clients connected (0 slaves), 1079056 bytes in use
[7681] 06 Feb 23:25:27 - DB 0: 23 keys (0 volatile) in 32 slots HT.
[7681] 06 Feb 23:25:27 - 0 clients connected (0 slaves), 1079056 bytes in use
[7681] 06 Feb 23:25:32 - DB 0: 23 keys (0 volatile) in 32 slots HT.
[7681] 06 Feb 23:25:32 - 0 clients connected (0 slaves), 1079056 bytes in use
[7681] 06 Feb 23:25:38 - DB 0: 23 keys (0 volatile) in 32 slots HT.
[7681] 06 Feb 23:25:38 - 0 clients connected (0 slaves), 1079056 bytes in use
```

Now once Redis is started, we can start the RhoSync server:

```
rake rhosync:start
```

```
[11:29:10 PM 2011-02-06] Rhosync Server v2.1.1 started...
[11:29:10 PM 2011-02-06] ************************************************************
*****

[11:29:10 PM 2011-02-06] WARNING: Change the session secret in config.ru from <c
hangeme> to something secure.
[11:29:10 PM 2011-02-06]   i.e. running `rake secret` in a rails app will genera
te a secret you could use.

[11:29:10 PM 2011-02-06] ************************************************************
```

The above command will start your RhoSync server on the default port i.e. `9292`. We can also specify the port number on which you want to start the RhoSync server using the following command:

```
Rackup config.ru -p <port number>
```

Example: To start RhoSync on port 8080, type:

```
rackup config.ru -p 8080
```

A RhoSync application exposes a web interface, which runs on `http://localhost:9292/console/` by default. We can also open the console by running the following command in your application directory:

```
rake rhosync:web
```

This web console is intended to be used for basic tests on your RhoSync application. The following login page will appear at the beginning. We can enter default credentials i.e. **rhoadmin** as login username with no password and then click **submit to log in**:

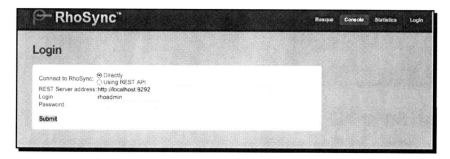

After logging in, we can see all the available devices for the application. Only 10 devices are available for development purposes. You can clear all the listed devices by clicking **reset**:

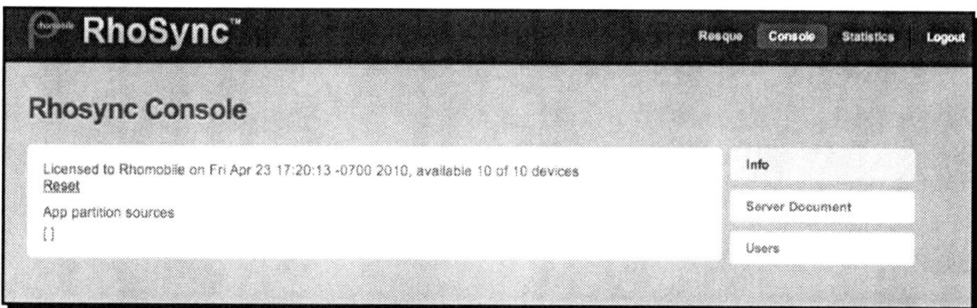

We can see the list of registered users by clicking the **Users** tab on the right. We can even create new users by clicking **Create User**:

We can see the list of database hash available by clicking the **Server Document** on the right:

What just happened?

We started theRedis and RhoSync server for running our Rhodes application. We looked into various options available in the Administration Console.

Have a go hero – Disable the web interface

Sometimes you may feel that the web interface is not required in your application. You can disable the interface by editing `config.ru`— rackup file.

```
# Setup the url map
run Rack::URLMap.new \
   "/"         => Rhosync::Server.new,
   "/resque"   => Resque::Server.new, # If you don't want resque
frontend, disable it here
   #"/console"  => RhosyncConsole::Server.new # If you don't want
rhosync frontend, disable it here
```

RhoSync source adapters

After creating our simple RhoSync application, we need a source adapter to integrate it with our backend application.

To define a RhoSync source, you just need to update a handful of operations such as login, query, sync, create, update, delete, and logoff, which would interact with your backend data source.

Time for action – Creating source adapter

We will now create a source adapter for our employee-server application that we created in the last section.

For creating a source adapter, we will use the RhoSync command utility. The following command will generate the employee source adapter:

```
rhosync source employee
    Generating with source generator:
         [ADDED]  sources/employee.rb
         [ADDED]  spec/sources/employee_spec.rb
```

We can see that two files are created by running the above mentioned command. The file `employee.rb` is the source adapter and the other file, `employee_spec.rb`, is a unit test file that we will discuss in detail in Chapter 8.

The above command will also edit `settings/settings.yml` and add the product adapter to the sources section with some default options:

```
:sources:
  Employee:
    :poll_interval: 300
```

This code means that `Employee` is our source adapter and its `poll_interval` is 300. `Poll interval` is the total seconds in which the corresponding source will synchronize with the device.

Inside `employee.rb`, there is a class `Employee` that is a subclass of `SourceAdapter`:

```
class Employee < SourceAdapter
  def initialize(source,credential)
    super(source,credential)
  end
```

```
  def login
    # TODO: Login to your data source here if necessary
  end

  def query(params=nil)
    # TODO: Query your backend data source and assign the records
    # to a nested hash structure called @result. For example:
    # @result = {
    #   "1"=>{"name"=>"Acme", "industry"=>"Electronics"},
    #   "2"=>{"name"=>"Best", "industry"=>"Software"}
    # }
    raise SourceAdapterException.new("Please provide some code to read
records from the backend data source")
  end

  def sync
    # Manipulate @result before it is saved, or save it
    # yourself using the Rhosync::Store interface.
    # By default, super is called below which simply saves @result
    super
  end

  def create(create_hash,blob=nil)
    # TODO: Create a new record in your backend data source
    # If your rhodes rhom object contains image/binary data
    # (has the image_uri attribute), then a blob will be provided
    raise "Please provide some code to create a single record in the
backend data source using the create_hash"
  end

  def update(update_hash)
    # TODO: Update an existing record in your backend data source
    raise "Please provide some code to update a single record in the
backend data source using the update_hash"
  end

  def delete(object_id)
    # TODO: write some code here if applicable
    # be sure to have a hash key and value for "object"
    # for now, we'll say that its OK to not have a delete operation
    # raise "Please provide some code to delete a single object in the
backend application using the object_id"
  end

  def logoff
```

```
    # TODO: Logout from the data source if necessary
  end
end
```

Your source adapter can use any of these methods to interact with your backend service:

- `Login`: Log in to your backend service (optional)
- `Logoff`: Logoff from your backend service (optional)
- `query(params = nil)`: Query your backend service and build a hash of hashes (required)
- `create(create_hash)`: Create a new record in the backend (optional)
- `update(update_hash)`: Update an existing record in the backend (optional)
- `delete(delete_hash)`: Delete an existing record in the backend (optional)

Similarly, we will create one more source adapter company:

```
rhosync source company
   Generating with source generator:
        [ADDED]  sources/company.rb
        [ADDED]  spec/sources/company_spec.rb
```

It is similar to what we did for the employee source adapter.

What just happened?

We just created two source adapters for employee and company using the `rhosync` command. We also understood the files that were created while running the command.

Configure the Rhodes application to connect to RhoSync

After creating the Rhodes application and the source adapter, now it's the time to connect the RhoSync application with your Rhodes application.

Time for action – Connecting the Rhodes application to RhoSync

As we have seen that RhoSync is a separate application hosted on some servers and the Rhodes application is a different one installed on the mobile client. Rhodes and RhoSync applications will interact with each other using the `https` protocol. RhoSync application runs on port 9292 unless specified.

Open `rhoconfig.txt` in your Rhodes application and add specify the URL for the RhoSync server:

```
syncserver = 'http://localhost:9292/application'
```

If you are developing your app for Android then you have to give the IP address instead of `localhost`. This is because Android simulator does not understand `localhost`.

Now, when you create a build for the phone, it will connect to your server.

To enable sync for your model, go to model `employee.rb` and `company.rb` and add:

```
enable :sync


class Employee
  include Rhom::PropertyBag
   belongs_to :company_id, 'Company'
  # Uncomment the following line to enable sync with Employee.
  enable :sync

  #add model specifc code here
end
Enable sync in company.rb
class Company
  include Rhom::PropertyBag
enable :sync
  #add model specifc code here
end
```

What just happened?

We have configured the Rhodes application to connect it with the RhoSync server. We also learned to enable sync for your model.

Placing data in the Rhodes application from RhoSync

We will now transfer data from the RhoSync server to our Rhodes application using the source adapter.

Time for action – Filling data from RhoSync

Let's understand how to transfer data to our employee application using the RhoSync server.

First, update the query method in your source adapter `company.rb`:

```
    def query(params=nil)
      # TODO: Query your backend data source and assign the records
      # to a nested hash structure called @result. For example:
  @result = {
        "1" => {"name" => "Google"},
        "2" => {"name" => "Microsoft"}
      }
  end
```

In `@result`, we have hash of hashes where the hash key of the outer hash is the ID of each object (as described above in the query method). Each hash key in the inner hash represents an attribute of an individual object. Whatever value we store in `@result`, the same values will be sync to device. Note that, all data types must be strings (so the hash values need to all be strings not integers). For example:

```
  @result = {
        "1" => {"name" => "Google"},
        "2" => {"name" => "Microsoft"}
      }
```

These values will be updated in the company model of Rhodes application.

Similarly, the update employee source adapter:

```
    def query(params=nil)
      # TODO: Query your backend data source and assign the records
      # to a nested hash structure called @result. For example:
  @result = {
        "1" => {
         "name" => "Abhishek Nalwaya",
   "company_id" =>"1",
  "address"=>"Chicago",
  "age"=>"25",
  "gender"=>"Male",
  "salary"=>"200000000"
  },
        "2" => {
  "name" => "John",
         "company_id" =>"1",
  "address"=>"India",
```

```
"age"=>"50",
"gender"=>"Male",
"salary"=>"100000000"}
          }
end
```

Now, start/restart RhoSync and Rhodes application.

When we change something in the RhoSync application, we have to restart the server to reflect the changes.

Click the **Login** title on the home page and enter any username and password, it will work as authentication hasn't been applied yet:

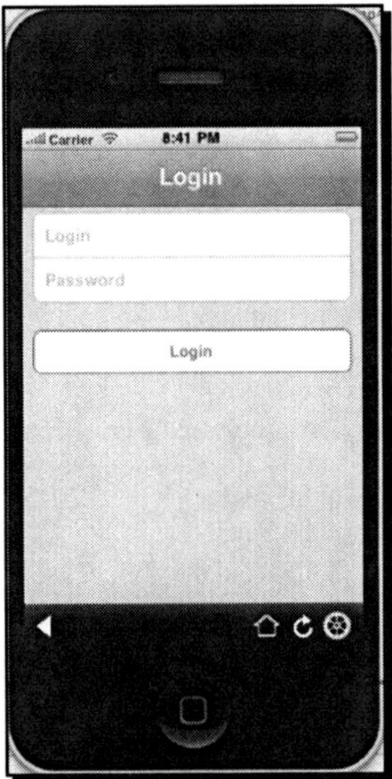

After login, you will get an option **Settings** screen by default, which can be customized to load some other pages too. This page is quite important for troubleshooting. If you want to clear all the data you can click on **Reset Database** or if you want to manually call the sync you can click **Perform Sync**.

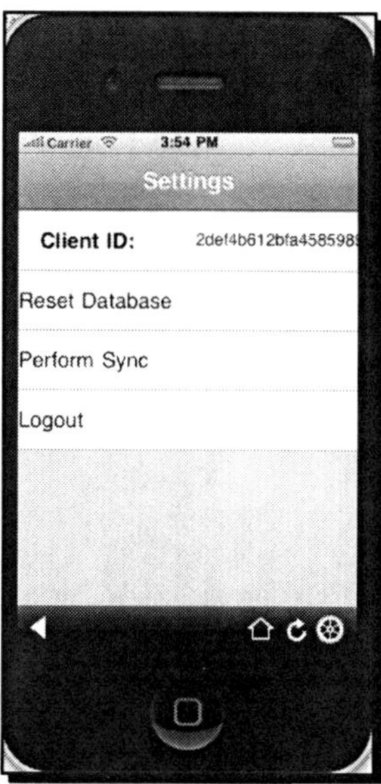

We will now go to the home page by clicking on **Home** in the menu.

We will now navigate to the **Employee** and **Company** pages. Here, the data is being loaded from RhoSync. As shown in the following image, both Companies and Employees values are populated on the device:

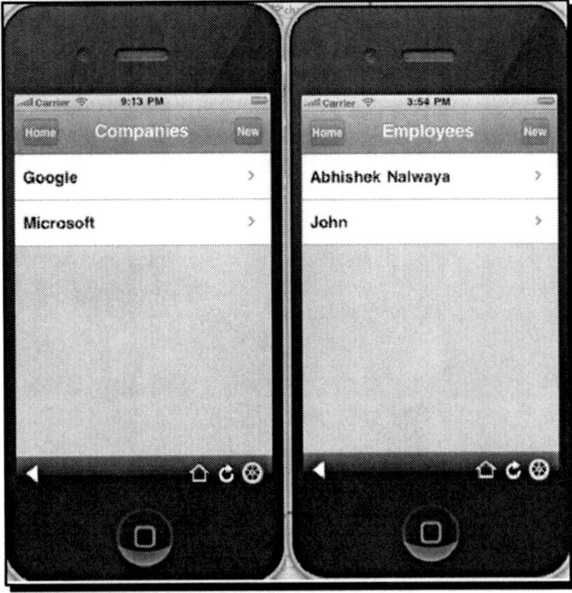

Once this synchronization is done, this data will be available even if we get disconnected. So, RhoSync has added offline capability to our application.

What just happened?

We have loaded the data in our client application from the RhoSync server and navigated through various pages present on the client application.

Connecting to Backend services

Now we will connect to our Backend service. To demonstrate this, I have created a Rails application that is hosted on Heroku. You can use this URL to fetch the data for your application:

```
http://employee-rails.heroku.com/employees
```

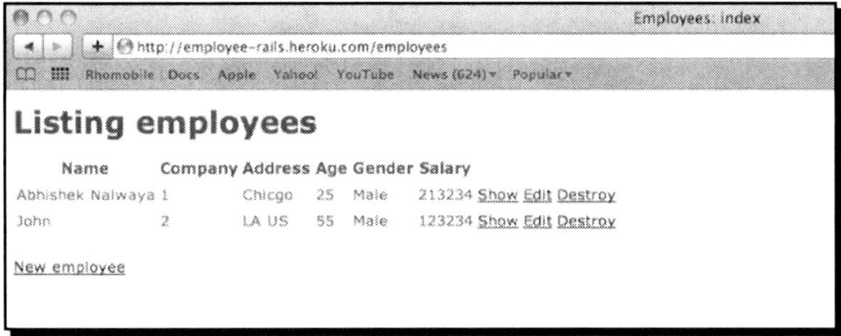

`http://employee-rails.heroku.com/companies`

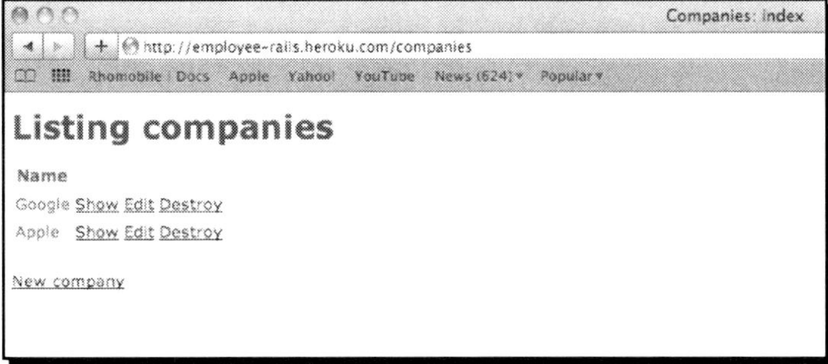

Our RhoSync application will dynamically fetch data from these applications with the help of a request in the JSON format. And then we will feed this data to our phone.

If you open `http://employee-rails.heroku.com/companies.json` you will receive the following data in JSON format:


```
[
{
"company":
{"name":"Google",
"created_at":"2011-02-11T10:51:10Z",
"updated_at":"2011-02-11T10:51:10Z","id":1}
},
{
"company":
{"name":"Apple",
"created_at":"2011-02-11T10:51:22Z",
"updated_at":"2011-02-11T10:51:22Z",
"id":2}
}
}
```

And, when you check `http://employee-rails.heroku.com/employees.json`:


```
[
{"employee":
{"name":"Abhishek Nalwaya",
"address":"Chicgo",
"created_at":"2011-02-11T10:52:11Z",
"updated_at":"2011-02-11T10:52:11Z",
"salary":213234,
"id":1,
"gender":"Male",
"company_id":1,
"age":25
}},
{"employee":{
"name":"John",
"address":"LA US",
"created_at":"2011-02-11T10:52:40Z",
"updated_at":"2011-02-11T10:52:40Z",
"salary":123234,
"id":2,
"gender":"Male",
"company_id":2,
"age":55
}}]
```


Now update the query and initialize methods in the `company.rb` file. Generally, if we have to use any variable in the source adapter, we pre-define it in the initialize method. So, we will define a variable `@base` for storing the URL.

```
def initialize(source,credential)
    @base = "http://employee-rails.heroku.com/companies"
    super(source,credential)
  end
```

Now, in query method we will send a request to the application present on Heroku. We will use the `RestClient` to request the output in JSON format. Then, we will parse it to create an array of Ruby key value pairs that will be stored in `@result`.

```
    def query(params=nil)
      parsed=JSON.parse(RestClient.get(@base +".json").body)
      @result={}
      parsed.each { |item|@result[item["employee"]["id"].to_
  s]=item["employee"] } if parsed
      @result
    end

    def initialize(source,credential)
      @base = "http://employee-rails.heroku.com/companies"
      super(source,credential)
    end


    def query(params=nil)
      parsed=JSON.parse(RestClient.get(@base +".json").body)
      @result={}
      parsed.each { |item|@result[item["company"]["id"].to_
  s]=item["company"] } if parsed
      @result
    end
```

Similarly we will do for employee.rb:

```
    def initialize(source,credential)
      @base = "http://employee-rails.heroku.com/employees"
      super(source,credential)
    end

    def query(params=nil)
      parsed=JSON.parse(RestClient.get(@base +".json").body)
      @result={}
      parsed.each { |item|@result[item["employee"]["id"].to_
  s]=item["employee"] } if parsed
      @result
    end
```

Now, we will start our Rhodes application and restart the RhoSync application. Then, after login, we will be able to see that the data is loaded to the employee and company model as shown in the following images:

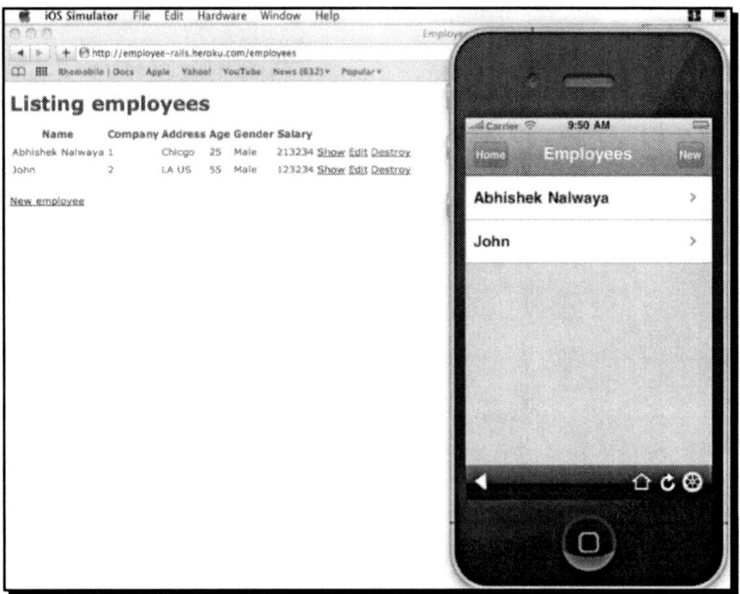

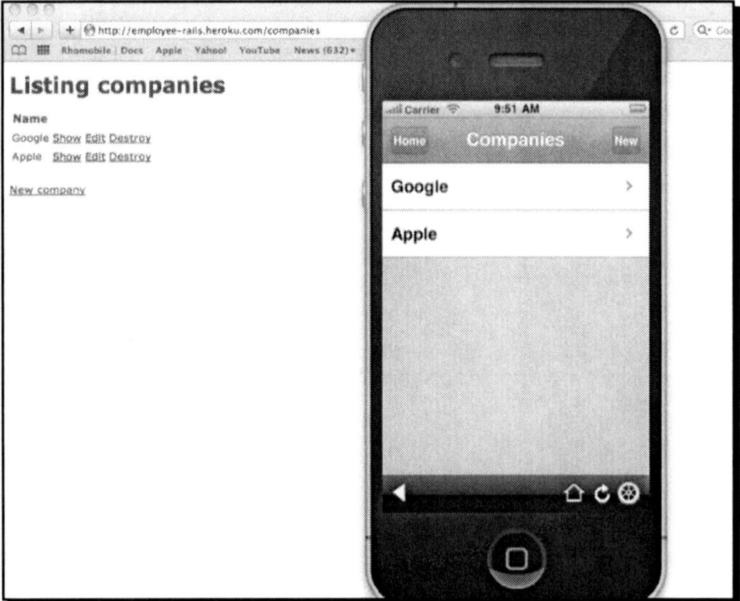

What just happened?

We have just connected our Rhodes application with Backend services using RhoSync.

CRUD operation using RhoSync

Now we will perform the basic CRUD operation to our employee application. RhoSync requires that you write a small amount of Ruby code for the query, create, update, and delete operations for your particular enterprise backend application. The collection of the Ruby code for these operations are referred to as a "source" or "source adapter".

Before starting, we need to understand these operations:

Operations	Verb	URL	Method used in RhoSync
`Create`	`POST`	`http://employee-rails.heroku.com/employees`	create
`Read`	`GET`	`http://employee-rails.heroku.com/employees/:id`	query
`Update`	`PUT`	`http://employee-rails.heroku.com/employees/:id`	update
`Delete`	`DELETE`	`http://employee-rails.heroku.com/employees/:id`	delete

Now update `employee.rb` file as shown below. We will use `RestClient` to request our Heroku application:

```
class Employee < SourceAdapter
  def initialize(source,credential)
    @base = "http://employee-rails.heroku.com/employees"
    super(source,credential)
  end

  def login
  end

  def query(params=nil)
    parsed=JSON.parse(RestClient.get(@base +".json").body)
    @result={}
    parsed.each { |item|@result[item["employee"]["id"].to_
s]=item["employee"] } if parsed
```

```
    @result
  end

  def sync
    super
  end

  def create(create_hash,blob=nil)
    result = RestClient.post(@base,:employee => create_hash)

    # after create we are redirected to the new record.
    # The URL of the new record is given in the location header
    location = "#{result.headers[:location]}.json"

    # We need to get the id of that record and return it as part of
create
    # so rhosync can establish a link from its temporary object on the
    # client to this newly created object on the server

    new_record = RestClient.get(location).body
    JSON.parse(new_record)["employee"]["id"].to_s
  end

  def update(update_hash)
    obj_id = update_hash['id']
    update_hash.delete('id')
    RestClient.put("#{@base}/#{obj_id}",:employee => update_hash)
  end

  def delete(object_id)
    RestClient.delete("#{@base}/#{object_id['id']}")
  end

  def logoff
    # TODO: Logout from the data source if necessary
  end
end
```

And now similarly we will edit for the company source adapter.

Operation	**Verb**	**URL**	**Method used in Rhosync**
Create	POST	http://employee-rails.heroku.com/companies	create
Read	GET	http://employee-rails.heroku.com/companies/:id	query
Update	PUT	http://employee-rails.heroku.com/companies/:id	update
Delete	DELETE	http://employee-rails.heroku.com/companies/:id	delete

Update the `company.rb` file as shown below:

```
class Company < SourceAdapter
  def initialize(source,credential)
    @base = "http://employee-rails.heroku.com/companies"
    super(source,credential)
  end

  def login
    # TODO: Login to your data source here if necessary
  end

  def query(params=nil)
    parsed=JSON.parse(RestClient.get(@base +".json").body)
    @result={}
    parsed.each { |item|@result[item["company"]["id"].to_
s]=item["company"] } if parsed
    @result
  end

  def sync
    # Manipulate @result before it is saved, or save it
    # yourself using the Rhosync::Store interface.
    # By default, super is called below which simply saves @result
    super
  end

  def create(create_hash,blob=nil)
    result = RestClient.post(@base,:company => create_hash)
```

```
    # after create we are redirected to the new record.
    # The URL of the new record is given in the location header
    location = "#{result.headers[:location]}.json"

    # We need to get the id of that record and return it as part of
create
    # so rhosync can establish a link from its temporary object on the
    # client to this newly created object on the server

    new_record = RestClient.get(location).body
    JSON.parse(new_record)["company"]["id"].to_s
  end

  def update(update_hash)
    obj_id = update_hash['id']
    update_hash.delete('id')
    RestClient.put("#{@base}/#{obj_id}",:company => update_hash)
  end

  def delete(object_id)
    RestClient.delete("#{@base}/#{object_id['id']}")
  end

  def logoff
    # TODO: Logout from the data source if necessary
  end
end
```

Restart the RhoSync and Rhodes applications after which we will check all the operations one by one:

Create

Testing the create functionality:

1. Log in to the device by entering any username or password.
2. Click on **Employee** link on home page.
3. Click on **New** in toolbar.
4. Enter some data in the form and click **create**.

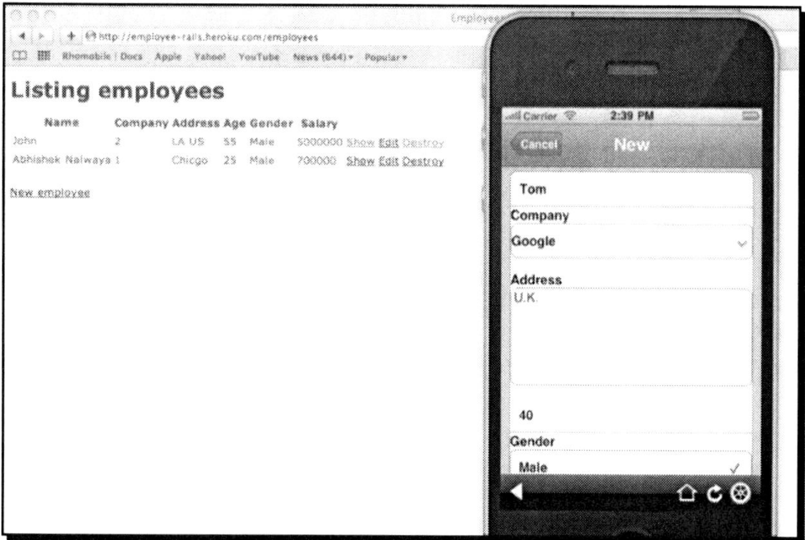

5. Go to the homepage and click **sync**. This will sync with the employees, which you created on the Heroku server.

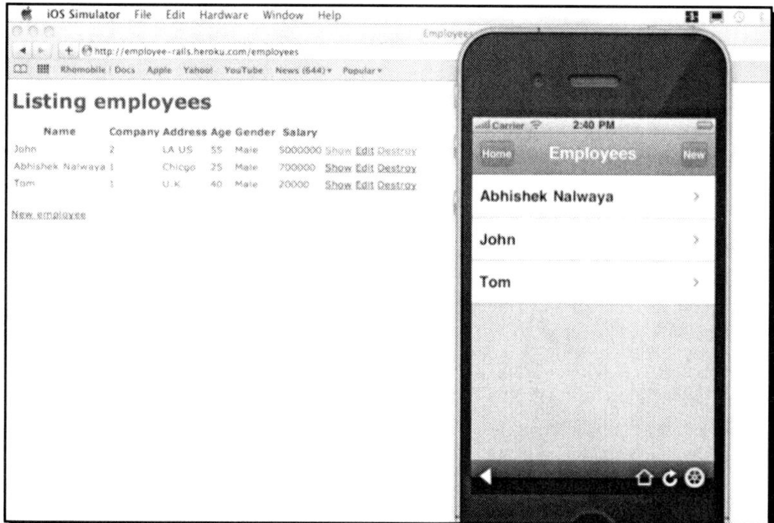

Update

Testing the update functionality:

1. Click on Employee link on the homepage.
2. Click on any employee listed.

3. Edit his detail and click **Update button.**
4. Click on **Sync** on the homepage. This will update the changes to the server.

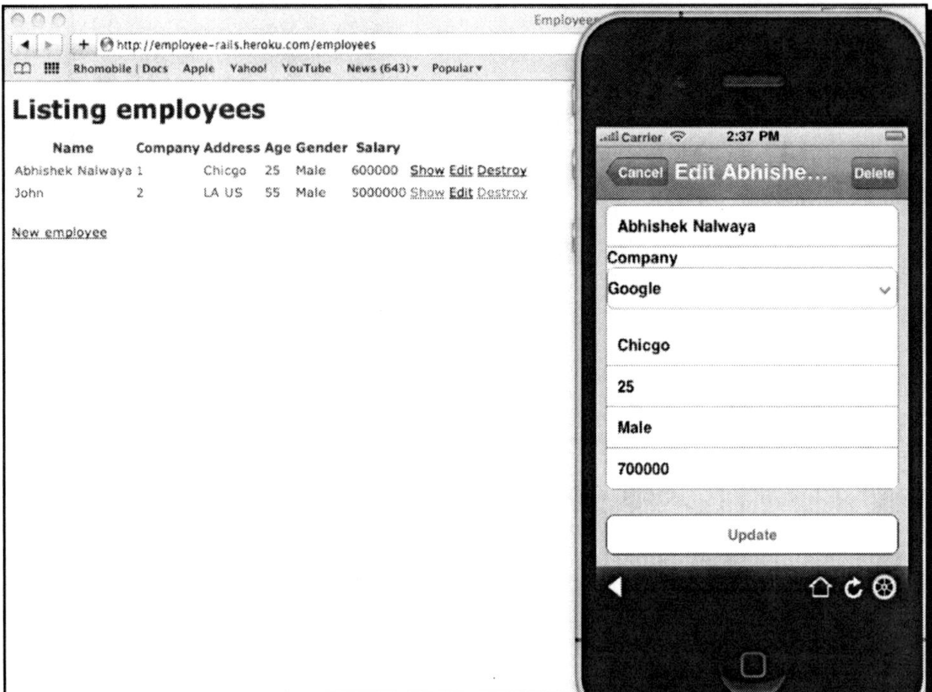

Delete

Testing the delete functionality:

1. Click on **Employee** link on the home page.
2. Click on any employee listed.
3. Click the **Delete** button at the top of page.

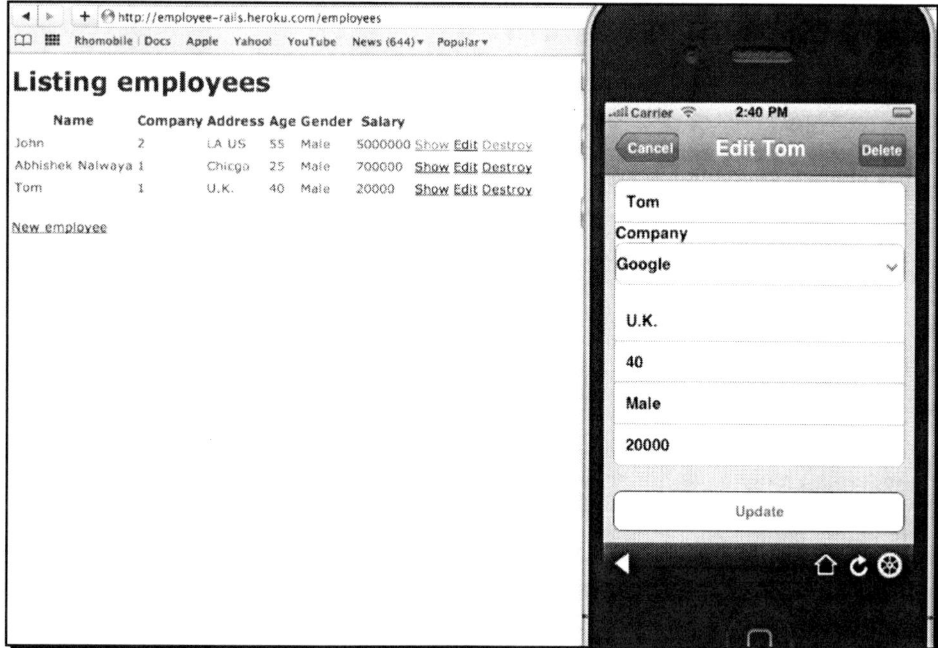

4. Click **Sync** on the home page.

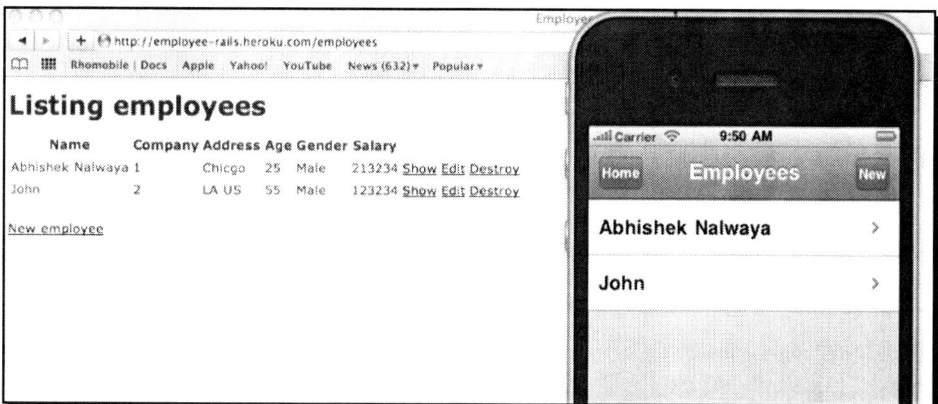

What just happened?

We performed the CRUD operations i.e. Create, Read, Update, and Delete using RhoSync. We connected the Rhodes application to our backend application, which gives the data in JSON format to the RhoSync application.

Filtering datasets with search

If you have a large dataset at your backend service, you don't have to synchronize everything with the SyncEngine. Instead you can filter the synchronized dataset using the SyncEngine's search functionality. Like everything else with the SyncEngine, the search requires a defined callback that is executed when the search results are retrieved from the RhoSync server.

We will use the search method available with Rhodes. The syntax for the search method is `ModelName.search` with a few additional parameters from the following:

- `:source_names` =>Sends a list of source adapter names to RhoSync to search across
- `:search_parms` => Contains the parameter that we want to send
- `:callback` => Contains the callback method that has to be called
- `:callback_param` => Parameter that will be passed to the callback method

Now, we will understand the Notification system that will be available in the callback. When the notification is called, it will receive a variable called `@params`, just like a normal Rhodes controller action.

These parameters are included in all notifications:

- `@params["source_id"]` – The ID of the current model that is being synchronized
- `@params["source_name"]` – Name of the model (i.e. `"Product"`)
- `@params["sync_type"]` – Type of sync used for this model: `"incremental"` or `"bulk"`
- `@params["status"]` – Status of the current sync process: `"in_progress"`, `"error"`, `"ok"`, `"complete"`, `"schema-changed"`

These are the possible values of status, which we can use in our callback:

- `"in_progress"` – incremental sync
    - `@params["total_count"]` – Total number of records that exist for this RhoSync source.
    - `@params["processed_count"]` – Number of records included in the sync page.
    - `@params["cumulative_count"]` – Number of records the SyncEngine has processed so far for this source.
- `"in_progress"` – bulk sync
    - `@params["bulk_status"]` – The state of the bulk sync process: "start", "download", "change_db"

- "error"
  - @params["error_code"] – HTTP response code of the RhoSync server error: 401, 500, 404, etc
  - @params["error_message"] – Response body (if any)
  - @params["error_type"] – Type of RhoSync adapter error (if exists): "login-error", "query-error", "create-error", "update-error", "delete-error", "logoff-error"
  - @params["create_error"] – Array of hashes each containing an "object" (that failed to create) and a corresponding "error_message"
- "ok"
  - @params["total_count"] – Total number of records that exist for this RhoSync source
  - @params["processed_count"] – Number of records included in the last sync page
  - @params["cumulative_count"] – Number of records the SyncEngine has processed so far for this source
- "complete"–This status is returned only when the SyncEngine process is complete.
- "schema-changed"–This status is returned for bulk-sync models that use FixedSchema when the schema has changed in the RhoSync server.

Time for action – Filtering data with search

After understanding the search functionality we will now include it in our employee application. We will search employees based on their name and then fetch the results.

To receive the entire data in JSON format, open the following link:

http://employee-rails.heroku.com/employees.json

To implement the search functionality of Rhodes, we will use the search method as mentioned earlier:

1. Add the following code in employee_controller.rb:

```
def search
    Employee.search(:from => 'search',
      :search_params => {:name => @params['query']},
      :callback => '/app/Employee/search_callback',
      :callback_param => "name=#{@params['query']}")
    @response['headers']['Wait-Page'] = 'true'
```

```
    render :action => :searching
  end

  def search_callback
    if @params['status'] == 'complete'
      @employees = Employee.find(:all, :conditions => {:name => @
params['name']})
      render_transition :action => :search
    else
      WebView.navigate url_for :action => :index
    end
  end
```

In search action of employee controller, we have used search method with the necessary `params` whereas in the `search_callback` action we have rendered the pages according to the status.

2. Create a file `search.erb` in Employee. This is the view file that will be shown after the search is complete.

```
<div class="pageTitle">
  <h1>Search</h1>
</div>

<div class="toolbar">
  <div class="leftItem regularButton">
    <a href="<%= Rho::RhoConfig.start_path %>">Home</a>
  </div>
  <div class="rightItem regularButton">
    <a href="<%= url_for :action => :new %>">New</a>
  </div>
</div>

<div class="content">
  <form method="POST" action="<%= url_for(:action => :search) %>">
    <ul>
      <li>
        <label for="query" class="fieldLabel">Query</label>
        <input type="text" name="query" <%= placeholder("Query")
%>/>
      </li>
    </ul>
    <input type="submit" class="standardButton" value="Search"/>
  </form>
  <div>
    <%= "Found #{@employees.length} customer(s)." %>
```

```
  </div>
  <% if !@employees.empty? %>
      <ul>
        <% @employees.each do |x| %>
            <li><%= link_to "#{x.name}", {:action => :show, :id =>
x.object} %></li>
        <% end %>
      </ul>
  <% end %>
</div>
```

3. Update `index.rb` file in the `Employee` folder. This will add a search box to the employee page:

```
<div class="pageTitle">
  <h1>Employees</h1>
</div>

<div class="toolbar">
  <div class="leftItem regularButton">
    <a href="<%= Rho::RhoConfig.start_path %>">Home</a>
  </div>
  <div class="rightItem regularButton">
    <a class="button" href="<%= url_for :action => :new %>">New</
a>
  </div>
</div>

<div class="content">

    <form method="POST" action="<%= url_for(:action => :search)
%>">
    <ul>
      <li>
        <label for="query" class="fieldLabel">Query</label>
        <input type="text" name="query" <%= placeholder( "Query" )
%>/>
      </li>
    </ul>
    <input type="submit" class="standardButton" value="Search"/>
  </form>

  <ul>
    <% @employees.each do |employee| %>
```

```
          <li>
            <a href="<%= url_for :action => :show, :id => employee.
object %>">
              <span class="title"><%= employee.name %></span><span
class="disclosure_indicator"></span>
            </a>
          </li>

    <% end %>
  </ul>
</div>
```

4. Add a file `searching.erb` in the `Employee` folder:

```
<div style="margin: 150px auto; width: 100px; font-weight: bold;
color: white;">
  Searching...
</div>
```

5. Now, update the source adapter `employee.rb` in the RhoSync application:

```
  def search(params)
    parsed=JSON.parse(RestClient.get(@base +".json").body)
    @result = {}
    parsed.each do |item|
      if item["employee"]["name"] == params['name']
        puts item["employee"]
        @result[item["employee"]["id"].to_s] = item["employee"]
      end
    end if parsed
    @result
end
```

6. Now, restart the RhoSync and Rhodes application.

7. After login, navigate to the Employee page by clicking **Employee** on the home page.

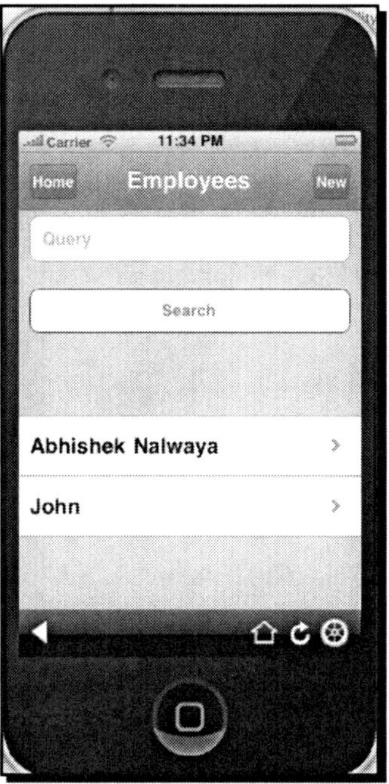

8. Enter someone's name for the search criteria and then click **Search**. The searching screen will be loaded:

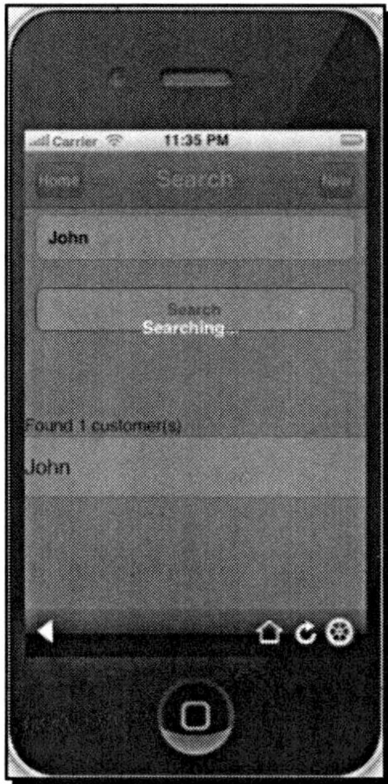

9. And then the result will be shown on the page:

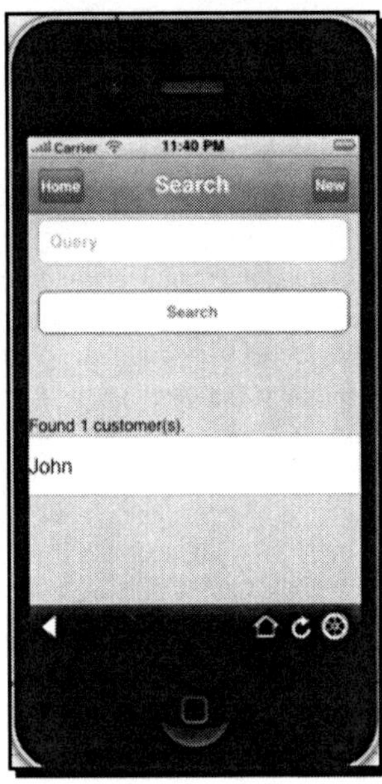

10. You can click on **Employee** to get his details with an option to edit it:

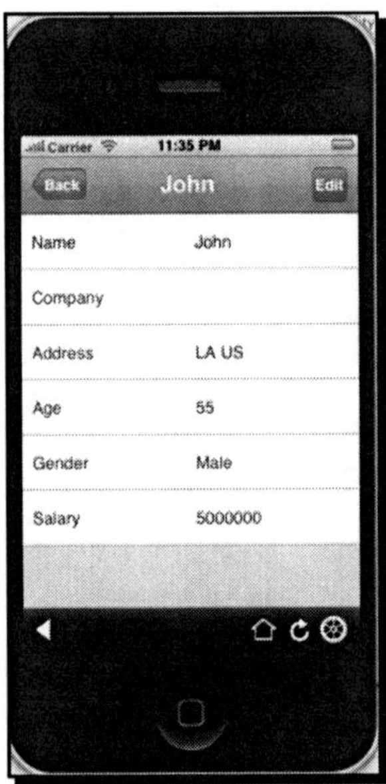

Authentication

Now, we will learn about authentication using RhoSync. We have a login page in Rhodes application, whatever username and password we enter they are accessible inside the authentication method in `application.rb` file of the RhoSync application. The RhoSync application code includes a file at the root called `application.rb` that contains an `authenticate` hook. This method is called when a device first connects to the RhoSync application and provides the username/password:

```
class Application < Rhosync::Base
  class << self

    def authenticate(username,password,session)
      true # do some interesting authentication here...
    end

def initializer(path)
      super
    end
def store_blob(object,field_name,blob)
      super #=> returns blob[:tempfile]
    end
  end
end
Application.initializer(ROOT_PATH)
```

If your backend web service requires authentication, simply add code to the authenticate method and return true if authentication was successful or false to deny access to the application from this client. For example:

```
def authenticate(username, password, session)
  # ... connect to backend using API and authenticate ...
  if success
    # save the data for later use in the source adapter
    Store.put_value("username:#{username}:token",username)
  end
  return success
end
```

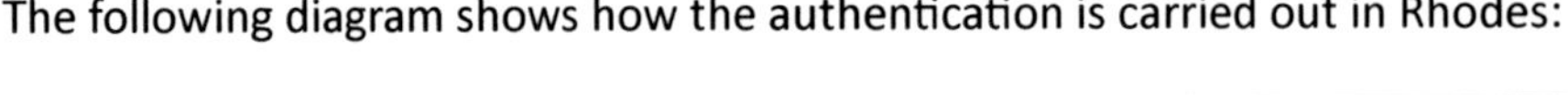

The following diagram shows how the authentication is carried out in Rhodes:

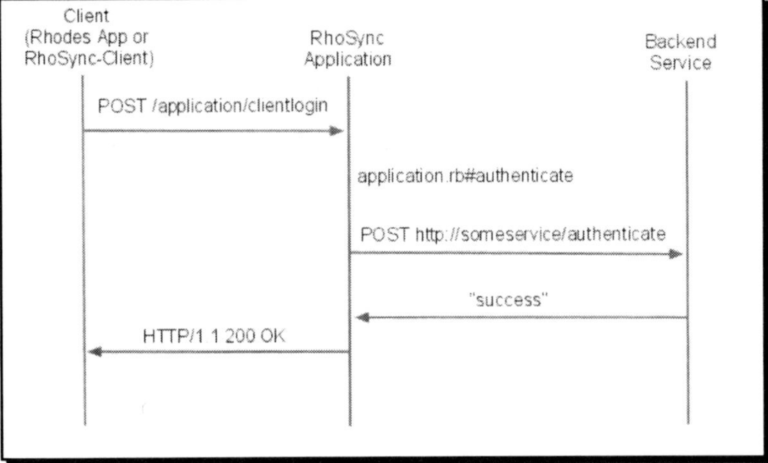

What just happened?

We just learned about the search method available with RhoSync and the various options available with this method. We also understood how the Authentication works in Rhodes.

RhoSync REST API

The RhoSync REST API allows you to control, monitor, and debug a running RhoSync application using a simple HTTP API:

- `get_api_token`: Before you can use RhoSync API you should get an API token:

```
require 'rest_client'
require 'json'
server = "http://localhost:9292"
login = "rhoadmin"
password = ""
res = RestClient.post("#{server}/login", { :login => login, :
password => password }.to_json, :content_type => :json)
token = RestClient.post("#{server}/api/get_api_token",'',{ :
cookies => res.cookies })
```

- `get_license_info` :Returns license information of the currently used license:

```
license_info = RestClient.post(
  "#{server}/api/get_license_info",
  {:api_token => token}.to_json, :content_type => :json
).body
```

- `reset`: Reset the server: flush db and re-bootstrap server:

```
RestClient.post("#{server}/api/reset",
  { :api_token => token }.to_json,
  :content_type => :json
)
```

- `ping`: Sends a PUSH message to all the devices of the specified user:

```
# :message - message which will be used to display notification
popup dialog on the device
# :badge - iphone specific badge
# :sound - name of the sound file to play upon receiving PUSH
notification
# :vibrate - number of seconds to vibrate upon receiving PUSH
notification
# :sources - list of data source names to be synced upon receiving
PUSH notification
ping_params = {
  :api_token => token,
  :user_id => user_id,
  :sources => source_name,
  :message => 'hello world',
  :vibrate => 2000,
  :sound => 'hello.mp3'
}

RestClient.post(
  "#{server}/api/ping",ping_params.to_json,
  :content_type => :json
)
```

- `list_users`: List users registered with this RhoSync application:

```
users = RestClient.post(
  "#{server}/api/list_users",
  { :api_token => token }.to_json,
  :content_type => :json
).body
```

- `create_user`: Create a user in this RhoSync application:

```
RestClient.post("#{server}/api/create_user",
  {
    :api_token => token,
    :attributes => {
      :login => login,
      :password => password
```

```
      }
    }.to_json,
    :content_type => :json
)
```

- `delete_user`: Delete User and all associated devices from the RhoSync application:

  ```
  RestClient.post(
    "#{server}/api/delete_user",
    {
      :api_token => token,
      :user_id => user_id
    }.to_json,
   :content_type => :json
  )
  ```

- `list_clients`: List clients (devices) associated with a given user:

  ```
  clients = RestClient.post("#{server}/api/list_clients",
    {
      :api_token => token,
      :user_id => user_id
    }.to_json,
   :content_type => :json
  ).body
  ```

  Returns a list of client IDs.

- `create_client`: Creates a client (device) for a given user:

  ```
  RestClient.post(
    "#{server}/api/create_client",
    {
      :api_token => token,
      :user_id => user_id
    }.to_json,
    :content_type => :json
  ).body
  ```

- `delete_client`: Deletes the specified client (device).

  ```
  RestClient.post(
    "#{server}/api/delete_client",
    {
      :api_token => token,
      :user_id => user_id,
      :client_id => client_id
    }.to_json,
  ```

```
  :content_type => :json
)
```

- `get_client_params`: Returns client (device) attributes, such as `device_type`, `device_pin`, `device_port`. These attributes are used by RhoSync push:

```
RestClient.post(
  "#{server}/api/get_client_params",
  {
    :api_token => token,
    :client_id => client_id
  }.to_json,
  :content_type => :json
).body
```

Summary

In this chapter, we have learned to:

- Create a RhoSync application
- Create a source adapter
- Perform CRUD operation using RhoSync
- Use search method to synchronize only the desired data
- Authenticate in Rhodes
- RhoSync REST API

In the next chapter, we will learn to create views dynamically using metadata and to push the data to phone.

6

Metadata and Push—Creating Agile Views

In the last chapter, we learned to connect to backend services through RhoSync. In this chapter, we will learn about a powerful feature of RhoSync called metadata.

Before understanding how to use metadata we should know what is metadata and when to use it.

Generally, the big enterprise application's structure keeps changing. How do you handle this with a native local smart phone app running on the device? The Rhodes Metadata Framework allows the changed metadata (not just data) to be synchronized to the device. When new fields get added to the backend enterprise app, they are available in forms and screens on the device right after a sync happens. The metadata framework is a RhoSync & Rhodes tool, which provides synchronized application layouts. For example, if your application has a model `Employee` with the fields `name` and `address`, metadata would allow you to add an additional field `phone` in the source adapter and this new field would automatically display in the Rhodes application.

In addition to adding/removing/updating fields, metadata also provides powerful features like handling field validations, data-binding, collections, repeatable elements, and much more.

Getting ready for Metadata

To get started with Metadata we have to understand how it works and how to install the prerequisites. Following are the steps that tell us how metadata work:

- Metadata is first defined in a source adapter by implementing an adapter method metadata that returns a JSON structure. The JSON structure may contain a hash of hashes and can also have child elements defined as arrays of hashes. The key in each object can be any string; however, there are some reserved labels, which are used by certain elements.

- The metadata for an adapter is synchronized to Rhodes along with the rest of the adapter dataset. Metadata is called before the query method in the SyncEngine workflow, so you can tailor your query method based on metadata.
- Rhodes uses the synchronized metadata definition to render views at runtime. These views are driven by the metadata definition, so when a new definition is synchronized, the views will automatically reflect the changes.

To use this powerful feature metadata we have to install and configure Rhodes-translator gem. If you are new to Ruby, gem is a Ruby library.

Time for action – Installing the Rhodes translator gem

To get started, we have to follow these steps:

1. The first step is to install the `rhodes-translator` gem. Go to the command prompt and type the following command:

   ```
   gem install rhodes-translator
   ```

2. Then, add `rhodes_translator` to your extensions in your Rhodes application's `build.yml` file:

   ```
   extensions: ["rhodes-translator"]
   ```

3. You need to make sure that sync is enabled on the model, which is using metadata:

   ```
   class Company
     include Rhom::PropertyBag

    enable :sync

   end
   ```

What just happened?

We just understood how metadata works and how to install the `rhodes-translator` gem, which is a prerequisite to using metadata. We also learned how to configure the `rhodes-translator` extension.

Creating the first view using metadata

We will now create the first view using metadata. You may be wondering what a view means. Basically, a view is an erb file, which contains HTML and a little bit of Ruby code. These views are traditionally meant to be at the client device but metadata allows you to have them at the server. The advantage of having these views at the server is: if you want to change any view, you just need to change it at the server and it would be reflected at the client without the need for reinstalling at the client.

Generally, we will use metadata when our views are not fixed and keep changing. For using metadata there are many templates available that can be used directly. A view can be a collection of a number of templates.

The following labels are reserved and used by the metadata framework for specifying the template to be used:

- `:type`: Type label is used to define the template which we want to use. There are various templates available with `rhodes-translator` gem, which can be used directly. Like form, text, select etc. We can also define our custom template which will be discussed later in the chapter
- `:children`: Children of an element are defined by an array of hashes. To specify the children of an element you add the `:children` label and the name of those children.
- `:repeatable`: Repeatable elements use data binding to specify an array of objects to iterate over. The children of the repeatable element are duplicated for each element in the object referred to by the repeatable hash key.
- `:validation`: Validation is use to add validation to the field.

Time for action – Creating an index page

We will create an index page of a company using metadata. Right now the view is displayed through the `index.erb` file. Now, we will use metadata to load this from RhoSync.

These are the steps:

1. Add the following code to the company source adapter in your RhoSync application. Edit `company.rb` and add following code:

```
def metadata
    objectlink = { :type => "linkli", :uri => "{{showuri}}", :text
=> "{{name}}" }
    list = { :type => "list", :children => [objectlink], :
repeatable => "{{@companies}}" }
    content = { :type => "content", :children => [ list ] }
    toolbar = { :type => "toolbar", :lefturi => "/app", :righturi
=> "/app/Company/new", :lefttext => "Home", :righttext => "New"}
    title = { :title => "Meta Company", :type => "title"}
    index = { :title => "index", :type => "view", :children =>
[title, toolbar, content]}
  {'index' => index }.to_json
end
```

2. Now, we will try to understand the above code step by step:

```
objectlink = {
        :type => "linkli",
        :uri => "{{showuri}}",
        :text => "{{name}}" }
```

3. Here, `linkli` is the default template available with the `rhodes-translator`. We can see all the available templates inside the template folder of the Rhodes-translator gem. `Uri` and `text` labels are available in the `linkli` template to define the URL and display the name respectively:

```
list = {
:type => "list",
 :children => [objectlink],
:repeatable => "{{@companies}}"
}
```

4. Also, `list` is a template name and `@companies` is a variable defined in the `incident_controller.rb` file, which has an array of company objects. Repeatable elements use data binding to specify an array of objects to iterate over. The children of the repeatable element are duplicated for each element in the object referred by the repeatable hash key. So, in this case, for each object of the company, the `objectlink` template would be called:

```
content = {
   :type => "content",
   :children => [ list ]
   }
```

5. Content is the template available with `Rhodes-translator`. This contains the content section, which is the main part of the screen:

```
toolbar = {
            :type => "toolbar",
            :lefturi => "/app",
            :righturi => "/app/Company/new",
            :lefttext => "Home",
            :righttext => "New"
}
```

6. This is the toolbar for your view, which has two links: one at the right and the other at the left. `:lefturi, :righturi` define the URL and `:lefttext, :righttext` define the display name for the links.

```
    title = {
     :title => "Meta Company",
     :type => "title"}
```

7. This is the title, which will be displayed on top of the page. In this case **Meta Company** will be shown at the top.

```
index = {
 :title => "index",
 :type => "view",
:children => [title, toolbar, content]
}
```

8. As we have already discussed each page has three sections: title, toolbar, and content. So, we can see that `view` template has three children: title, toolbar, and content, which have already been defined earlier.

9. Edit `index` action in `incident_controller.rb`:

```
  def index
    @companies = Company.find(:all)
       @companies.each do |company|
      company.showuri = url_for :action => :show, :id => company.
object
    end
    render
  end
```

We have created a link for each company.

10. Restart your Rhodes and RhoSync applications.

11. Log in with any username and password.

12. Click on **Company**, and you can now see the list of companies using metadata. The page coming from metadata would have the page title as **Meta Company**.

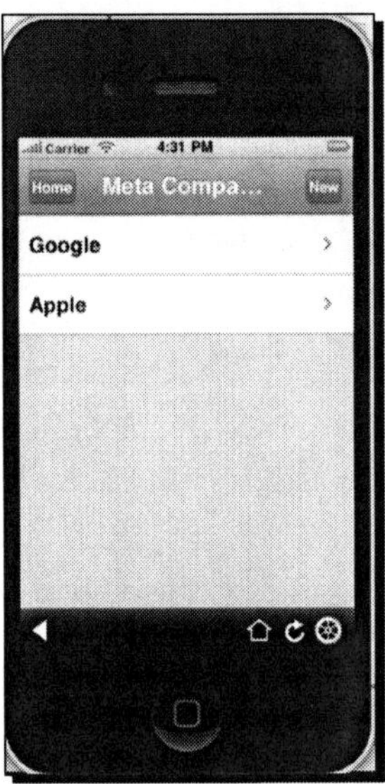

What just happened?

We have just created an index view using metadata on the RhoSync application, which was present on the Rhodes application.

Have a go hero

Now, in the same view, we will display the same company's details two times. This time we will not change any code in the Rhodes application. We will only add it in the RhoSync application and the changes would be automatically reflected once we log in or sync our Rhodes application.

```
def metadata
    objectlink = { :type => "linkli", :uri => "{{showuri}}", :text =>
"{{name}}" }
    list = { :type => "list", :children => [objectlink], :repeatable
=> "{{@companies}}" }
    content = { :type => "content", :children => [ list, list ] }
    toolbar = { :type => "toolbar", :lefturi => "/app", :righturi =>
"/app/Company/new", :lefttext => "Home", :righttext => "New"}
    title = { :title => "Meta Company", :type => "title"}
    index = { :title => "index", :type => "view", :children => [title,
toolbar, content]}
```

```
    {'index' => index }.to_json
  end
```

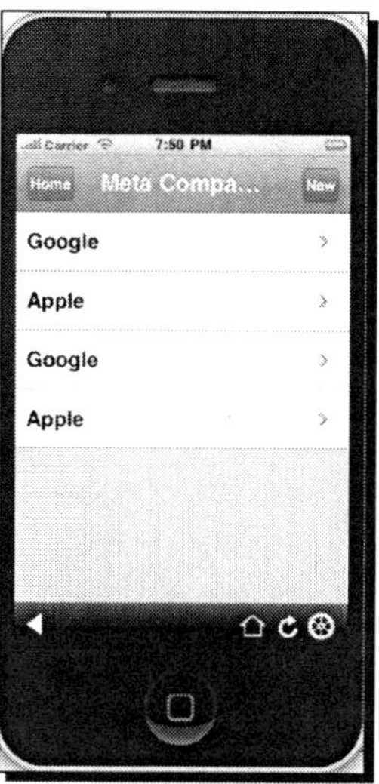

We can observe that the companies are shown twice for which we did not have to restart the simulator. So we have changed the view of our application without changing the Rhodes code.

Getting all the views for company from Metadata

As we created the index page using metadata, now we will create views for new, edit, and show page.

1. We have to update `metadata` action in `company.rb` of the RhoSync application:

```
def metadata

    objectlink = { :type => "linkli", :uri => "{{showuri}}", :text
=> "{{name}}" }
    list = { :type => "list", :children => [objectlink], :
repeatable => "{{@companies}}" }
    content = { :type => "content", :children => [ list ] }
    toolbar = { :type => "toolbar", :lefturi => "/app", :righturi
=> "/app/Company/new", :lefttext => "Home", :righttext => "New"}
    title = { :title => "Meta Company", :type => "title"}
    index = { :title => "index", :type => "view", :children =>
[title, toolbar, content]}
```

```
## NEW

###Shared with NEW and EDIT
companyname = { :type => 'labeledinputli',
  :label => 'Name',
  :name => 'company[name]',
  :value => '{{@company/name}}' }

##End Shared

newlist = { :type => 'list',
  :children => [ companyname ] }

newsubmit = { :type => 'submit',
  :value => 'Create' }

newhiddenid = { :type => 'hidden',
  :name => 'id',
  :value => '{{@company/object}}' }

newform = { :type => 'form',
  :action => '/app/Company/create',
  :method => 'POST',
  :children => [newhiddenid, newlist, newsubmit] }

newcontent = { :type => 'content',
  :children => [ newform ] }

newtoolbar = { :type => 'toolbar',
  :lefturi => '/app/Company',
  :lefttext => 'Cancel',
  :leftclass => 'backButton',
  :righturi => '/app',
  :righttext => 'Home' }

newtitle = { :title => 'New',
  :type => 'title' }

new = { :title => 'index',
  :type => 'view',
  :children => [newtitle,newtoolbar,newcontent] }
##END NEW

##SHOW
```

```
showcompanyname = { :type => 'labeledvalueli',
  :label => 'Name c',
  :value => '{{@company/name}}' }


showlist = { :type => 'list',
  :children => [ showcompanyname ] }


showcontent = { :type => 'content',
  :children => [ showlist ] }

showtoolbar = { :type => 'toolbar',
  :lefturi => 'index',
  :lefttext => 'Back',
  :leftclass => 'backButton',
  :righturi => 'edit',
  :righttext => 'Edit' }

showtitle = { :title => '{{@company/name}}',
  :type => 'title' }

show = { :title => 'view',
  :type => 'view',
  :children => [showtitle,showtoolbar,showcontent] }
## END SHOW

## edit

editsubmit = { :type => 'submit',
  :value => 'Update' }


#NOTE: see that we reuse newhiddenid and newlist components
editform = { :type => 'form',
  :action => '/app/Company/update',
  :method => 'POST',
  :children => [newhiddenid, newlist, editsubmit] }

editcontent = { :type => 'content',
  :children => [ editform ] }

edittoolbar = { :type => 'toolbar',
  :lefturi => '/app/Company',
```

```
            :lefttext => 'Cancel',
            :leftclass => 'backButton',
            :righturi => '{{@company/deleteuri}}',
            :righttext => 'Delete' }

          edit = { :title => 'index',
            :type => 'view',
            :children => [showtitle,edittoolbar,editcontent] }
          ## END UPDATE

          {'index' => index, 'new' => new, 'show' => show, 'edit' =>
    edit }.to_json


        end
```

2. Restart your Rhodes and RhoSync applications.
3. Log in with any username and password.
4. Navigate through the **company** link to see all the screens.

Understanding the code

Now it's the time to understand the code for new, show, and the edit page.

Digging the code for the new page

The following code was written for the new page. As already discussed, the page is divided into three sections: content, toolbar, and title:

- `Content`: This is the code for the content part:

```
companyname = { :type => 'labeledinputli',
      :label => 'Name',
      :name => 'company[name]',
      :value => '{{@company/name}}' }

    newlist = { :type => 'list',
      :children => [ companyname ] }
```

```
newsubmit = { :type => 'submit',
  :value => 'Create' }

newhiddenid = { :type => 'hidden',
  :name => 'id',
  :value => '{{@company/object}}' }

newform = { :type => 'form',
  :action => '/app/Company/create',
  :method => 'POST',
  :children => [newhiddenid, newlist, newsubmit] }

newcontent = { :type => 'content',
  :children => [ newform ] }
```

First line of this code will create the input box for the new and edit page. `Labeledinputli` is the template name that is provided by the rhodes_translator. `:label` is used to specify the display name that will appear for the input textbox. `:name` is the variable that stores the value of the textbox and `:value` is the corresponding value of the field.

The template `submit` will create a submit button with the display name Create. We have to pass a hidden field object, which will be a primary key for the row. Then, the template `form` will create a submit form. We can define the action and method of action by `:action` and `:method label`.

- `Toolbar`: This will create a toolbar with two buttons:

```
newtoolbar = { :type => 'toolbar',
  :lefturi => '/app/Company',
  :lefttext => 'Cancel',
  :leftclass => 'backButton',
  :righturi => '/app',
  :righttext => 'Home' }
```

- `Title`: This section of code will give a title `New` to the page.

```
newtitle = { :title => 'New',
  :type => 'title' }
```

And finally linking the three sections:

```
new = { :title => 'index',
      :type => 'view',
      :children => [newtitle,newtoolbar,newcontent] }
```

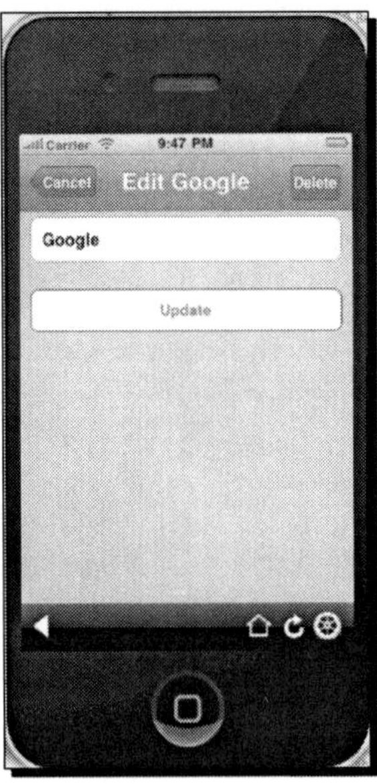

Digging the code for the show page

The following code was written for the show page. As already discussed, the page is divided into three sections: content, toolbar, and title.

- `Content`: This is the code for the content part:

```
showcompanyname = { :type => 'labeledvalueli',
  :label => 'Name',
  :value => '{{@company/name}}' }


showlist = { :type => 'list',
  :children => [ showcompanyname ] }


showcontent = { :type => 'content',
  :children => [ showlist ] }
```

The `labeledvalueli` template will show the text and value as defined in the label and value hash key respectively. `@company/name` is data binding that contains the name of the company. So, the `@company` variable is defined in the `show` action of `company` controller. If we write `@company/name` in RhoSync, this means `@company["name"]`.

- `Toolbar`: This will create a toolbar with two buttons:

```
showtoolbar = { :type => 'toolbar',
  :lefturi => 'index',
  :lefttext => 'Back',
  :leftclass => 'backButton',
  :righturi => 'edit',
  :righttext => 'Edit' }
```

- `Title`: This section of the code will give a title to the `Show` page:

```
showtitle = { :title => '{{@company/name}}',
  :type => 'title' }
```

- And finally, linking the three sections:

```
show = { :title => 'view',
  :type => 'view',
  :children => [showtitle,showtoolbar,showcontent] }
```

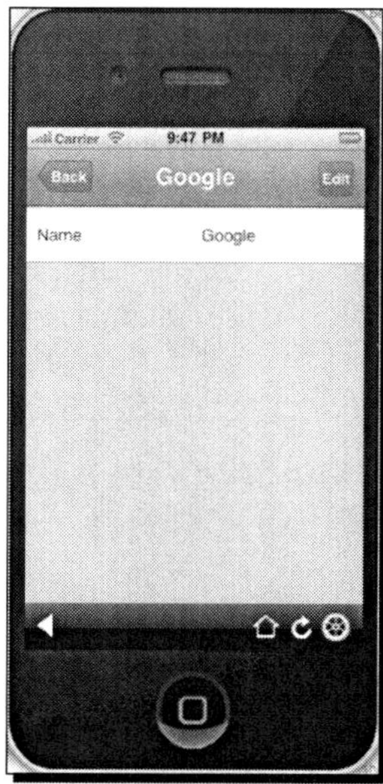

Digging the code for the edit page

The following code was written for the edit page. As already discussed, the page is divided into three sections: content, toolbar, and title.

- `Content`: This is code for the content part:

```
companyname = { :type => 'labeledinputli',
      :label => 'Name',
      :name => 'company[name]',
      :value => '{{@company/name}}' }

    editsubmit = { :type => 'submit',
      :value => 'Update' }


    #NOTE: see that we reuse newhiddenid and newlist components
    editform = { :type => 'form',
      :action => '/app/Company/update',
      :method => 'POST',
      :children => [newhiddenid, newlist, editsubmit] }

    editcontent = { :type => 'content',
      :children => [ editform ] }
```

  The first line of this code will create an input box for the new and edit page as we discussed earlier. `Labeledinputli` is the template name that is provided by rhodes_translator. `:label` is used to specify the display name that will appear for the input textbox. `:name` is the variable that stores the value of the textbox and `:value` is the corresponding value of the field.

  The template `submit` will create a submit button with the display name `Update`. We have to pass a hidden field `object` that will be a primary key for the row. Then the template `form` will create a submit form. We can define the action and method of action by `:action` and `:method label`.

- `Toolbar`: This will create a toolbar with two buttons on the right and left:

```
edittoolbar = { :type => 'toolbar',
  :lefturi => '/app/Company',
  :lefttext => 'Cancel',
  :leftclass => 'backButton',
  :righturi => '{{@company/deleteuri}}',
  :righttext => 'Delete' }
```

- `Title`: This section of code will give a title `New`.

```
    edit = { :title => 'index',
      :type => 'view',
}
```

- And finally, linking the three sections:

```
    edit = { :title => 'index',
      :type => 'view',
      :children => [showtitle,edittoolbar,editcontent] }
```

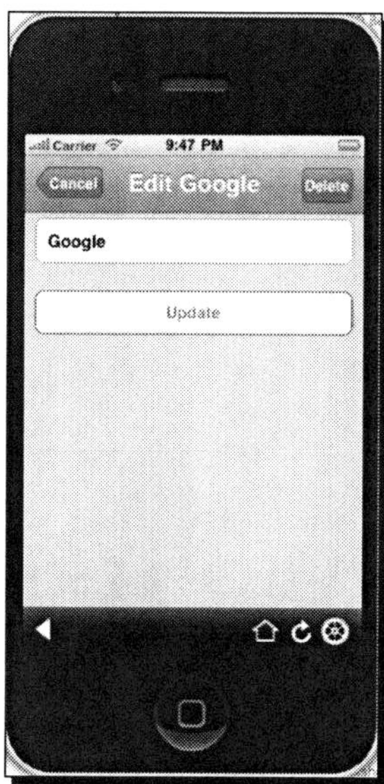

Metadata validation

In the earlier section, we have learned to create input fields using metadata, but an application would definitely need validation checks to be implemented to make it less prone to errors. Metadata provides an easy way to implement validation in the RhoSync application. Validation is expressed as a key added to an existing metadata definition. Below is a sample showing all of the validations that can be used.

Following options are available with Validation:

- `:regexp`
- `:validators`
- `:min_len`
- `:max_len`

- :min_value
- :max_value

This is the simple code that we have to add validation:

```
:validation => {
   :regexp = "^.+$",
   :validators = [:required, :number, :currency, :email, :phone],
   :min_len = 0,
   :max_len = 100,
   :min_value = 10,
   :max_value = 1000
}
```

Now, to get the errors while validating, use the following code:

```
errors = validate(SourceName.metadata['validation'],@params)
```

`validate` method is available with `rhodes-translator`, which will form custom error messages depending on the validations.

Custom templates

Templates can be overridden by placing the ERB files in the `app/templates` folder in your Rhodes application. They will be used before using any of the built-in templates.

Push data to your phone

RhoSync has a simple Ruby API for sending push notifications to a user's device. This API can be called directly, queued as a resque job, or called remotely via the RhoSync REST API. The push message can trigger the following actions in the Rhodes application: alert with a message, sync one or more sources, vibrate, display a badge, play a sound file.

We will now show you how to use the RhoSync application to deliver push messages on each platform and how you can handle the push notification in your Rhodes application.

Set up the Rhodes application for Push

First, enable push in your Rhodes application in `build.yml`:

```
capabilities:
  - push
  - vibrate #=> if you want to enable vibrate in your push messages
```

Next, your RhoSync application should be running on a network that is accessible to your device. For example, you might have your RhoSync application running on a LAN with IP 192.168.1.40, PORT 9292. Then make sure your device is connected to the same LAN and set up your `syncserver` inside `rhoconfig.txt` file as follows:

```
syncserver = 'http://192.168.1.40:9292/application'
```

Now, your Rhodes application is configured to receive push messages.

Push for iOS

To set up your RhoSync application for iOS push, you will need to update `settings/settings.yml` to include the following:

```
:development:
  :redis: localhost:6379
  :iphonecertfile: settings/apple_push_cert.pem
  :iphonepassphrase: #=> empty or put password for your certificate
  :iphoneserver: gateway.sandbox.push.apple.com
  :iphoneport: 2195
  :syncserver: http://localhost:9292/application/
  :licensefile: settings/license.key
```

This is for running your application in development mode, for production you will need all of the iPhone settings, and change the `:iphoneserver` to:

```
:iphoneserver: gateway.push.apple.com
```

iPhone PUSH support uses the Apple Push Notification Service (APNS) introduced in iPhone SDK 3.0. In order to use the service, you will need to obtain a push-enabled provisioning profile and a server-side push certificate used for encrypting RhoSync->APNS traffic.

The first step to setting up your environment is to create an APNS push certificate. To create the SSL certificate, follow the *Creating the SSL Certificate and Keys* section on the `http://developer.apple.com/library/ios/#documentation/NetworkingInternet/Conceptual/RemoteNotificationsPG/ProvisioningDevelopment/ProvisioningDevelopment.html`.

Once you have the certificate, you will need to export it to a `.pem` format using these instructions. Make sure to name the output file `apple_push_cert.pem` file from these instructions, since this is what we configured in our RhoSync application.

Once you have this file, copy it to your RhoSync application directory under the `settings` folder:

```
$ cd myrhosyncapp
$ cp /path/to/apple_push_cert.pem settings/apple_push_cert.pem
```

Now, your RhoSync application is ready to send APNS messages.

Push for Android

To set up your RhoSync application for Android push, you will need to update `settings/settings.yml` to include the following:

```
:development:
  :redis: localhost:6379
  :syncserver: http://localhost:9292/application/
  :licensefile: settings/license.key
  :authtoken: authtoken
```

Android PUSH support uses the Android Cloud to Device Messaging (AC2DM) system introduced in Android 2.2 (Froyo). In order to use the service, you will need to register your role-based Google account (or use the existing one) and then register this account in Google C2DM program.

As the first step, register your role-based Google account for your application. Here for example it will be referred to as push-app@gmail.com. You should have different accounts for sending and receiving push messages.

Then, modify your application's `build.yml` and specify there the Google account used to send PUSH messages:

```
android:
  push:
    sender: push-app@gmail.com
```

This is the same address used by RhoSync to retrieve authtoken.

Push for Blackberry

To set up your RhoSync application for BlackBerry push, you will need to update `settings/settings.yml` to include the following:

```
:development:
  :redis: localhost:6379
  :mdsserver: 192.168.1.110
  :mdsserverport: 8080
  :syncserver: http://localhost:9292/application/
  :licensefile: settings/license.key
```

Replace `:mdsserver:` and `:mdsserverport:` with the hostname/IP and port of your machine (default port is 8080).

Notifications to BlackBerry are sent using PAP 2.0 message through a BES/MDS server.

On the simulator, this is done via the MDS simulator tool.

Setting up the MDS simulator

Make sure you close the BlackBerry simulator and MDS simulator before continuing for your changes to take effect!

To enable the push port in your MDS simulator, edit the following file: `C:\Program Files\Research In Motion\BlackBerry JDE <VERSION YOU ARE BUILDING>\MDS\config\rimpublic.property`

Uncomment the last line of the file, which should be:

```
push.application.reliable.ports=100
```

To listen for incoming messages on the BlackBerry, the Rhodes application will start when device powers is on and will run a listener thread in the background. You will use the `push_port` option in the `rhoconfig.txt` to specify the listening port for incoming push messages. If `push_port` is not specified, the default will be 100 as shown in the previous section.

Testing Push in the Web Console

The RhoSync Web Console includes a utility for testing push to make sure everything is wired up correctly.

1. Make sure you've logged in and performed a sync on the device/simulator you are going to test.
2. Open the RhoSync console by:
   `http://localhost:9292/console`
3. Log in to the console.
4. Navigate to the user's page you used to log into the Rhodes application. For example in our case it is **John and admin:**

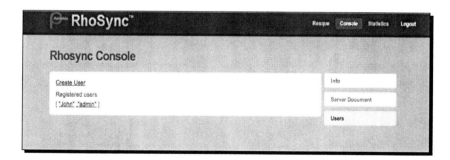

5. For example, if you logged in as user **admin**, the URL would be:

   `http://localhost:9292/console/user?user_id=admin`

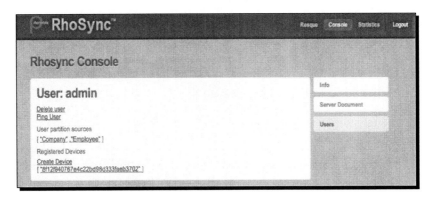

6. You should see a registered device for this user, for example: "**8f12f940767e4c22bd98d333faeb3702**". Click on the link for this device and you will see the device attributes:

```
device_type: APPLE
device_pin:
10fd92abfa8ee48155d9af6e7329086322b323fd0d18fdbd19e92d03c0fef7c8
device_port: 100
user_id: t
app_id: application
```

   If you don't see all of these attributes, then something is incorrect in your Rhodes application settings. Please verify that you've followed the Rhodes application push setup.

7. Now that the device is registered, go back to the **Users** page and click **Ping User**:

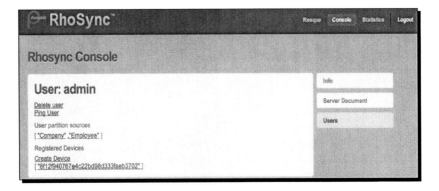

8. Enter in some values or try the defaults, you should see a push message on the device when you click **Ping!**

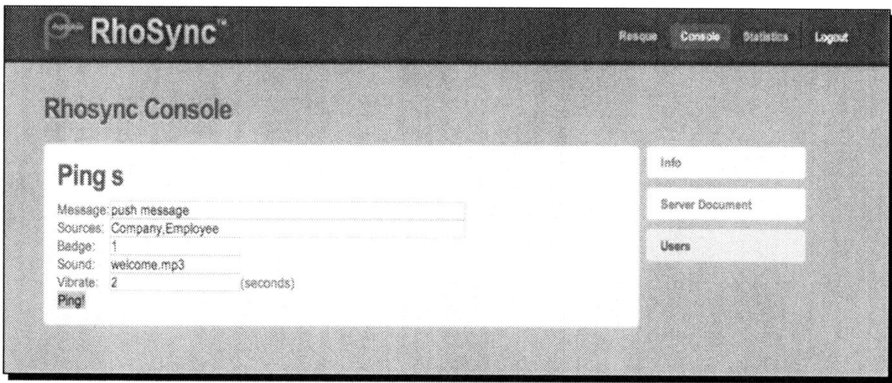

Here you can specify an alert message, sources array to sync, badge value (iOS only), sound file to play, and duration to vibrate.

By default, the sources list will be a comma-separated list of your RhoSync application's sources. This sources list will be sent in the push message to trigger a sync. You can specify one or more sources, or 'all' to trigger a sync of all sources.

Summary

In this chapter, we have learnt about:

- Installing and configuring the Rhodes-translator gem for using metadata
- How to create a view using metadata
- Using validation
- Push for iPhone, Blackberry, and Android

In the next chapter, we will learn about iPhone, Android, and Blackberry Native User Interface.

7

Native User Interface—Cosmetics for Your Smart Phones

In the last chapter, we learned how to create views using metadata and push data to the client through RhoSync. In this chapter we will learn about Native User Interface for different phones. We will perform device-specific operations to give a more native look to our application. First, we will understand how Rhodes handles the native look for different devices. The Rhodes framework includes cascading stylesheets, which are customized for each device to give your applications a native look and feel.

Many of the custom styles required on one platform have no counterpart on other platforms. For example, while the iPhone supports several toolbar button styles, there are no corresponding styles in the Android or Windows Mobile platforms. As a result, the iPhone stylesheet provides custom styles for each of these button types, while the remaining devices apply the same style definition to all four-button styles, which we shall discuss in detail later in this chapter.

Device-specific style

There are a lot of differences in the way the screen layout is sliced on different devices whether it's a header, footer, toolbar, or buttons. The nomenclature is the same for all the devices the only difference is the way they are displayed on the screen of each device. This will be clear from the following snapshots.

The following image shows how the Native UI looks on the iPhone:

The following image shows how the Native UI looks on Android:

The following image shows how the Native UI looks on the Blackberry:

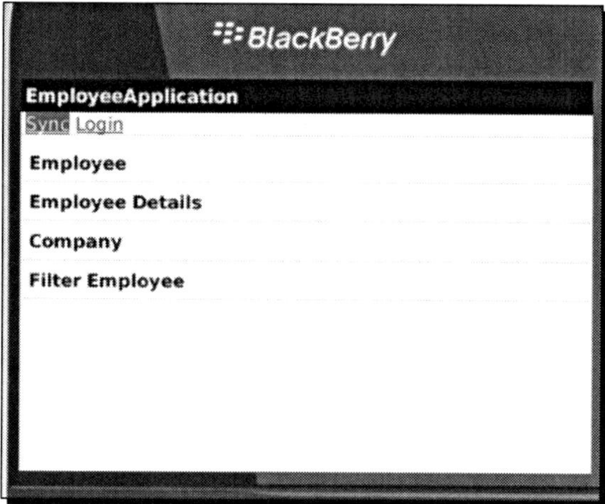

The Rhodes framework includes stylesheets customized for each device to give your applications a native look and feel. These stylesheets are included by default in generated Rhodes applications (`public/css/`), and are included in the application layout file (`app/layout.erb`).

Time for action – Adding device-specific style

Rhodes supports a layout mechanism based on ERB templates. The default layout template is called `layout.erb` and is located in the application root folder. Unless overridden, this layout is rendered on all non-Ajax requests. You may use `layout.erb` to load CSS and favorite JavaScript frameworks and libraries. Generated `layout.erb` loads Rhomobile CSS framework and modified JQTouch library. JQTouch is loaded by default; in case you want to use other frameworks like JQMobile it can be replaced.

If we open `layout.erb` it looks like this:

```
<!DOCTYPE html PUBLIC "-//W3C//DTD XHTML 1.0 Strict//EN"
        "http://www.w3.org/TR/xhtml1/DTD/xhtml1-strict.dtd">
<html xmlns="http://www.w3.org/1999/xhtml">

<head>

<title>Test</title>
<meta name="viewport" content="width=device-width;
height=device-height; initial-scale=1.0;
maximum-scale=1.0; user-scalable=0;"/>
```

```
<% is_bb6 = System::get_property('platform') == 'Blackberry' &&
        (System::get_property('os_version') =~ /^6\.0/) %>

<% if System::get_property('platform') == 'APPLE' ||
        System::get_property('platform') == 'ANDROID' || is_bb6 %>
<script src="/public/jqtouch/jquery.1.3.2.min.js"
type="text/javascript"></script>
<script src="/public/jqtouch/jqtouch.js"
type="text/javascript"></script>
<link href="/public/jqtouch/jqtouch.css"
type="text/css" rel="stylesheet"/>
<% if System::get_property('platform') == 'APPLE' %>
<link href="/public/jqtouch/jqtouch-iphone.css"
type="text/css" rel="stylesheet"/>
<% end %>
<script>$.jQTouch();</script>
<% end %>

<% if System::get_property('platform') == 'APPLE' %>
<link href="/public/css/iphone.css"
type="text/css" rel="stylesheet"/>
<% elsif System::get_property('platform') == 'ANDROID' %>
<link href="/public/css/android.css"
type="text/css" rel="stylesheet"/>
<% elsif is_bb6 %>
<link href="/public/css/android.css"
type="text/css" rel="stylesheet"/>
<% elsif System::get_property('platform') == 'Blackberry' %>
<link href="/public/css/blackberry.css"
type="text/css" rel="stylesheet"/>
<% else %>
<link href="/public/css/windows_mobile.css"
type="text/css" rel="stylesheet"/>
<% end %>
</head>

<body>
<%= @content %>
</body>

</html>
```

`System::get_property('platform')` dynamically assigns the value of the current platform. That is if the device is Blackberry then its value will be Blackberry. So if we want device-specific code we can put an if else condition to check the code. For example, we will have different stylesheets for each device so that we have to place checks for each device to include their corresponding stylesheet in the layout.

To render content in a specific platform, you can include conditional statements within your views. For example, this code can be used to conditionally display the name of the phone's operating system in your model views:

```
<% if platform == 'APPLE' %>
iPhone
<% elsif  platform == 'ANDROID' %>
    Android
<% elsif platform == 'Blackberry' %>
    BlackBerry
<% else %>
     Windows Mobile
<% end %>
```

What Just happened

We have seen how Rhodes handles templating system for each device. We have learned that each device-specific stylesheet is included in layout.erb by putting a platform check.

Customizing layouts

If you would like to override or customize the layout behavior, you can call the `render` function with the following parameters:

```
render :action => 'index',
:layout => 'mycustomlayout', :use_layout_on_ajax => false
```

We can pass various arguments as a key value pair in render. The `:action` argument is the action you would like to render. Next is the layout name, which assumes the application root as a base directory. In the above example, Rhodes would look for a file called `mycustomlayout.erb` in the application root directory (you may also disable the use of a layout template by specifying `:layout => false`). The `use_layout_on_ajax` argument tells Rhodes whether or not to use the layout on AJAX calls (default is false).

You can call the layout method on the controller to overwrite the default layout name:

```
layout :mycustomlayout
```

This will force the render call to use `mycustomlayout.erb` in place of the default layout file for all the actions of this controller.

Dynamic loading of custom view files based on the current platform

For a simple application the erb files can be common for all devices, but for device-specific applications we can customize the views independently. Rhodes supports platform-specific loading of view (erb) files. At compile time, the application detects the current platform, and checks first for a platform-specific file before loading the default view file.

To create a platform-specific file, simply name the file using the following convention [action_name].[platform_abbreviation].`erb` (e.g.`index.bb.erb`, `show.wm.erb`). It will work for all the files that are in the app and public folder. These are the different abbreviations for the different devices:

Device	Abbreviation	File name
Android	Android	`index.android.erb`
Blackberry	bb	`Index.bb.erb`
iPhone	iphone	`index.iphone.erb`
Windows Mobile	wm	`index.wm.erb`

As an example, the BlackBerry browser has severely limited support for modern CSS. In order to take full advantage of the capabilities of the more advanced browsers found on iPhone, Android, and Windows Mobile devices, the views generated via the `rhogen` command include custom BlackBerry view files, which are loaded while running on a BB device. As described above, the files customized for the BlackBerry are designated by including "bb" before the standard erb extension (e.g. `app/index.bb.erb`).

Keep in mind that any changes made to the standard view files are not incorporated into the custom views, so if you're developing custom views for a specific platform, ensure that any necessary changes are applied to all the relevant view files.

Standard smart phone CSS/HTML architecture

If you use the default generated code, every page in a Rhodes application is divided into three sections:

1. Title: Header of the view.
2. Toolbar: For navigation and different actions for application.
3. Content: Body of the view.

Advanced users can use their own arbitrary HTML. Now, we will discuss these three sections in detail:

pageTitle (<div id="pageTitle">)

The pageTitle div contains the title of the current page, wrapped in an h1 tag. The page title will be displayed in the appropriate location for each device.

The code for the title looks like:

```
<div class="pageTitle">
<h1>EmployeeApplication</h1>
</div>
```

Now, we will see how it looks on different phones:

- This is how it looks on the iPhone:

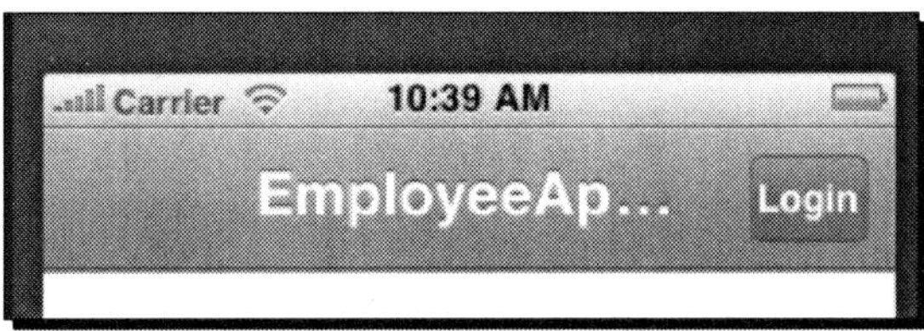

- This is how it looks on the Android:

- This is how it looks on the Blackberry:

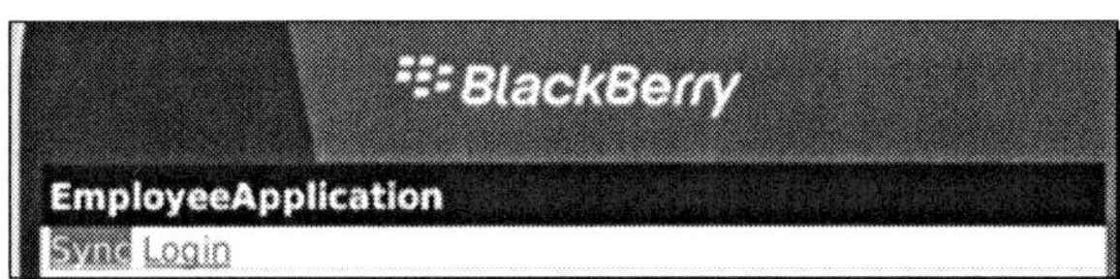

The pageTitle div is not displayed on Windows Mobile devices.

toolbar (<div id="toolbar">)

The toolbar div contains interaction elements that allow users to perform actions and navigate through the application. Most frequently, these elements are links styled as buttons.

The toolbar div is displayed at the top of the page on standard smart phones.

You can read more about the conflict between viewports and fixed positioning at the end of this document.

```
<div class="toolbar">
<% if SyncEngine::logged_in > 0 %>
<div class="leftItem blueButton">
<a href="<%= url_for :controller => :Settings, :action => :do_sync
%>">Sync</a>
</div>
<div class="rightItem regularButton">
<a href="<%= url_for :controller => :Settings, :action => :logout
%>">Logout</a>
</div>
<% else %>
<div class="rightItem regularButton">
<a href="<%= url_for :controller => :Settings, :action => :login
%>">Login</a>
</div>
<% end %>
</div>
```

The toolbar `div` supports three positions:

- `leftItem`
- `rightItem`
- `centerItem`

Note that placing an item in the `#centerItem` div will prevent the page title from being displayed on the iPhone, and is not in compliance with Apple's human interface guidelines. If you wish to include more than two items in an application targeting iPhone, you may wish to add a secondary toolbar directly below the application toolbar.

This is how it looks on the different devices:

- iPhone: On the iPhone, the content of the toolbar is overlaid on top of the `pagetitle` div:

- Android: The size of the button in Android is set automatically.
    - In the case of One Button, it looks like the following:

    - In the case of Two Buttons, it looks like the following:

- In the case of Blackberry, it will appear as links as shown below:

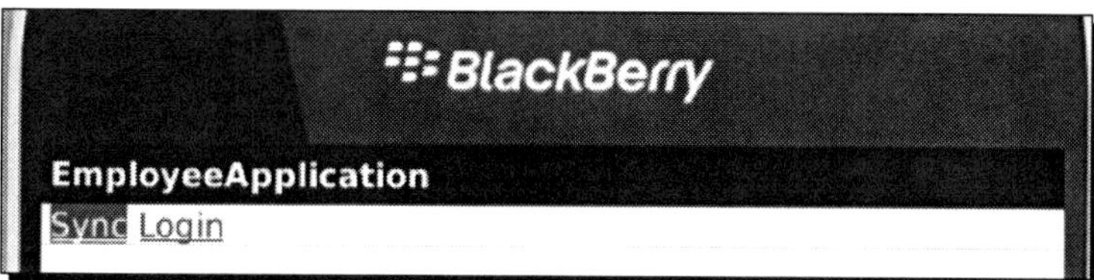

Toolbar button styles

Four button styles are supported for the toolbar. Note that variation in height and width are due to variation in the toolbar height between the platforms. Additionally, in Blackberry and Windows Mobile, the button is a simple text-based link.

IPhone

There are four types of buttons:

- This is how a `.regularButton` style button looks:

- This is how a `.blueButton` style button looks:

- This is how a `.backButton` style button looks:

- This is how a `.deleteButton` style button looks:

Android

For Android, the button is the same for all classes. The variation in width of the buttons for Android is due to the length of the text in the button, and should not be attributed to the classes described in this section. This is how it looks on Android:

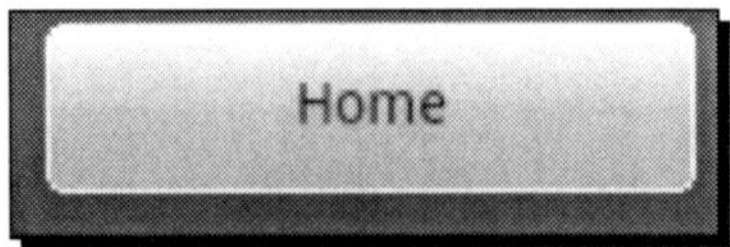

Blackberry

For Blackberry, the button is a simple text-based link. This is how it looks on Blackberry:

Content (<div id="content">)

The features described below are only accessible when they are used inside the `content` div.

The `content` div includes support for native-styled forms and lists. The content div contains the main body of your application. So, in the following code, it shows the various navigation links created:

```
<div class="content">
<ul>
<li>
<a href="<%= url_for :controller => :Employee %>"><span class="title">
Employee</span><span class="disclosure_indicator"/></a>
</li>
<li>
<a href="<%= url_for :controller => :Employee, :action => :employee_
details %>"><span class="title"> Employee Details</span><span
class="disclosure_indicator"/></a>
</li>
<li>
<a href="<%= url_for :controller => :Company %>"><span class="title">
Company</span><span class="disclosure_indicator"/></a>
</li>
<li>
<a href="<%= url_for :controller => :Employee, :action => :filter_
employee_form %>"><span class="title"> Filter Employee </span><span
class="disclosure_indicator"/></a>
</li>
</ul>
</div>
```

- This is how the content part will look on the iPhone:

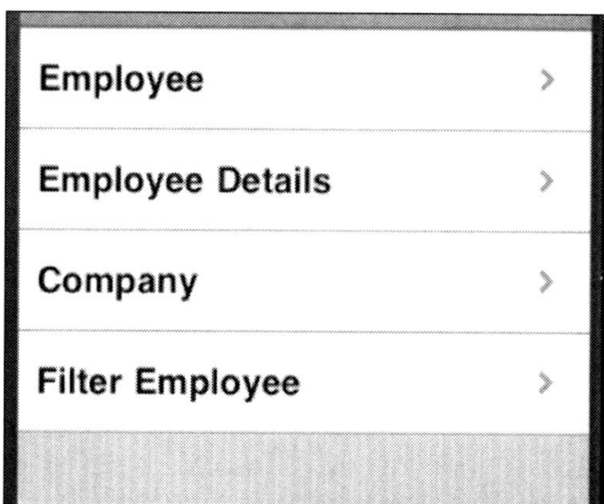

- This is how the content part looks on Android:

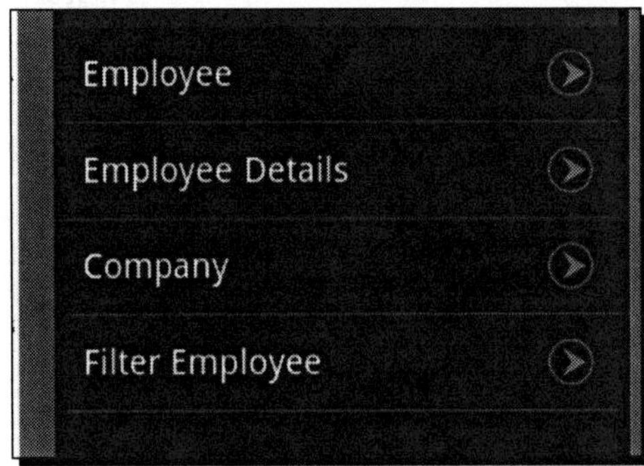

- And this is how it looks on the Blackberry:

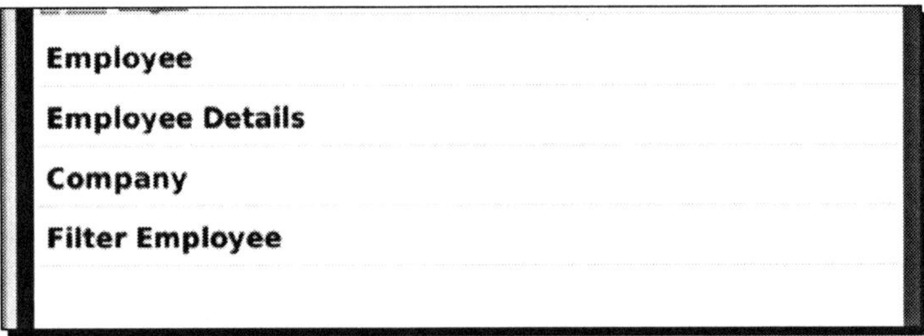

Application menu

Application menus not only help us navigate easily but also give a native look and feel to the application. For platforms that support menus Rhodes framework provides the ability to change the native application menu options through the simple API. So, in this section, we will create a default menu, which will appear on each page of our application. And in the next section, we will create a Controller Action Menu.

Time for action – Default menu

We can set the default menu for all the pages in our application.

To change the default menu (in `application.rb`):

```
class AppApplication < Rho::RhoApplication
def initialize
super
    @default_menu = {
      "Go Home" => :home,
```

```
        "View Employee" => "/app/Employee",
        "Do Refresh" => :refresh,
        "Perform Sync" => :sync,
        "App Options" => :options,
        "View Log" => :log
      }
  end
  end
```

`@default_menu` is hash with key as label and value as action. So, this code will create a menu on Blackberry as shown below:

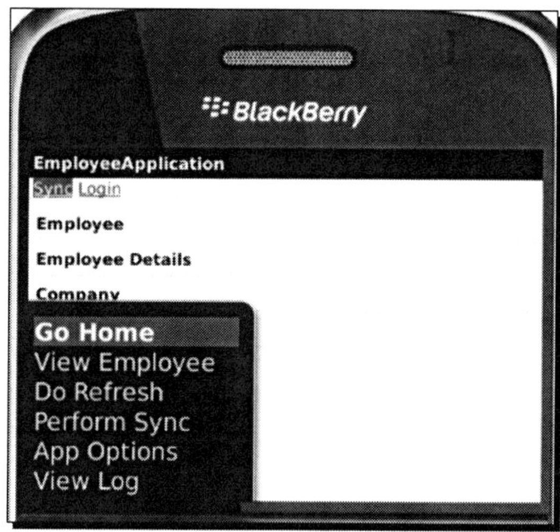

This will create a default menu with the following items (in top-down order):

- **Go Home**
- **View Employee**
- **Do Refresh**
- **Perform Sync**
- **App Options**
- **View Log**

All of these menu items, with the exception of **View Employee,** call a reserved menu item. The **View Employee** item will navigate to the path specified by the hash value, in this case `/app/Employee`.

What just happened?

We have learned to create the default menu for our application. This menu will appear on all the actions.

Controller action menu

In the last section, we have learnt to create the default menu. Now, we will create an action-specific menu.

Time for action – Creating an action menu

We can also change the menu for a specific action (in `controller.rb`).

```
def index
  @accounts = Employee.find(:all)
  @menu = {
    "Go Home" => :home,
    "Refresh" => :refresh,
    "Options" => :options,
:separator => nil,
    "Log" => :log,
    "New Employee" => "/app/Employee/new"
  }
render
end
```

If there is no menu defined in the action then it will have the default menu, which is defined in `application.rb`.

What just happened?

We have created action-specific menus. This menu will appear only on a specific action.

Native tab bar

Rhodes supports displaying a native looking 'tab bar'.

The tab bar is a set of different UI views associated with each tab, so that selecting any tab will display the associated view. There is no ability to define custom actions for the tab bar like you can do for the toolbar. The only action when a tab is selected is to switch to another UI view.

The tab bar is supported on iPhone and Android.

You can use VerticalTab Bar control on iPad (specific control for iPad). It is like the tab bar, but the tabs in it are located on the left side and each item has horizontal orientation. Tab items can have an Icon image and text. You can customize `toolbars/tabbars` during runtime also.

Time for action – Creating tabs

Each tab bar item defined in the above sample defines the following tab elements:

```
require 'rho/rhoapplication'

class AppApplication < Rho::RhoApplication
def initialize
    # Tab items are loaded left->right, @tabs[0] is leftmost tab in
the tab-bar
    # Super must be called *after* settings @tabs!
    @tabs =  [
{ :label => "Home", :action => '/app',
:icon => "/public/images/whiteButton.png", :reload => true, :web_bkg_
color => 0x7F7F7F },
{ :label => "Employees",  :action => '/app/Employee',
:icon => "/public/images/whiteButton.png" },
{ :label => "Companies",  :action => '/app/Company',
:icon => "/public/images/whiteButton.png" },
{ :label => "Settings",   :action => '/app/Settings',
:icon => "/public/images/whiteButton.png" }
    ]

    @@tabbar = nil
```

```
super

    # Uncomment to set sync notification callback to /app/Settings/
sync_notify.
    # SyncEngine::set_objectnotify_url("/app/Settings/sync_notify")
    # SyncEngine.set_notification(-1, "/app/Settings/sync_notify", '')
end
end
```

Now, we can see how it appears on the different devices:

- For iPhone, the tab bar menu will look like the following:

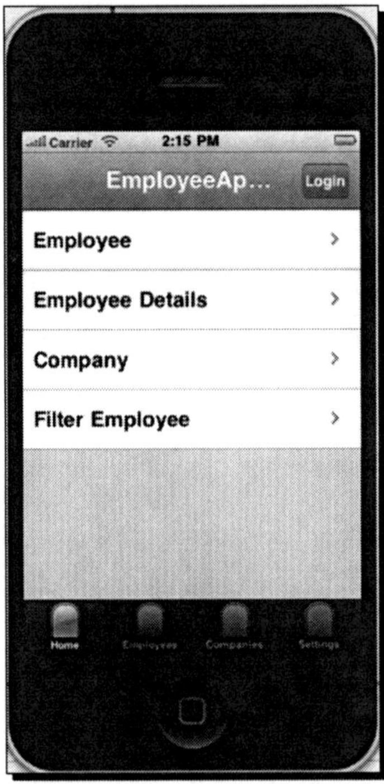

- For Android, it will look like the following:

These are the options available to create a label:

- `:label` – It is the visible label to display on the tab bar (required).
- `:action` – It is the path to your Rhodes action; i.e. `/app/Account` would load the Account index action (required).
- `:icon` – It is the relative path to the tab bar item icon in your Rhodes app; typically located in `/public/images/` (required).
- `:reload` – It is the optional argument that tells Rhodes to reload the tab's `:action`, it defaults to false.
- `:selected_color` – It is an optional parameter for changing the selected color of these tabs (if you use it on Android—you should define it for all tabs! And also define `:background_color` for Tab Bar!).
- `:disabled` – It is an optional parameter to disable this tab.
- `:web_bkg_color` – It is the background color for the tab (use when your app background is not white to remove the blink during switching between tabs). Its value is int hex value (like HTML color).
- `:use_current_view_for_tab` – It is an optional argument that tells Rhodes to smoothly transfer `WebView` from current view into this tab and make this tab active. It defaults to `false`. Only one tab can have this parameter!

Behind the scenes, `Rho::RhoApplication` will detect the `@tabs` array in its initialize method and build the native bar through the following function:

```
require 'rho/rhotabbar'
Rho::NativeTabbar.create(bar_items_array)
```

To disable the tab bar entirely:

```
class AppApplication < Rho::RhoApplication
def initialize
    @tab = nil
super
end
end
```

What just happened?

We have just created a tab bar for Android and iPhone.

BlackBerry CSS/HTML architecture

The BlackBerry Browser version 4.2—the version available to native BlackBerry applications built for Blackberry devices prior to version BB 6.0—has extremely limited support for modern CSS, most notably the key styles applied to divs, like floats, which are used in the standard views. Instead, the view files loaded when your application runs on the BlackBerry use a table-based layout.

Please refer to Blackberry HTML and CSS for a discussion of the styles used for BB.

Loading screen

We can set the loading screen while your application is launching. The loading screen is located at `/app/loading.html`.

Alternatively, you can replace `loading.html` with an image named `loading.png` if you just want a simple image to be displayed.

You can control how images are presented by modifying the `splash_screen` options in `rhoconfig.txt`:

- `delay` – how long the splash screen should be displayed (in seconds)
- `center,vcenter,hcenter` – picture alignment
- `zoom,vzoom,hzoom` – scaling options

Time for action – Setting the loading Image

Place the splash screen in the center and show it for 5 seconds:

```
splash_screen='delay=5;center'
```

Center the splash screen horizontally, scale it vertically to fill all available space, and show it for 5 seconds:

```
splash_screen='delay=5;hcenter;vzoom'
```

You can customize your loading image (shown on the start of the application) for each platform-by-platform suffix:

- Android loading.android.png
- iPhone loading.iPhone.png
- WM loading.wm.png
- BB loading.bb.png

If the application doesn't have a platform specific loading image, then Rhodes will try to load default loading.png.

What just happened?

We have just set loading images for different phones

Adding transition styles for iPhone/Android

We can add various transition styles for links on iPhone/Android.

Transitions between screens are 'slide' by default. You can override the animation on a link by setting a specific animation class. Valid animation classes are:

- slide (default)
- fade
- dissolve
- flip
- slideup
- swap
- cube
- pop

Note that animations other than slide may not work so well on Android devices as they do on the iPhone.

Time for action – Adding transaction animation

Now we will add transaction animation to our home page. Go and edit `index.rb`

```
<div class="pageTitle">
<h1>EmployeeApplication</h1>
</div>

<div class="toolbar">
<% if SyncEngine::logged_in > 0 %>
<div class="leftItem blueButton">
<a class="swap" href="<%= url_for :controller => :Settings, :action =>
:do_sync %>">Sync</a>
</div>
<div class="rightItem regularButton">
<a class="flip" href="<%= url_for :controller => :Settings, :action =>
:logout %>">Logout</a>
</div>
<% else %>
<div class="rightItem regularButton">
<a href="<%= url_for :controller => :Settings, :action => :login
%>">Login</a>
</div>
<% end %>
</div>

<div class="content">
<ul>
<li>
<a class="swap" href="<%= url_for :controller => :Employee %>">
<span class="title"> Employee</span><span class="disclosure_
indicator"/></a>
</li>
<li>
<a class="slideup" href="<%= url_for :controller => :Employee, :action
=> :employee_details %>">
<span class="title"> Employee Details</span><span class="disclosure_
indicator"/></a>
</li>
<li>
```

```
<a class="pop"href="<%= url_for :controller => :Company %>">
<span class="title"> Company</span><span class="disclosure_
indicator"/></a>
</li>
<li>
<a class="cube" href="<%= url_for :controller => :Employee, :action =>
:filter_employee_form %>">
<span class="title"> Filter Employee </span><span class="disclosure_
indicator"/></a>
</li>
</ul>
</div>
```

What just happened?

We have just added various transaction animations to different links.

Pop Quiz

1.) Which of the CSS/JavaScript framework does Rhomobile supports?

a. jQtouch

b. JQuery Mobile

c. Both

d. None

2.) Which of the following platform does not supports Native tabbar?

a. iPhone

b. Android

c. Blackberry

3.) Which of the following platform does not supports Menus?

a. iPhone

b. Android

c. Blackberry

Summary

In this chapter we have learnt about :

- Adding device specific style
- Dynamic loading of custom view files based on the current platform
- Standard Smartphone CSS/HTML architecture
- Application menu
- Tabs and tab bar
- Loading screen
- Added transaction animation

In the next chapter we will learn about Unit testing, debugging, and logging.

8

Unit Testing and Logging—Writing Better Code

In the last chapter, we learned about the Native User Interface for different devices. In this chapter we will learn about testing and logging. Testing plays a very crucial role in the process of software development. It is important to write test cases in order to have good, maintainable, and bug free code. To start with we will learn to write a unit test for our code.

Unit testing

Unit testing is a method by which individual units of source code are tested to determine whether they are fit for use. A unit is the smallest testable part of an application. These are written for each method. Unit tests are created by programmers or occasionally by white box testers during the development process.

Rhodes provides a good way to write `spec` using `msepc`. Rhodes makes it super easy to write your tests. It starts by producing a skeleton test code in the background while you are creating your models and controllers.

We will write a unit test for both Rhodes and RhoSync application's. To write a unit test case for Rhodes we will use `mspec` and for RhoSync we will use `rspec`. First, we will start with our `employee` Rhodes application.

Time for action – Getting ready for testing the Rhodes application

Now, we will configure `mspec` to write a unit test for our Rhodes application. We have to generate a few files using the `rhogen` generator.

Run the following command in your `application` directory:

```
$ rhogen spec
```

We can see the following files being created using the `rhogen` command:

```
Generating with spec generator:
     [ADDED]  app/SpecRunner
     [ADDED]  app/spec
     [ADDED]  app/mspec.rb
     [ADDED]  app/spec_runner.rb
```

It has created a folder `SpecRunner`, which contains a controller and an `index` file. These files will help us to run and check the test result from the simulator.

It also creates the mspec test files `mspec.rb` and `spec_runner.rb`, which will help to run the unit test.

To use these Ruby extensions in our application we need to add `fileutils` and `mspec` in `build.yml`:

```
extensions: ["fileutils", "mspec"]
```

Now, we have to add a link to run these tests. So, we will add a link to the `SpecRunner` controller:

```
<li><a href="SpecRunner"><span class="title"> Run Test</span><span
class="disclosure_indicator"/></a></li>
```

We will now build the code and start our simulator:

```
rake run:iphone
```

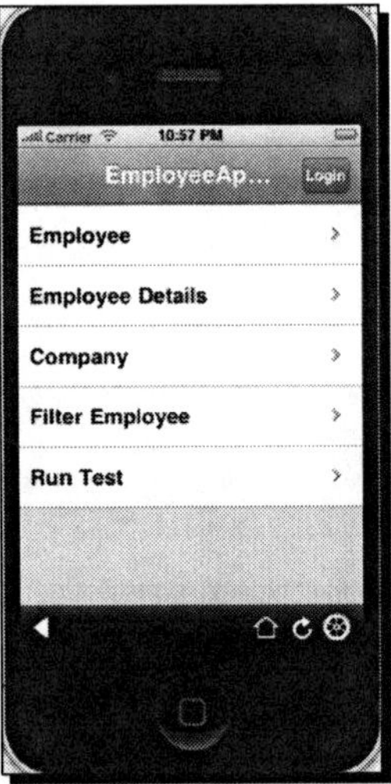

We can see in the screenshot that a link **Run Test** is created.

Now, click on the **Run Test** link that we have created. On clicking this link, all the unit tests will be executed and we can check the status on the next page. We see that a total of two tests ran and both failed. As this test failed, it is shown in red:

From this screenshot, it is clear that a total of two tests ran and both failed.

We can also trace this in the log of our applications.

The log file shows:

- Total unit test executed
- Total passed tests
- Total failed tests

From the log, we can also trace the reason for the failure of the test. This is how the log file looks:

```
I 03/31/2011 23:02:30:419 b0353000                RhoRuby| require_
compiled: test/employee_spec
I 03/31/2011 23:02:30:419 b0353000                    APP| describe
"Employee"
I 03/31/2011 23:02:30:419 b0353000                    APP| - it "should
have tests"
```

```
I 03/31/2011 23:02:30:420 b0353000                APP| FAIL:
Employee - Expected true
 to equal false

lib/mspec/expectations/expectations.rb:15:in `fail_with'
lib/mspec/matchers/base.rb:8:in `=='
apps/app/test/employee_spec.rb:5:in `block (2 levels) in <main>'
lib/mspec/runner/mspec.rb:88:in `instance_eval'
lib/mspec/runner/mspec.rb:88:in `protect'
lib/mspec/runner/context.rb:137:in `block in protect'
lib/mspec/runner/context.rb:137:in `each'
lib/mspec/runner/context.rb:137:in `all?'
lib/mspec/runner/context.rb:137:in `protect'
lib/mspec/runner/context.rb:165:in `block in process'
lib/mspec/runner/context.rb:157:in `each'
lib/mspec/runner/context.rb:157:in `process'
lib/mspec/runner/mspec.rb:57:in `describe'
lib/mspec/runner/object.rb:11:in `describe'
apps/app/test/employee_spec.rb:1:in `<main>'
lib/mspec/runner/mspec.rb:76:in `load'
lib/mspec/runner/mspec.rb:76:in `block (2 levels) in files'
lib/mspec/runner/mspec.rb:88:in `instance_eval'
lib/mspec/runner/mspec.rb:88:in `protect'
lib/mspec/runner/mspec.rb:76:in `block in files'
lib/mspec/runner/mspec.rb:70:in `each'
lib/mspec/runner/mspec.rb:70:in `files'
lib/mspec/runner/mspec.rb:62:in `process'
apps/app/spec_runner.rb:28:in `run'
apps/app/SpecRunner/controller.rb:12:in `index'
lib/rho/rhocontroller.rb:65:in `serve'
lib/rho/rhoapplication.rb:111:in `serve'
lib/rho/rho.rb:539:in `serve'
I 03/31/2011 23:02:30:420 b0353000   APP| ***Total:  2
I 03/31/2011 23:02:30:420 b0353000   APP| ***Passed: 0
I 03/31/2011 23:02:30:420 b0353000   APP| ***Failed: 2
```

The log file shows that two unit tests were executed and both failed. You might be wondering why,even though we have not written any test case, it still shows the failure of two test cases. Actually, a default false test case is generated when we create a model using the `rhogen` command. The test files that are generated by Rhogen command are `employee_spec.rb` and `company_spec.rb`, which can be located in `test` folder.

Open the `employee_spec.rb` file located in the `test` folder:

```
describe "Employee" do
  #this test always fails, you really should have tests!

  it "should have tests" do
    true.should == false
  end
end
```

We can see that a false test is already present in the test file. These tests always start with `it` followed by a simple English statement beginning with `should`, describing the purpose of the test.

What just happened?

We have configured and learned how to run the test using `mspec`. We saw the output result in the device as well as in the log file. After this we know how to get started, where to write the test, and how to run them.

Writing your first Rhodes unit test

Now it's time to write the first test for our code. We will create a method in the model and then write the test code for it.

Time for action – Writing the first test

We will first write a method `lower_case` that will down case the name and then write its unit test.

Create a method `lower_case` in the model `employee.rb`. This method will down case the name of the employee:

```
class Employee
  include Rhom::PropertyBag
   belongs_to :company_id, 'Company'
  # Uncomment the following line to enable sync with Employee.
  enable :sync


def lower_name
self.name.downcase
end

end
```

Now, we will write a unit test case for the method `lower_name`:

```
describe "Employee" do

   before :each do
      Employee.delete_all
      Employee.create "name" => "John", "company"=>"1" ,"age" =>
"23","gender" => "male", "salary"=>"20000"
   end

   it "should lower case name" do
      Employee.find(:all)[0].name.should == "John"
      Employee.find(:all)[0].lower_name.should == "john"
   end

end
```

The Rhodes application interacts with the database and, as a result, your tests will need a database to interact with as well. So, we may want to have some initial data seeded before writing a test for a model method. To do so, we will create a `before` filter:

```
before :each do
      Employee.delete_all
      Employee.create "name" => "John", "company"=>"1" ,"age" =>
"23","gender" => "male", "salary"=>"20000"
   end
```

`Employee.delete_all` will delete all the data in the employee table and `Employee.create` will seed an employee row.

Now, the actual test, `lower_name` method:

```
it "should lower case name" do
      Employee.find(:all)[0].name.should == "John"
      Employee.find(:all)[0].lower_name.should == "john"
   end
```

`Employee.find(:all)` is an array of objects storing all employees and `Employee.find(:all)[0]` will have the first row of `employee` table. The method `lower_name` will down case all the letters.

Now, build the application and run the simulator:

```
rake run:iphone
```

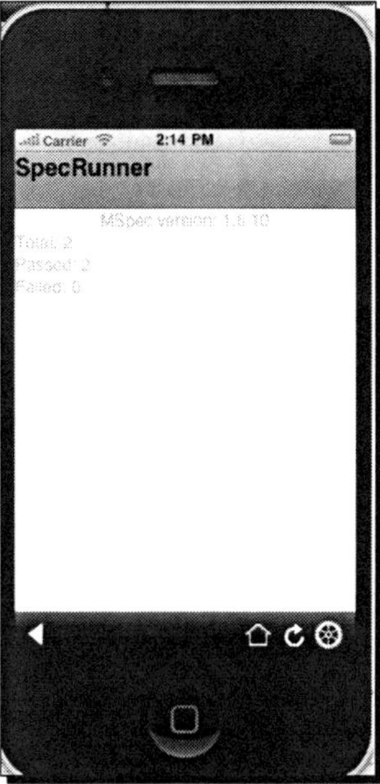

What just happened?

We have written a unit test for a model method using `mspec`, where we first seeded a dummy data and then compared the results with and without the method that was to be tested.

Testing the RhoSync application

RhoSync provides a spec framework for behavior-driven development of your application. We can use the popular test framework `rspec` for writing the unit test case. When your application and source adapters are generated, you will see spec files being generated in the top-level `spec` folder of your application. We will now run the default unit test.

Time for a Action – Running the default test

To run the test case, we will use the `rake` command. We can use the following command to run your test:

```
$ rake rhosync:spec
(in /Users/ employee-server)
```

```
[10:29:21 PM 2011-04-06] Rhosync Server v2.1.1 started...
Company
  should process Company query (PENDING: TODO)
  should process Company create (PENDING: TODO)
  should process Company update (PENDING: TODO)
  should process Company delete (PENDING: TODO)
Employee
  should process Employee query (PENDING: TODO)
  should process Employee create (PENDING: TODO)
  should process Employee update (PENDING: TODO)
  should process Employee delete (PENDING: TODO)

Pending:

Company should process Company query (TODO)
./spec/sources/company_spec.rb:10

Company should process Company create (TODO)
./spec/sources/company_spec.rb:14

Company should process Company update (TODO)
./spec/sources/company_spec.rb:18

Company should process Company delete (TODO)
./spec/sources/company_spec.rb:22

Employee should process Employee query (TODO)
./spec/sources/employee_spec.rb:10

Employee should process Employee create (TODO)
./spec/sources/employee_spec.rb:14

Employee should process Employee update (TODO)
./spec/sources/employee_spec.rb:18

Employee should process Employee delete (TODO)
./spec/sources/employee_spec.rb:22

Finished in 0.228515 seconds

8 examples, 0 failures, 8 pending
```

Actually, when we create a source adapter it also creates a `spec` for that source adapter.

If you check the `spec` folder in the application you will see `employee_spec.rb` and `company_spec.rb`:

```
require File.join(File.dirname(__FILE__),'..','spec_helper')

describe "Employee" do
  it_should_behave_like "SpecHelper"

  before(:each) do
    setup_test_for Employee,'testuser'
  end

  it "should process Employee query" do
    pending
  end

  it "should process Employee create" do
    pending
  end

  it "should process Employee update" do
    pending
  end

  it "should process Employee delete" do
    pending
  end
end
```

By default status, all the tests are pending.

Pop Quiz – Spec

1. If we have to write a test for the employee source, where can we write the test?
    a. In the `employee.rb` file
    b. In the `employee_spec.rb` file in the Employee folder
    c. In the `employee_spec.rb` file in the spec folder
    d. In the `spec.rb` file

2. What can be the output of a test when it is run?
   a. Fail
   b. Pending
   c. Pass
   d. All of the Above

What just happened?

We ran the default unit test using the rake task for our RhoSync application.

Creating the first unit test for the RhoSync application

In the last section, we learned to run the unit test. Now, we will write the unit test for a source adapter.

Time for action – Creating a unit test for the source adapter

Now, we will write a unit test for the source adapter `product.rb`. There are four actions defined in the source adapter: `query`, `create`, `delete`, and `update`. We will write a unit test for each action.

Open the `product_spec.rb` file and write the following code:

```
require File.join(File.dirname(__FILE__),'..','spec_helper')

describe "Employee" do
  it_should_behave_like "SpecHelper"

  before(:each) do
    setup_test_for Employee,'testuser'

    @employee = {
      'name' => 'John',
     'company'=>'1' ,
     'age' => '23',
     'gender' => 'male',
     'salary'=>'20000'

    }
  end

  it "should process Employee query" do
```

```
    test_create(@employee)
    test_query.size.should > 0
    query_errors.should == {}
  end

  it "should process Employee create" do
    new_employee_id = test_create(@employee)
    new_employee_id.should_not be_nil
    create_errors.should == {}
    md[new_employee_id].should == @employee
  end

  it "should process Employee update" do
    employee_id = test_create(@employee)
    md.should == {employee_id => @employee}
    test_update({employee_id => {'age' => '55'}})
    update_errors.should == {}
    test_query
    md[employee_id]['age'].should == '55'
  end

  it "should process Employee delete" do
    employee_id = test_create(@employee)
    md.should == {employee_id => @employee}
    test_delete(employee_id => @employee)
    delete_errors.should == {}
    md.should == {}
  end
end
```

In `before(:each)` block we will write the code that we want to execute before running the test:

```
  before(:each) do
    setup_test_for Employee,'testuser'

    @employee = {
     'name' => 'John',
    'company'=>'1' ,
    'age' => '23',
    'gender' => 'male',
    'salary'=>'20000'

    }
  end
```

Here, we initialized the source adapter for `testuser` and seeded some initial data.

Before understanding the test for each action of the source adapter, we need to understand the various test APIs that we have used:

- `setup_test_for(Employee,'testuser')`: Initializes the source adapter.
- `test_query`: Executes the adapter's `query` method and returns the master document (`:md`) stored in Redis.
- `test_create(record)`: Executes the adapter's `create` method with a provided record and returns the object string from the `create` method. If the `create` method returns a string, then a link will be saved for the device the next time it synchronizes. This link can be tested here.
- `create_errors`: This will return the result of the adapter's `create` method. The master document `(:md)` should also contain the new record. Returns any errors stored in Redis from the previous source adapter `create` (same structure as query errors).
- `test_update(record)`: Execute the source adapter's `update` method. Takes a record as hash of hashes `(object_id => object).`
- `update_errors`: Returns any errors stored in Redis from the previous source adapter update (same structure as query errors).
- `test_delete(record)`: Execute the source adapter's `delete` method. Takes a record as hash of hashes `(object_id => object).`
- `delete_errors`: Returns any errors stored in Redis from the previous source adapter delete (same structure as query errors).
- `md`: Returns the master document `(:md)` for the source adapter stored in Redis. This is equivalent to the `@result` hash of hashes structure.

Now we will understand the specs, which we have written for `query`, `create`, `update`, and `delete`.

Query

This action will get an array of `employee` object. The spec for the query looks like:

```
it "should process Employee query" do
  test_create(@employee)
  test_query.size.should > 0
  query_errors.should == {}
end
```

`test_create` will call the `create` action for the `employee` source adapter and `test_query` will execute the `query` action. `test_query.size` and `query_errors` will return the count of employees and errors while executing the `query` action respectively. For a successful test, `query_errors` should return a blank array.

Create

This action is called when the `employee` object is created. The code for this spec looks like:

```
it "should process Employee create" do
  new_employee_id = test_create(@employee)
  new_employee_id.should_not be_nil
  create_errors.should == {}
  md[new_employee_id].should == @employee
end
```

`test_create(@employee)` will return the `id` of the created `employee` object. For running the test successfully `new_employee_id` should not be `nil`. `create_error` and `md[new_employee_id]` will return the error message and `employee` object respectively. For the test to have run successfully the error should be a blank array and the `employee` object should be updated to Redis. To test whether the `employee` object has been successfully updated to Redis, we compare it with `@employee`.

Update

This action is called when `employee` is updated. The code for this spec looks like the following:

```
it "should process Employee update" do
  employee_id = test_create(@employee)
  md.should == {employee_id => @employee}
  test_update({employee_id => {'age' => '55'}})
  update_errors.should == {}
  test_query
  md[employee_id]['age'].should == '55'
end
```

We have first created the employee object using `test_create` and updated the age to 55 using the `test_update` method.

`Update_error` will return the array of errors during updating an `employee` record. If it is successfully updated it will return a blank array. We can check the updated value of age from Redis using `md[employee_id]['age']`.

Delete

`Delete` action is called when we delete an employee. The code for this spec looks like:

```
it "should process Employee delete" do
  employee_id = test_create(@employee)
  md.should == {employee_id => @employee}
  test_delete(employee_id => @employee)
  delete_errors.should == {}
  md.should == {}
end
```

We first created an employee using `test_create`. After which we checked whether the employee is successfully created using `md.should == {employee_id => @employee}`.

Then, we delete the employee using `test_delete(employee_id => @employee)` and we check for errors while deleting the record using `delete_error`.

What just happened?

We created specs for all the actions of the RhoSync source adapter. We also understood the various API methods available for writing tests.

Have a go hero – Creating a test for the company model

In the previous example, we created a test for the employee source adapter. I think we are now clear on how to write a unit test. As we have one more source adapter `company.rb` in our application, now you can write a similar unit test for this source adapter.

Logging

We may want to see logs for different devices to troubleshoot the issues in our application. Before checking the location of the log file that is created for different devices, we have to configure the generation of logs.

Time for action – Configure logs for the Rhodes application

We can configure different levels of logs in our Rhodes application. We can configure this in `rhoconfig.txt` in the Rhodes `application` folder. We have to set the value of a property named `MinSeverity` for different levels of logging.

The different log levels for `MinSeverity` are:

- 0-trace
- 1-info(app level)
- 3-warnings
- 4-errors

For the development set:

```
MinSeverity = 0
```

It is recommended to set it to `3` for production so as to minimize logging and increase performance due to limited log output.

What just happened?

We configured and understood the various options for generating logs for a Rhodes application.

Where to find logs:

Logs for each device are stored at different locations:

iPhone

Logs for iPhone are stored in `rholog.txt` inside the `application` directory.

Android

Logs for Android are stored in the directory where the Rhodes gem is installed. `rhobuild.txt` file is also present in the same directory.

To get the application logs from the device or emulator, type the following command from your `application` folder or from the root folder of your Rhodes gem (the place where `rhobuild.yml` is located):

```
$ rake device:android:getlog
```

Or:

```
$ rake emulator:android:getlog
```

The application log will be pulled from the device/emulator and stored in your `application` directory with the name `RhoLog.txt`.

To see all emulator messages, run `adb logcat` and start the application on emulator.

To see all the device messages, run `adb -d logcat` and start the application on device.

Blackberry

You can see the logs where the Blackberry simulator is installed. Run your application and see the log file at `<simulator folder>\sdcard\rho\<app_name>\RhoLog.txt`.

If your Blackberry simulator hangs, or for any troubleshooting, you can reset the simulator from **File | Reset**.

You can also clear all simulator data by running `clean.bat` in `<simulator folder>\simulator`, which is mostly `C:\Program Files\Research In Motion\BlackBerry JDE 4.6.0\simulator`.

Pop quiz- Logging

1. If we have two JDE installs for Blackberry then where will the `Rholog.txt` file be stored?
   a. In both the JDE folders
   b. In the JDE that is configured in `rhobuild.yml`
2. If you see that only warning is logged in your log file, what can be the reason for this?
   a. `MinSeverity` in `rhoconfig.txt` is set to 0
   b. `MinSeverity` in `rhoconfig.txt` is set to 1
   c. `MinSeverity` in `rhoconfig.`txt is set to 3
   d. Some issues with the simulator

See the device log on the device

Now we know where the log files are located when you are running the application on simulator. But what if we are running on the device?

To show the application logs on the device we can use the following method available with Rhodes:

```
Rho::RhoConfig.show_log
```

You may also send the log to the log server URL, defined in `rhoconfig.txt`:

```
Rho::RhoConfig.send_log = "some URL"
```

The URL format will be:

```
<logserver>/client_log?client_id=<client_id>&device_pin=<device_
pin>&log_name=<logname>
```

RhoError class

It is important to understand the RhoError class because you may find access to the error class useful in logging and reporting:

- RhoError class contains error codes. Currently, RhoError contains the following error codes:

  ```
  ERR_NONE = 0
  ERR_NETWORK = 1
  ERR_REMOTESERVER = 2
  ERR_RUNTIME = 3
  ERR_UNEXPECTEDSERVERRESPONSE = 4
  ERR_DIFFDOMAINSINSYNCSRC = 5
  ERR_NOSERVERRESPONSE = 6
  ERR_CLIENTISNOTLOGGEDIN = 7
  ERR_CUSTOMSYNCSERVER = 8
  ERR_UNAUTHORIZED = 9
  ```

  You can get a list of all the error codes available from www.doc.rhomobile.com.

- A method message(): It translates the error code to a text message.

Summary

We have learned the following things in this chapter:

- Writing mspec for Rhodes application
- Writing rspec for Rhosync application
- Configuring various logging options
- Checking logs in different devices
- Learned about the RhoError class

In the next chapter, we will learn to deploy our RhoSync application and to build the Rhodes code for different devices using Rhohub.

9
RhoHub—Deploying to Cloud

In the last chapter, we have learned about the unit test and logging. In this chapter, we will learn about hosting solutions for RhoMobile called RhoHub. RhoHub provides a hosting solution for your RhoSync application and also creates builds of your Rhodes application for different smart phones. It makes each process easier, reducing the overhead of getting started as well as streamlining the ongoing development effort. RhoHub eliminates the requirement for every smart phone SDK. RhoHub provides hosted builds of Rhodes-based apps, version control, collaboration, and a hosted runtime RhoSync server. Writing a project on RhoHub consists of creating a client side Rhodes app and a server side RhoSync app.

Installation and configuration

So before starting, we have to install Git and configure it with the RhoHub account. Git is used for version control and it will also push the code to Cloud.

Time for action – Installation and configuration

To get started, follow these steps:

- **Install Git**: Install Git using the Rhomobile Windows installer for Windows and for other platforms; you can install it by downloading it from `http://git-scm.com/`.
- **Register on RhoHub**: Create a RhoHub account or log in if you already have one. To create an account you have to register at `https://rhohub.com`.
- **Confirm email**: After signing up, you will receive an email containing a link directing you to `http://app.rhohub.com/your-user-name`. Open the link to confirm your email address.
- **Setting SSH key**: Create the SSH key by typing the following command in the terminal for Mac and Linux and for Windows in Git shell:

  ssh-keygen -t rsa -C your_email@youremail.com

- `SSH-Keygen` is a UNIX utility that is used to generate, manage, and convert authentication keys for SSH authentication. The `SSH-keygen` tool stores the private key in `$HOME/.ssh/id_rsa` and the public key in `$HOME/.ssh/id_rsa.pub` in the user's home directory. When we set the key using `ssh-keygen` it will ask for the file to store the key. You can keep it blank. By default, the file name `$HOME/.ssh/id_rsa`, which represents an RSA v2 key, appears in parentheses:

  Enter the file in which to save the key (/Users/abhisheknalwaya/.ssh/id_rsa):

- Now, you need to enter a passphrase. The passphrase you will enter will be used for encrypting your private key. A good passphrase should be alphanumeric having 10-30 character length. You can also use the null passphrase, however, it can be a loophole in the security:

  ```
  Enter passphrase (empty for no passphrase):
  ```

  Enter the same passphrase again:

  It will set the key and will give the following output:

  ```
  Your identification has been saved in /Users/abhisheknalwaya/.ssh/
  id_rsa.
  Your public key has been saved in /Users/abhisheknalwaya/.ssh/
  id_rsa.pub.
  The key fingerprint is:
  af:3f:fe:82:ec:56:aa:bd:0f:ab:98:17:7f:3c:c7:1e nalwayaabhishek@
  gmail.com
  The key's randomart image is:
  +--[ RSA 2048]----+
  |                 |
  |                 |
  |                 |
  |                 |
  |        S        |
  |      .   ..     |
  |       +.=..E    |
  |     o..*+* o.   |
  |    o.o=**+Bo    |
  +-----------------+
  ```

- The private key was saved in the `.ssh/id_rsa` file, which is a read-only file. No one else should see the content of that file, as it is used to decrypt all correspondence encrypted with the public key. The public key is saved in the `.ssh/id_rsa.pub` file.
- **Login to RhoHub**: Enter the username and password to log in to the RhoHub account.

- **Copy SSH key**: Copy the key that we generated. You can copy from the file directly or you can copy from the terminal by:

  pbcopy < ~/.ssh/id_rsa.pub

- **Add SSH key**: Add your SSH public key in the RhoHub SSH Keys page. From `http://rhohub.com`, click **My Account**. Click the **SSH Keys** link in the right top navigation. Click **Add Public Key**:

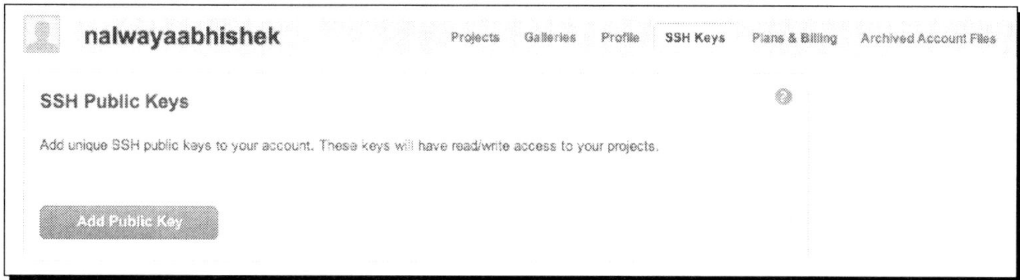

- Add the **Title** and **Public Key** that you have copied from your machine and then click on **Add Public Key**:

- Set the username or email address of RhoHub using the following command:

  ```
  git config --global github.user username
  ```

  or:

  ```
  git config --global user.email you@yourdomain.example.com
  ```

Each commit has an author and a committer field that record who created the change, when the change was created, and who committed it.

What just happened?

We have installed Git and set up the keys it requires for encryption.

Understanding basic Git

Before going further we need to understand Git. It is a free and open source, distributed version control system designed to handle everything from small to very large projects with speed and efficiency. Every Git clone is a fully-fledged repository with complete history and full revision tracking capabilities, not dependent on network access or a central server. Branching and merging are fast and easy to do.

It is a version control system allowing us to track changes to our project's code, collaborate more easily, and roll back any inadvertent errors (such as accidentally updating or deleting files).

Now, we will see a few Git commands:

- `git init`: It will initialize the working directory—you may notice a new directory created, named `.git`
- `git add`: It will add all the files under the current directory
- `git commit`: This commit will create the initial import, given that repositories are coupled with working copies
- `git diff`: This will show you any changes that you've made but not yet added
- `git add file1 file2 file3`: Modify some files, then add their updated contents to the index

There are lots of commands available, which you can refer from `http://git-scm.com/`.

Creating a RhoHub project

In the last section, we have set up Git and understood how it works. Now, we will create a RhoHub project.

Time for action – Creating a RhoHub project

We will create an employee project on RhoHub. It will be a combination of Rhodes and RhoSync applications. Follow these steps:

1. Log in to RhoHub with the login and password that you created during registration.

2. Click on **Create Project**:

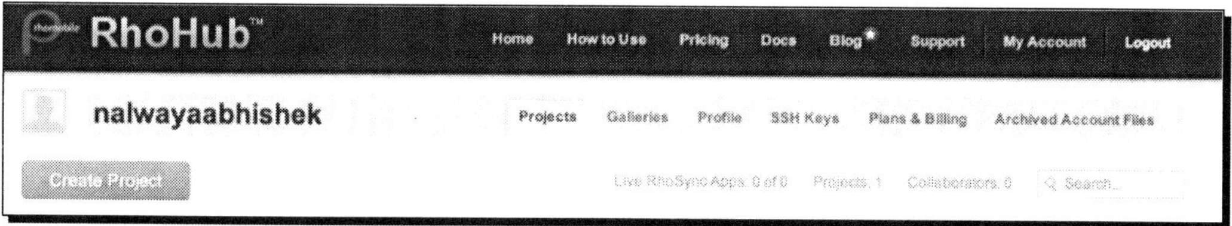

3. A dialog box will appear for creating a project. Enter your project name and description. Uncheck **Generate Apps** as we already have an application that we will deploy. If you are generating an application you can also select the RhoSync version otherwise it will take that information from the configuration files:

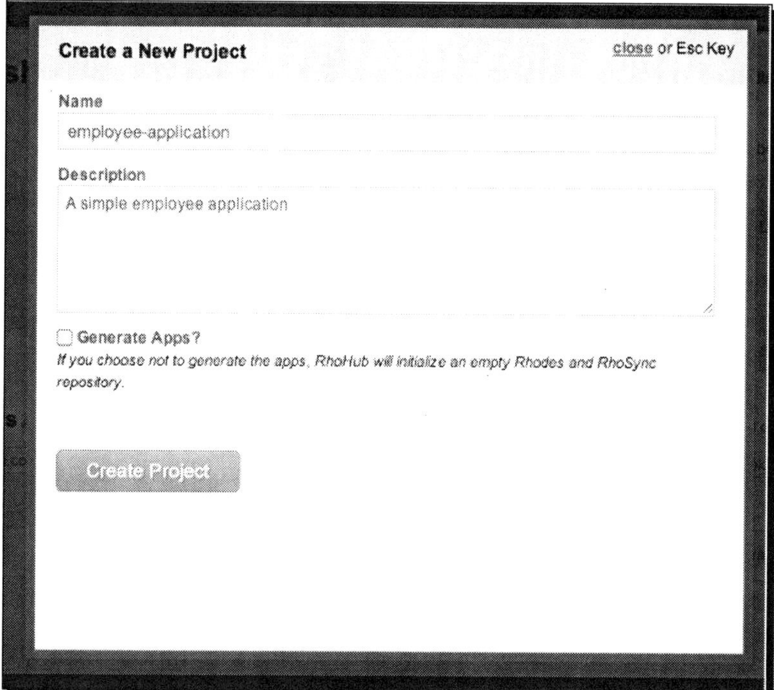

4. Your project detail will pop up on the screen that has all the Git commands to manage your application:

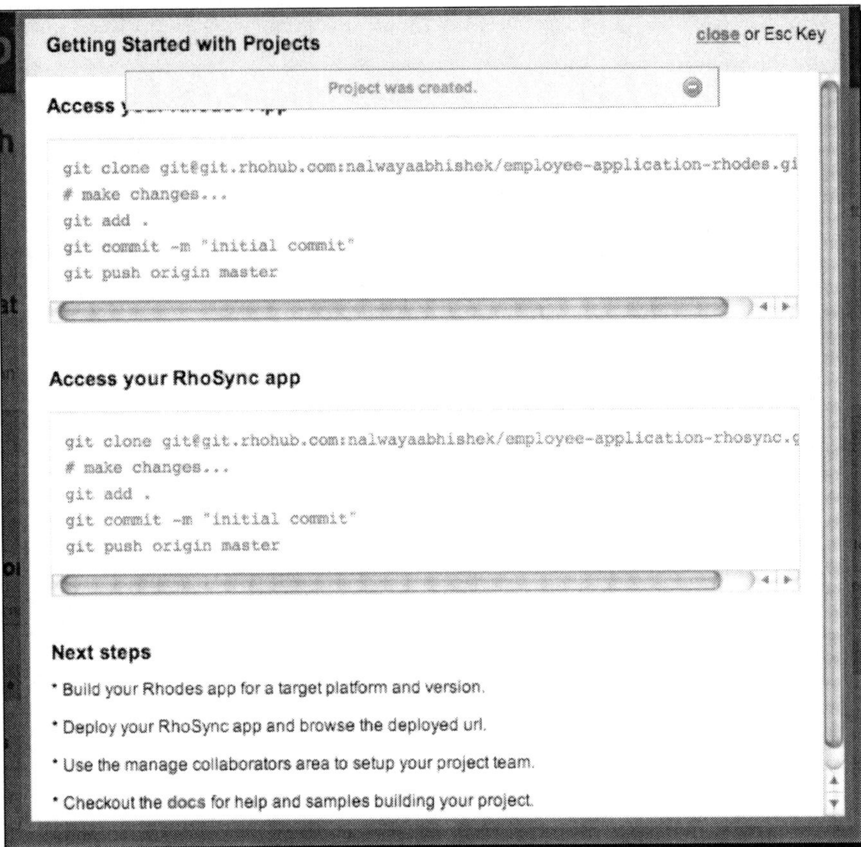

What Just Happened?

We have created an employee project in RhoHub. This contains a Rhodes and a RhoSync application.

Pop Quiz

1. Where can we host the RhoSync server?
    a. We can host it on Heroku
    b. We can host it on Amazon S3
    c. We can host it on our own server.
    d. All of the above

2. Can more than one developer work on the same project simultaneously on RhoHub?

    a. True

    b. False

Cloning and committing your Rhodes application

We have created an account and project in RhoHub in the last section. Now, we can clone the empty employee Rhodes application to our local machine and then push our application code to this project.

Time for action – Pushing Rhodes application

We will clone the Rhodes application and then commit our code from the local machine. Follow these steps:

1. We will clone the repository to our local machine. Clone means it will copy all the files on the server to our local machine. The clone is on an equal footing with the original project, possessing its own copy of the original project's history:

    ```
    git clone git@git.rhohub.com:nalwayaabhishek/employee-application-rhodes.git
    ```

    Please do not copy the same code. As your Git repository will have a different Git URL.

    This creates a new directory `employee-application-rhodes` containing a clone of the RhoHub employee Rhodes application repository. You will get the following output:

    ```
    >>$ git clone git@git.rhohub.com:nalwayaabhishek/employee-application-rhodes.git
    Cloning into employee-application-rhodes...
    ```

    warning: You appear to have cloned an empty repository

    As we have an empty directory, it will clone an empty directory with the name `employee-application-rhodes`.

2. Copy your Rhodes application to this directory.

3. Go to the terminal and from the application directory run the following command:

    ```
    git add .
    ```

4. From the application directory, run the following command to commit your changes:

```
git commit -m "my first commit"
```

You will get the following output:

```
[master (root-commit) 987ea53] first commit
 128 files changed, 4324 insertions(+), 0 deletions(-)
 create mode 100644 Rakefile
 create mode 100644 app/Company/company.rb
 create mode 100644 app/Company/company_controller.rb
 create mode 100644 app/Company/edit.bb.erb
 create mode 100644 app/Company/edit.erb
 create mode 100644 app/Company/index.bb.erb
 create mode 100644 app/Company/index.erb
 create mode 100644 app/Company/new.bb.erb
 create mode 100644 app/Company/new.erb
….
…..
….
 create mode 100755 public/images/toolbar.png
 create mode 100755 public/images/whiteButton.png
 create mode 100755 public/jqtouch/jqtouch-iphone.css
 create mode 100755 public/jqtouch/jqtouch.css
 create mode 100755 public/jqtouch/jqtouch.js
 create mode 100755 public/jqtouch/jqtouch.transitions.js
 create mode 100755 public/jqtouch/jquery.1.3.2.min.js
 create mode 100755 public/js/application.js
 create mode 100755 public/js/rho.js
 create mode 100755 public/js/rhogeolocation-wm.js
 create mode 100755 public/js/rhogeolocation.js
 create mode 100644 rhoconfig.txt
 create mode 120000 rholog-4.0.2.txt
 create mode 120000 sim-public-4.0.2
```

5. From the application directory, run the following command:

```
git push origin master
```

You will get the following output:

```
Counting objects: 137, done.
Delta compression using up to 2 threads.
Compressing objects: 100% (135/135), done.
Writing objects: 100% (137/137), 253.09 KiB, done.
Total 137 (delta 22), reused 0 (delta 0)
To git@git.rhohub.com:nalwayaabhishek/employee-application-rhodes.
git
 * [new branch]      master -> master
```

Your code is now pushed to the server.

What Just Happened?

In this section we have cloned the Rhodes application to our local machine using Git. We have also learned to commit the Code using Git.

Have a go hero – Commit the code

As you have understood the basics of Git, now make changes in your Rhodes application and then commit these changes using Git. In the process you can explore the numerous commands available with Git.

Deploying the RhoSync application

Now, we will deploy the RhoSync code similar to the Rhodes code, which we did in the last section.

Time for action – Pushing the RhoSync application

We will clone the empty RhoSync application from RhoHub and then commit the code.

1. Clone the repository to our local machine using the following command:

   git clone git@git.rhohub.com:nalwayaabhishek/employee-application-rhosync.git

   Please do not copy the same code. As your Git repository will have a different Git URL.

2. This creates a new directory `employee-application-rhosync` containing a clone of RhoHub employee, RhoSync application repository. The clone is on an equal footing with the original project, possessing its own copy of the original project's history. You will get following output:

```
>>$ git clone git@git.rhohub.com:nalwayaabhishek/employee-
application-rhosync.git
Cloning into employee-application-rhosync...
```

   Warning: You appear to have cloned an empty repository.

As we have an empty directory, it will clone an empty directory with the name employee-application-rhosync.

3. Copy your RhoSync application to this directory.
4. Go to the terminal and from the application directory run the following command:

```
git add .
```

5. From the application directory, run the following command:

```
git commit -m "my first commit"
```

You will get the following output:

```
[master (root-commit) 8a26b44] first commit
 24 files changed, 1998 insertions(+), 0 deletions(-)
 create mode 100644 Rakefile
 create mode 100644 application.rb
 create mode 100644 config.ru
 create mode 100644 coverage/application_rb.html
 create mode 100644 coverage/index.html
 create mode 100644 coverage/jquery-1.3.2.min.js
 create mode 100644 coverage/jquery.tablesorter.min.js
 create mode 100644 coverage/print.css
 create mode 100644 coverage/rcov.js
 create mode 100644 coverage/screen.css
 create mode 100644 coverage/sources-company_rb.html
 create mode 100644 coverage/sources-employee_rb.html
 create mode 100644 nbproject/private/private.properties
 create mode 100644 nbproject/private/private.xml
 create mode 100644 nbproject/private/rake-d.txt
 create mode 100644 nbproject/project.properties
 create mode 100644 nbproject/project.xml
 create mode 100644 settings/license.key
 create mode 100644 settings/settings.yml
 create mode 100644 sources/company.rb
 create mode 100644 sources/employee.rb
 create mode 100644 spec/sources/company_spec.rb
 create mode 100644 spec/sources/employee_spec.rb
```

create mode 100644 spec/spec_helper.rb

6. From the application directory, run the following command:

```
Git push origin master
```

You will get the following output:

```
Counting objects: 33, done.
Delta compression using up to 2 threads.
Compressing objects: 100% (33/33), done.
Writing objects: 100% (33/33), 35.59 KiB, done.
Total 33 (delta 5), reused 0 (delta 0)
To git@git.rhohub.com:nalwayaabhishek/employee-application-rhosync.git
 * [new branch]      master -> master
```

What just happened?

In this section, we have learnt to clone the RhoSync application to our local machine using Git. We have also learned to commit the Code using Git.

RhoHub online editor

RhoHub 3.0 has an HTML5 project editor complete with a Git interface. We can edit the code directly from the web interface and commit that code.

RhoHub editor supports:

- Editing Ruby/HTML/CSS/JavaScript files
- Viewing image files
- Uploading of local files into the editor
- Adding, removing, and renaming of files and directories
- Git commit and reset actions to files

To open the editor, click on the **Launch Editor** link on your current project:

It will open the code for both the Rhodes and the RhoSync applications:

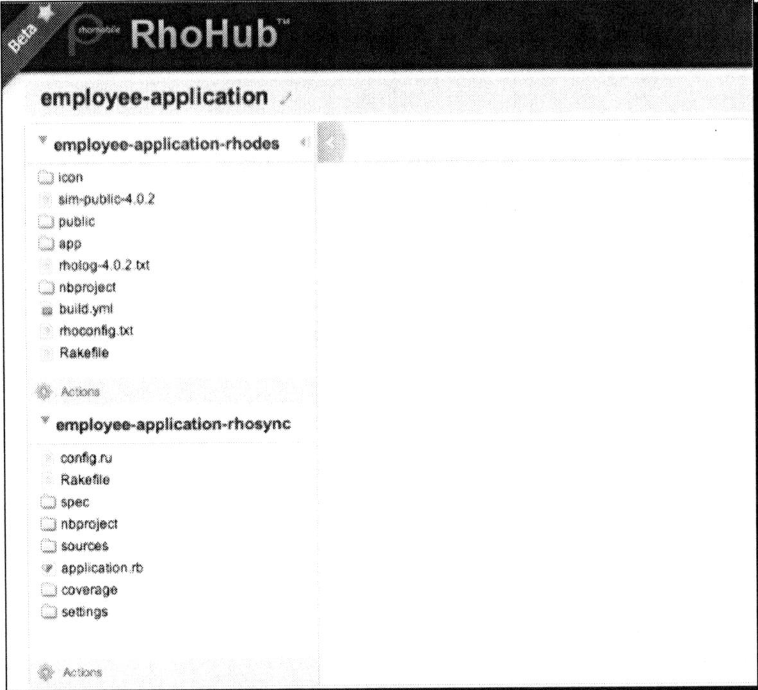

We can observe that on the left-hand side there is a full menu showing our Rhodes and RhoSync application files. We can open these files by clicking them and we can also edit them. We can even open multiple files together. The RhoHub editor also allows you to perform the following tasks with your Rhodes and RhoSync applications:

- Creation of Models for your Rhodes application
- Creation of Builds of your Rhodes application for various platforms
- Creation of a source adapter for your RhoSync application
- Deploying your RhoSync application
- Adding the test framework for your Rhodes application

Creating builds for different phones from RhoHub

Once you have your application working well locally in the simulator for a specific platform, you will want to test across all of the platforms that you plan to support. Using RhoHub, you can build for iPhone, Android, BlackBerry, or Windows Mobile.

We can directly create build for different devices right from your RhoHub account.

Time for action – Three steps to build the Rhodes code

First, make sure that all your latest changes have been committed to the remote repository:

```
git push origin master.
```

We will create build for different devices from the RhoHub account in three easy steps:

Step 1) Click Build: Click on **Build** at the top of your Rhodes application, a Dialog Box will open:

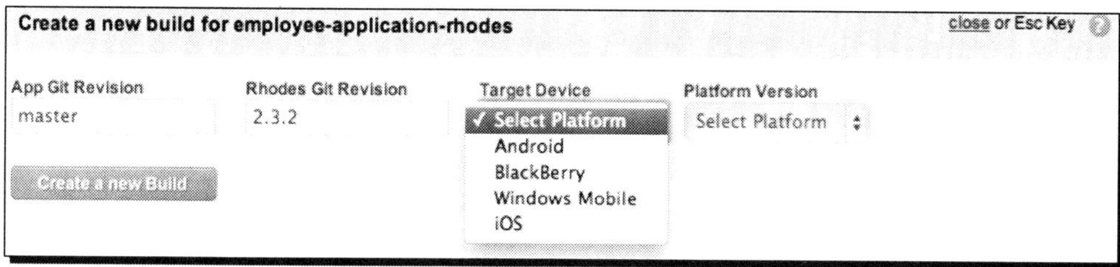

Step 2) Fill the form: Select the target Device and OS version in the form and click **Create a New Build:**

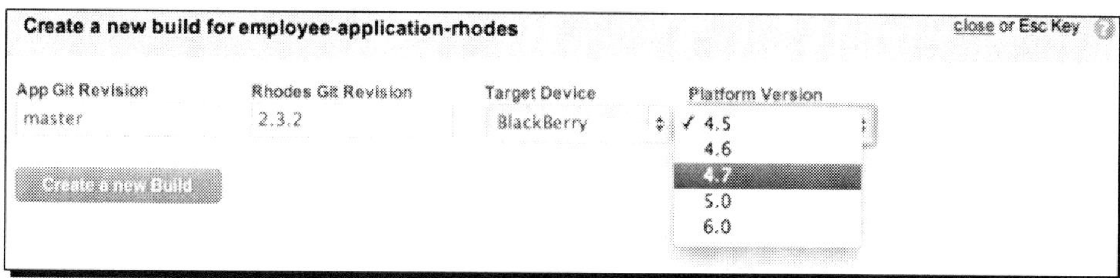

Step 3) Yippee! There is no step 3. Wait for the build to complete as it may take a few minutes to complete. Once the build is finished, you will see a green button. Click on the green button to download a zipped file containing an `.apk` file. The `.apk` file is an Android executable. All you need to do is to put the `.apk` on an http server and browse to it from a device and you will be prompted to install the application.

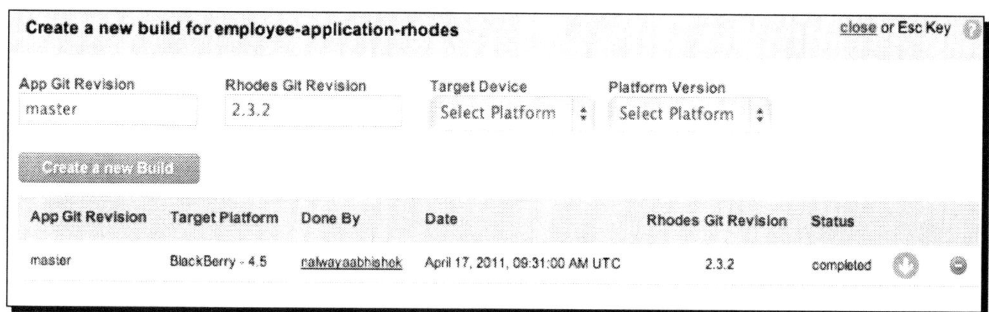

What Just Happened?

In this section, we have learned to create build for different devices and versions from your RhoMobile account.

Deploying the RhoSync application to RhoHub

We can deploy the RhoSync application to Heroku using Rhohub.

Time for action – Three steps to deploy RhoSync

We can deploy the Rhosync application to Rhohub by following three simple steps:

Step 1: In your RhoHub account ,click on **Deploy**:

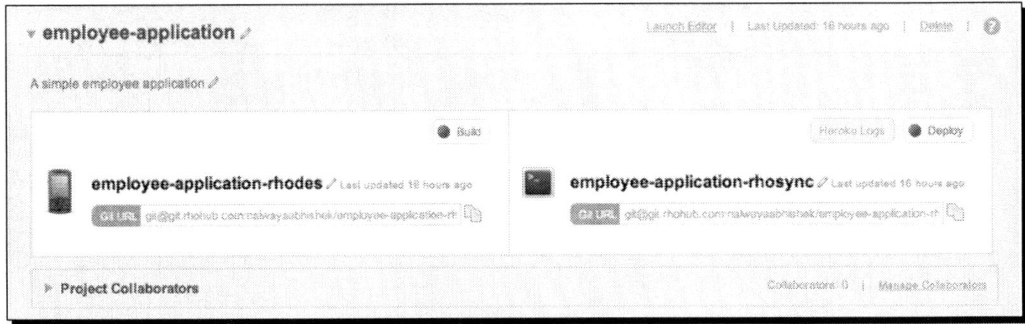

Step 2: Click **Deploy:**

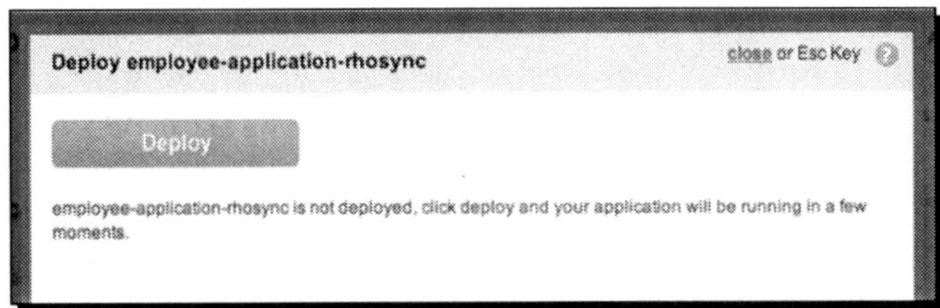

Step 3: Yippee! There is no step 3. Your code is deployed to Heroku using RhoHub. We can see how easy it is to deploy your code using RhoHub.

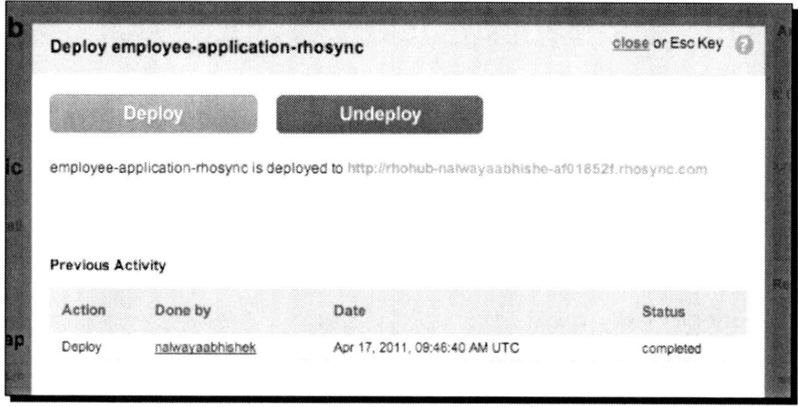

If you want to undeploy your application you can do by clicking **Undeploy** on the same screen from where we deployed it.

What Just Happened?

In this section, we have learned to deploy and undeploy the RhoSync application to Heroku from the RhoHub RhoMobile account.

RhoGallery

RhoGallery is the first hosted mobile app management solution. It allows administrators to manage apps exposed to their employees, making it easy for them to get mobile apps onto their devices. It gives users a single place to launch all of their important enterprise apps. RhoGallery lets you manage collections of apps (whether or not they are Rhodes apps) as "galleries" which you can then invite users and groups of users to access. Users then automatically have the appropriate apps downloaded to their device. New apps and updates are pushed to users and you can de-provision them as well. RhoGallery is the first hosted mobile app management solution.

Key features of RhoGallery:

- Administrator management of exposed apps, end consumers, and groups of consumers
- Central launchpad for exposed apps (coming soon)
- Automatic provisioning of exposed apps for end consumers

Now, we will create a gallery for an employee application.

Time for action – Creating a gallery

To get started with RhoGallery, follow these steps:

1. Create a new gallery by clicking **Create Gallery**.
2. A dialog box will be open; enter **Name**, **Description**, and choose an **Icon** for your gallery and then click **Create Gallery**:

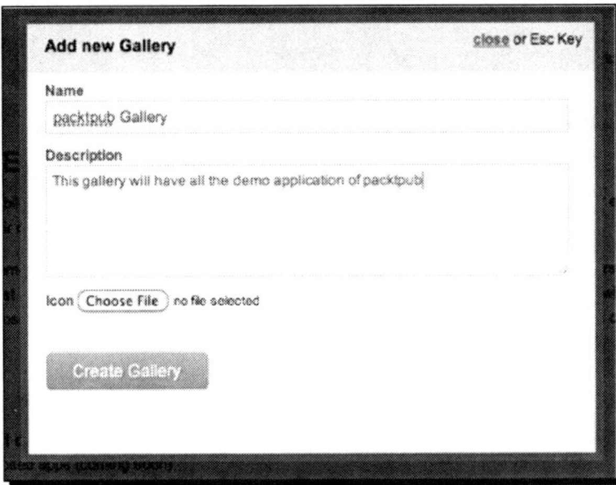

3. Add a new application to your gallery by clicking **Add a new App**:

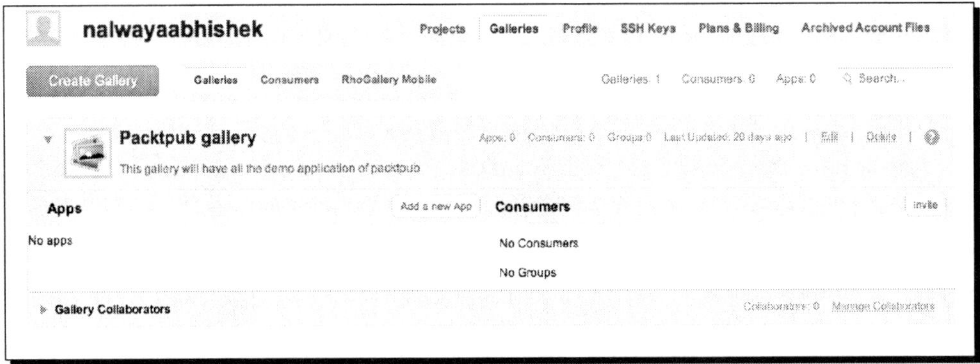

4. Now, there are four steps to create an application. In the first step, enter your **App Name**, **Description**, and **Icon** for your application:

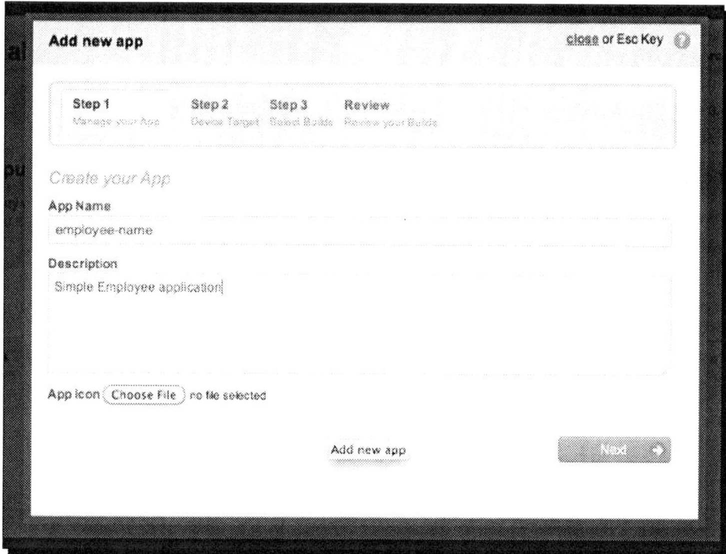

5. Now, specify the **target device**, Application **Version**, Application **ID, Security Token**, and click **Next**. Here, the target device is the platform for which we want to generate the build. Application Version is for the versioning of your application. **App ID** is generated by Apple and **Security Token** is for restricting the access to the application which is the same as that mentioned in your application's `build.yml`:

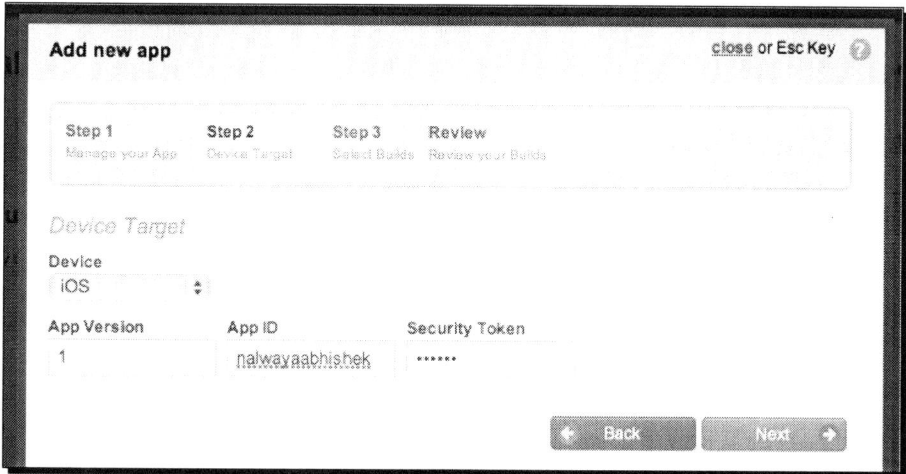

6. Upload build files, link to external builds, or add existing RhoHub builds to your application:

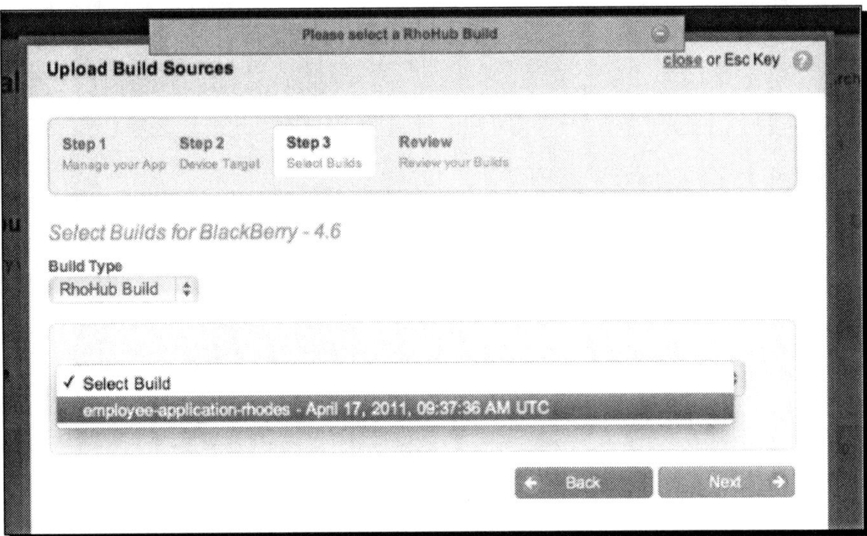

7. Go to `http://bit.ly/getrho` on your mobile device to install the RhoGallery Mobile application.

8. Invite some consumers to the gallery. They will automatically receive an email or SMS with credentials to use the RhoGallery Mobile application and access the gallery.

What just happened?

We have learned to create a gallery in RhoHub. We have also added an employee application to that gallery.

Summary

In this chapter we have learnt:

- To install Git and configure RhoHub on your local machine
- Understand the basic Git command
- Create a basic RhoHub project
- Clone and commit the Rhodes application
- Clone and commit the RhoSync application
- RhoHub online editor
- Creating build for different smart phones
- Deploying the RhoSync application to RhoHub
- What is RhoGallery?

In the next chapter, we will learn about the different device capabilities of the Rhodes application.

10

Rhodes power unleashed

In the last chapter, we learnt about RhoHub, a deploying solution for RhoMobile. By now we have learned the basic lifecycle of a RhoMobile application from zero to deployment. Now, in this chapter, we will learn about the Rhodes competence to access device specific capabilities such as GPS, PIM, camera, SMS, video player, accelerometer, proximity detector, and many more functionalities. Using Rhodes extensions we can use a lot of device capabilities but in this chapter we will discuss a few of them. To start with, we will learn to access device-specific properties using the System class.

System class

We may need to access a device-specific property at runtime. This device-specific property means Device name, checking the presence of camera, screen width, and many more things. Rhodes provides a System Ruby class that provides access to system-specific information.

The basic syntax for using `System` class is:

```
System.get_property(system_property)
```

Here, `system_property` is the property that you want to access. These are a list of properties we can use:

- `platform` – It returns the device name. For example: APPLE, Blackberry, WINDOWS, ANDROID, SYMBIAN.
- `has_camera` – It will check whether a camera is available on the device.
- `screen_width` – It returns the screen width in pixels.
- `screen_height` – It returns the screen height in pixels.
- `screen_orientation` – It returns the screen orientation. For example: portrait, landscape, etc.

- `ppi_x` – It returns the horizontal PPI (Pixels Per Inch)
- `ppi_y` – It returns the vertical PPI (Pixels Per Inch)
- `has_network` – It checks whether the device is connected to the network
- `phone_number` – It returns the device phone number
- `device_id` – It returns the device ID, which may be used to receive push messages
- `full_browser` – It checks whether the full browser is available on Blackberry.
- `device_name` – It checks for the name of the device on which the application is running. Examples: 9000(BB), iPhone, Dream (Android).
- `os_version` – It checks for the version of OS on the device. Examples: 4.6.0.192 (BB), 3.0 (iPhone), 1.6 (Android).
- `locale` – It returns the current language. For example: en, ru
- `country` – It returns the country abbreviation.
- `is_emulator` – It returns `true` if the application is running on an emulator.
- `has_calendar` – It returns `true` if calendar support is available.

These are the basic properties available with the `System` class.

Time for action – Using the System class

We have understood the basic options available in the `System` class. Now it's time to explore the `System` class using our application. We will create a new page in our employee application in which we will display most of the system properties available. Follow these steps:

1. Create a folder `SystemExamples` in the `app` folder of your application.
2. Create a file `controller.rb` in the `SystemExamples` folder.
3. Add the following code in `controller.rb`:

```
require 'rho/rhocontroller'

class SystemExamplesController < Rho::RhoController

  def index
    // This is no code in this action
  end
end
```

We have created a controller called `SystemExample`. All the controllers in Rhodes are a subclass of `RhoController`, so `SystemExample` will be a subclass of `RhoController`.

4. Create a file `index.rb` in the `SystemExamples` folder and add the following code:

```
<div class="pageTitle">
  <h1>
  System Examples
  </h1>
</div>
<div class="toolbar">
  <div class="leftItem regularButton">
    <a href="<%= Rho::RhoConfig.start_path %>">Home</a>
  </div>
</div>

<div class = "content">
  <br/>
  platform : <%=System.get_property('platform') %> <br/>
  has_network : <%=System.get_property('has_network') %> <br/>
  locale : <%=System.get_property('locale') %> <br/>
  country: <%=System.get_property('country') %> <br/>
  screen_width : <%=System.get_property('screen_width') %> <br/>
  screen_height : <%=System.get_property('screen_height') %> <br/>
  screen_orientation : <%=System.get_property('screen_
orientation') %> <br/>
  ppi_x : <%=System.get_property('ppi_x') %> <br/>
  ppi_y : <%=System.get_property('ppi_y') %> <br/>
  has_camera : <%=System.get_property('has_camera') %> <br/>
  phone_number : <%=System.get_property('phone_number') %> <br/>
  device_id : <%=System.get_property('device_id') %> <br/>
  full_browser : <%=System.get_property('full_browser') %> <br/>
  device_name : <%=System.get_property('device_name') %> <br/>
  os_version : <%=System.get_property('os_version') %> <br/>
  rhodes_port : <%=System.get_property('rhodes_port') %> <br/>
  is_emulator : <%=System.get_property('is_emulator') %> <br/>
  has_calendar : <%=System.get_property('has_calendar') %> <br/>
  get_start_params : <%=System.get_start_params() %> <br/>
  has_touchscreen : <%=System.get_property('has_touchscreen') %>
<br/>

</div>
```

We have used `System` class to fetch all the properties. We can use the `System.get_property(system_property)` command both in the controller and view to get the property.

5. We will add a link to the `index` action that we created. Open `index.erb` in the app folder and add the following code:

```
<li>
<a href="SystemExamples">
<span class="title"> System Examples</span>
<span class="disclosure_indicator"/></a>
</li>
```

6. Now build the application and start the simulator with:

```
rake run:iphone
```

7. Now, navigate to the System Example page:

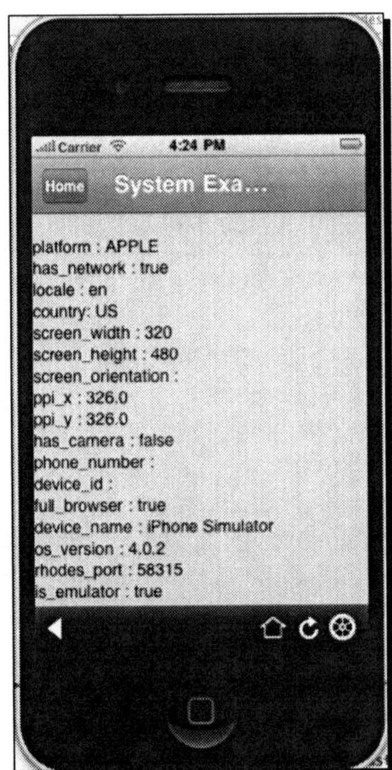

We can see that all the `System` properties are displayed on the screen.

What just happened?

We have created a page in our application, which displays the device-specific property using `System` class.

Doing more things with System class

There are many more things that we can do with the `System` class. We will explore a few of these one by one:

Exit application

We can completely exit the application using:

```
System.exit
```

Generally, if we close the application it runs in the background. However, if we use this command, it will exit the application completely from the device.

Enable\disable phone sleep

We can enable and disable phone sleep by:

```
System.set_sleeping
```

This will enable/disable phone sleep and return it to the previous state.

Managing other applications

We can do the following operations on another application installed on your device:

- Run a specified application:

  ```
  System.run_app(appname, params)
  ```

  where `appname` is platform dependent.
- Install the application from a specified `url`:

  ```
  System.app_install(url)
  ```

- Is the specified application installed on a device?

  ```
  System.app_installed?(appname)
  ```

- Uninstall the specified application:

  ```
  System.app_uninstall(appname)
  ```

These are the various options available in the `System` class.

Time for action – Starting other applications

We will now try these class methods in our application on the same page that we created in the last section.

Follow these steps:

1. Add the following code to the `controller.rb` in the `SystemExample` folder:

```
require 'rho/rhocontroller'

class SystemExamplesController < Rho::RhoController

  def index

  end
  def app_exit
    System.exit
  end

  def start_test_app

    if System::get_property('platform') == 'ANDROID'
      System.run_app('com.rhomobile.store', "security_token=123")
    elsif System::get_property('platform') == 'APPLE'
      System.run_app('store', "security_token=123")
    elsif System::get_property('platform') == 'Blackberry'
      System.run_app('store', "security_token=123")
    else
      System.run_app('rhomobile store/store.exe', "security_
token=123")
    end
  end
  //This action will start the Skype application.
  def start_skype_app
    System.run_app('skype', nil)
    redirect :action => :index
  end
//This action will check if Skype is installed on the device
  def is_skype_app_installed
    installed = System.app_installed?('skype')
    Alert.show_popup(installed ? "installed" : "not installed")
    redirect :action => :index
  end
end
```

We can see that we created four more actions in the `SystemExample` controller. `App_exit` action will exit the application. `Start_test_app` will open an application that is already installed on the device. We have to pass a security token to open an application that is provided by the application. To restrict access to the application, it could be built with a security token. Specify a security token in the `build.yml` and build the application. If it is not defined, we can keep it at nil. `Start_skype_app` will open Skype on your device and `is_skype_app_installed` will check whether Skype is installed on your system.

2. Add the following code to `index.erb`:

```
<%= link_to 'Exit application', url_for(:action => :app_exit) %>
<br/>
  <% if System::get_property('platform') == 'APPLE' %>
<br>
<%= link_to 'Is Skype app installed?', url_for(:action => :is_
skype_app_installed) %> <br/>
<%= link_to 'Start Skype app', url_for(:action => :start_skype_
app) %> <br/>
```

We have added links in the `index` page to open the action that we created.

3. Start the simulator:

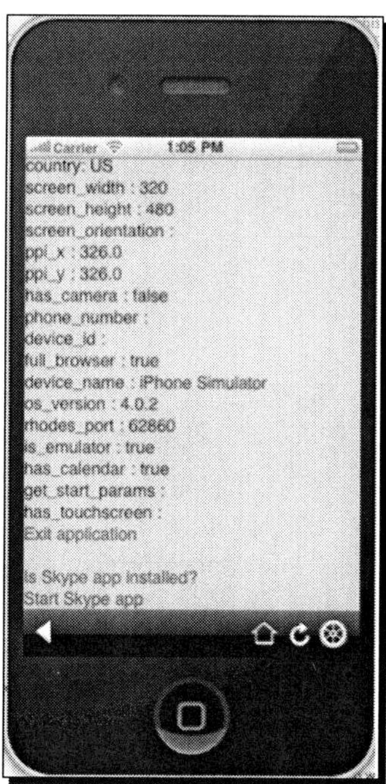

Now, we can click on these links and test all the actions that we created.

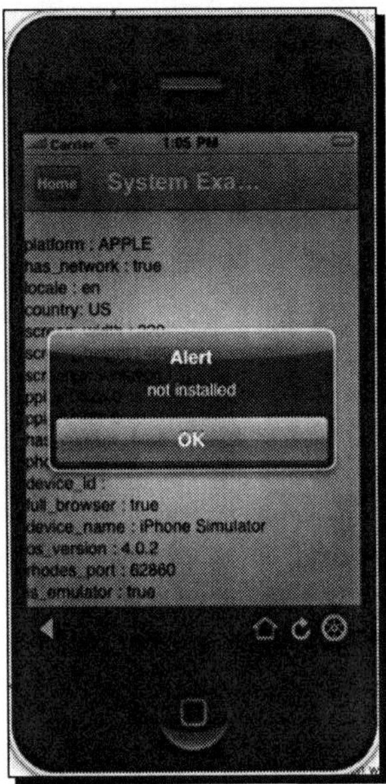

We can see that Skype is currently not installed on this device.

What just happened?

We have just explored `System` class methods in more detail. We have learned to exit from our application, open a new application, and check whether an application is installed on it.

PIM contacts

We can access a local phone book of our device and stored contacts to Rhom via the Ruby class `RhoContact`. We can perform basic CRUD i.e. Create, Read, Update, and Destroy operations on the phone contacts. The following methods are available in the RhoContact class:

Create

We can create a new contact in the phonebook with the following command:

```
Rho::RhoContact.create!(@params['contact'])
```

We can set the properties of the contact passed as parameter hash, and save the created phonebook records (create):

Read

We can get all the device contacts using the following command:

```
Rho::RhoContact.find(:all)
```

It will return hash of hashes of all contacts stored in the phonebook.

If we want to get only one specific contact, we may use the following command:

```
Rho::RhoContact.find(@params['id'])
```

It will return hash of all the properties of the contact identified by the provided ID.

Update

We can update a device contact by using the following command:

```
Rho::RhoContact.update_attributes(@params['contact'])
```

It will find the contact record in the phonebook, update that record with parameter hash passed, and save the updated record. We have to pass `Contact_id` in the updated hash.

Destroy

We can delete a contact using the following command:

```
Rho::RhoContact.destroy(@params['id'])
```

It will delete the contact for which we are passing the ID.

On all devices, properties currently supported are:

- `id`
- `first_name`
- `last_name`
- `mobile_number`
- `home_number`
- `business_number`
- `email_address`
- `company_name`

However, for the iPhone, additional contact properties are supported like `birthday`, `anniversary`, `job_title`, `assistant_name`, `assistant_number`, `spouse_name`, `person_note`, etc.

Time for action – CRUD operations on contacts

We will now perform all the CRUD operations on contacts. This means we will add, read, update, and delete the contact of our device from the Rhodes application.

Follow these steps:

1. Create a model contacts using the `rhogen` command:

   ```
   rhogen model contacts first_name, last_name, mobile_number, home_
   number, business_number, email_address, company_name
   ```

   You will get the following output:

   ```
   Generating with model generator:

       [ADDED]  app/Contacts/index.erb
       [ADDED]  app/Contacts/edit.erb
       [ADDED]  app/Contacts/new.erb
       [ADDED]  app/Contacts/show.erb
       [ADDED]  app/Contacts/index.bb.erb
       [ADDED]  app/Contacts/edit.bb.erb
       [ADDED]  app/Contacts/new.bb.erb
       [ADDED]  app/Contacts/show.bb.erb
       [ADDED]  app/Contacts/contacts_controller.rb
       [ADDED]  app/Contacts/contacts.rb
       [ADDED]  app/test/contacts_spec.rb
   ```

2. Open the `contacts_controller.rb` file in the `Contacts` folder generated by the `rhogen` command and update the following actions:
   - `index`: This action will retrieve all the contacts from your device:

```
def index
    @contacts = Rho::RhoContact.find(:all)
    @contacts = {} unless @contacts
    @contacts = @contacts.sort do |x,y|
      res = 1 if x[1]['first_name'].nil?
      res = -1 if y[1]['first_name'].nil?
      res = x[1]['first_name'] <=> y[1]['first_name'] unless res
      res
    end
    render :back => '/app'

  end
```

- `show`: This action will retrieve all the information of a specific contact:

```
def show
    @contact =  Rho::RhoContact.find(@params['id'])

  end
```

- `new`: This action will create a form for adding a new contact:

```
def new
    @contact = Contacts.new
    render :action => :new
  end
```

- `edit`: This action will create an edit form for editing an existing contact:

```
def edit
    @contact = Rho::RhoContact.find(@params['id'])

  end
```

- `create`: This action will create a contact using the `params` passed through the `new` action:

```
def create
    @contact = Rho::RhoContact.create!(@params['contact'])
    redirect :action => :index
  end
```

- `update`: This action will update a specific contact that is passed from the `edit` action:

```
  def update
    Rho::RhoContact.update_attributes(@params['contact'])
    redirect :action => :index
  end
```

- `delete`: This action will delete the specified contact:

```
def delete
    Rho::RhoContact.destroy(@params['id'])
    redirect :action => :index
  end
```

We have to add `require 'rho/rhocontact'` to use the basic CRUD methods.

3. Update the div of class `content` in the `index.erb` file present inside the `Contacts` folder:

```
<div class="content">
  <ul>

    <%@contacts.each do |contact|%>
      <li> <%=link_to "#{contact[1]['first_name']}
#{contact[1]['last_name']}", :action => :show, :id =>
contact[1]['id']%>  </li>
    <%end%>
  </ul>
</div>
```

It will display concatenated first name and last name as a link for all the contacts, which on clicking would open the show page of a particular contact.

```
Update the div of class content in the edit.erb file present
inside the Contacts folder:
<div class="content">
  <form method="POST" action="<%= url_for :action => :update %>">
// We have to pass hidden id to create contact.

    <input type="hidden" name="contact[id]" value="<%=@
contact['id']%>"/>
    <ul>
      // Creating text box for all the fields.
          <li>
            <label for="contact[first_name]"
class="fieldLabel">First name</label>
            <input type="text" name="contact[first_name]"
value="<%= @contact['first_name'] %>" <%= placeholder( "First
name" ) %> />
          </li>

          <li>
            <label for="contact[last_name]"
class="fieldLabel">Last name</label>
            <input type="text" name="contact[last_name]"
value="<%= @contact['last_name'] %>" <%= placeholder( "Last name"
) %> />
          </li>

          <li>
            <label for="contact[mobile_number]" class="fieldLabel"
>Mobile number</label>
```

```
            <input type="text" name="contact[mobile_number]"
value="<%= @contact['mobile_number'] %>" <%= placeholder( "Mobile
number" ) %> />
          </li>

          <li>
            <label for="contact[home_number]"
class="fieldLabel">Home number</label>
            <input type="text" name="contact[home_number]"
value="<%= @contact['home_number'] %>" <%= placeholder( "Home
number" ) %> />
          </li>

          <li>
            <label for="contact[business_number]" class="fieldLabe
l">Business number</label>
            <input type="text" name="contact[business_number]"
value="<%= @contact['business_number'] %>" <%= placeholder(
"Business number" ) %> />
          </li>

          <li>
            <label for="contact[email_address]"
class="fieldLabel">Email address</label>
            <input type="text" name="contact[email_address]"
value="<%= @contact['email_address'] %>" <%= placeholder( "Email
address" ) %> />
          </li>

          <li>
            <label for="contact[company_name]" class="fieldLabel">
Company name</label>
            <input type="text" name="contact[company_name]"
value="<%= @contact['company_name'] %>" <%= placeholder( "Company
name" ) %> />
          </li>

    </ul>
//creating submit button
    <input type="submit" class="standardButton" value="Update"/>
  </form>
</div>
```

This will create a form to edit a contact.

4. Update the div of class `content` in the `new.erb` file present inside the `Contacts` folder:

```
<div class="content">
// Creating a form which will create a Contact.
  <form method="POST" action="<%= url_for :action => :create %>">
    <input type="hidden" name="id" value="<%= @contact['id']
%>"/>
    <ul>

          <li>
            <label for="contact[first_name]"
class="fieldLabel">First name</label>
            <input type="text" name="contact[first_name]" <%=
            placeholder("First name") %> />
          </li>

          <li>
            <label for="contact[last_name]"
class="fieldLabel">Last name</label>
            <input type="text" name="contact[last_name]" <%=
            placeholder("Last name") %> />
          </li>

          <li>
            <label for="contact[mobile_number]" class="fieldLabel"
>Mobile number</label>
            <input type="text" name="contact[mobile_number]" <%=
            placeholder("Mobile number") %> />
          </li>

          <li>
            <label for="contact[home_number]"
class="fieldLabel">Home number</label>
            <input type="text" name="contact[home_number]" <%=
            placeholder("Home number") %> />
          </li>

          <li>
            <label for="contact[business_number]" class="fieldLabe
l">Business number</label>
            <input type="text" name="contact[business_number]" <%=

            placeholder("Business number") %> />

          </li>
```

```
          <li>
            <label for="contact[email_address]"
class="fieldLabel">Email address</label>
            <input type="text" name="contact[email_address]" <%=
            placeholder("Email address") %> />
          </li>

          <li>
            <label for="contact[company_name]" class="fieldLabel">
Company name</label>
            <input type="text" name="contact[company_name]" <%=
            placeholder("Company name") %> />
          </li>

    </ul>
    <input type="submit" class="standardButton" value="Create"/>
  </form>
</div>
```

5. Add a link to the `index.erb` in the `app` folder:

```
<li><a href="Contacts"><span class="title"> Contacts</span><span
class="disclosure_indicator"/></a></li>
```

6. Start the simulator:

```
rake run:iphone
```

This will list all the contacts on your device.

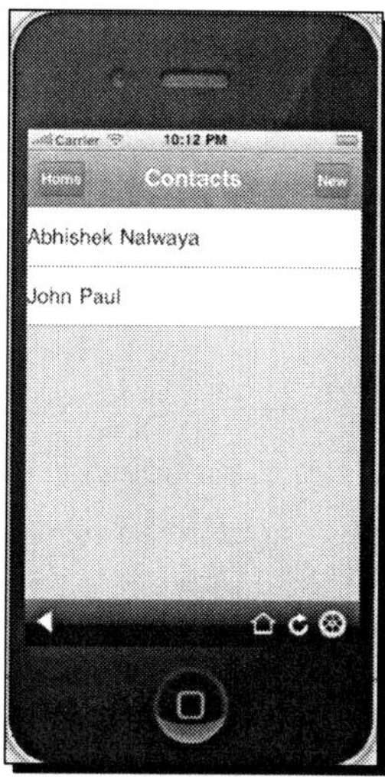

Now, you should be able to perform the following tasks on the simulator:

- List all the contacts by clicking **Contact link present on the home page**
- Update any contact details by clicking **Edit**
- Delete any contact by clicking **Delete**
- Create a new contact by clicking **New**

What just happened?

We have accessed the device contacts using the `Rhocontact` extension. Using the `Rhocontact` extension, we have learned to create, update, list, and delete the contacts.

Have a go hero – CRUD operations for Calendar/Events

As you have understood how PIM contact works with RhoContact API, now you can similarly create CRUD operations for PIM Calendar/Events using the RhoEvent API.

To give you a heads up about RhoEvent API, let's go through a few methods available in it.

Check if the device has a calendar:

```
System::get_property('has_calendar')
```

The following methods are available in the RhoContact class:

- **Get(find)**: We can find the Calendar event using the following command:

  ```
  Rho::RhoEvent.find(:all)
  ```

  It will return hash of hashes of all events stored in the calendar

  To get a specific event, we can use the following command:

  Rho::RhoEvent.find(@params['id'])

  We can get all the properties of the events found by specified parameters:

  ```
  Rho::RhoEvent.find(:all, :start_date=>start,

      :end_date => endtime, :find_type=>'starting', :include_
  repeating => true )
  ```

- **Create**: To create a event we can use following command:

  ```
  created_event = Rho::RhoEvent.create!(@params['event'])
  ```

- **Update**: To update RhoEvent, we can use the following command:

  ```
  Rho::RhoEvent.update_attributes(@params['event'])
  ```

- Destroy: To remove an event identified by the provided ID from the calendar:

```
Rho::RhoEvent.destroy(@params['id'])
```

Camera

Native applications can access the camera of the phone and perform operations like taking the picture, uploading it, and so on.

To check whether the device has a camera we can use following command:

```
System::get_property('has_camera')
```

The Camera API provides the following functionality:

Taking a picture

To take a picture, use the following command:

```
Camera::take_picture('/app/model/camera_callback')
```

This method will take the picture and once the picture is taken it will call `camera_callback`.

Choosing a picture from an album

We can choose a picture using the following command:

```
Camera::choose_picture('/app/model/camera_callback')
```

Once the user has taken/chosen a picture, the callback URL you specified will be called. The callback is a `POST` message; the body of the message contains the `status` and `image_uri`.

`status` can have: ok, cancel, or error value.

`image_uri` points to the taken/chosen image stored in the `/public/db-files` folder; the image file will have an auto-generated name.

Time for action – Capturing images

We will now create a page in the employee application, which will capture an image.

1. Create a folder called `Image` in the app folder.

2. Create a file called `controller.rb` and write the following code:

```
require 'rho/rhocontroller'

class ImageController < Rho::RhoController
  //index action will find all the images
  def index
    @images = Image.find(:all)
    render :back => '/app'
  end
//new action will take a picture from the camera and then will
call  camera_callback
  def new
    Camera::take_picture(url_for :action => :camera_callback)
    redirect :action => :index
  end
//edit action will choose a picture from device and then call
camera_callback
  def edit
    Camera::choose_picture(url_for :action => :camera_callback)
    ""
  end
 // delect action will remove a image
  def delete
    @image = Image.find(@params['id'])
    @image.destroy
    redirect :action => :index
  end

  def camera_callback
    if @params['status'] == 'ok'
      #create image record in the DB
      image = Image.new({'image_uri'=>@params['image_uri']})
      image.save
      puts "new Image object: " + image.inspect
    end
    WebView.navigate( url_for :action => :index )
    ""
  end

end
```

3. Create a model `image.rb` and write the following code:

```
class Image
  include Rhom::PropertyBag

  enable :sync

  property :image_uri, :blob
end
```

4. Create and write the following code in the `index.erb` inside the `Image` folder:

```
<div class="pageTitle">
  <h1>Image Capture</h1>
</div>

<div class="toolbar">
  <div class="leftItem regularButton">
    <a href="<%= Rho::RhoConfig.start_path %>">Home</a>
  </div>
</div>
<div class = "content">
   <%= link_to '[Choose Picture]', { :action => :edit }%><br/>
   <% if System::get_property('has_camera') %>
       <%= link_to '[Take Picture]', { :action => :new }%>
    <% end %>

    <br/>
   <% @images.reverse_each do |x|%>
       <img src="<%=Rho::RhoApplication::get_blob_path(x.image_
uri)%>" width='300px'></img><a href="<%=url_for(:action => :
delete, :id =>x.object)%>">Delete</a><br/>
   <% end %>
</div>
```

5. Add a link to `index.erb` in the app folder:

```
<li><a href="Image"><span class="title"> Camera</span><span
class="disclosure_indicator"/></a></li>
```

6. Start the simulator:

```
rake run:iphone
```

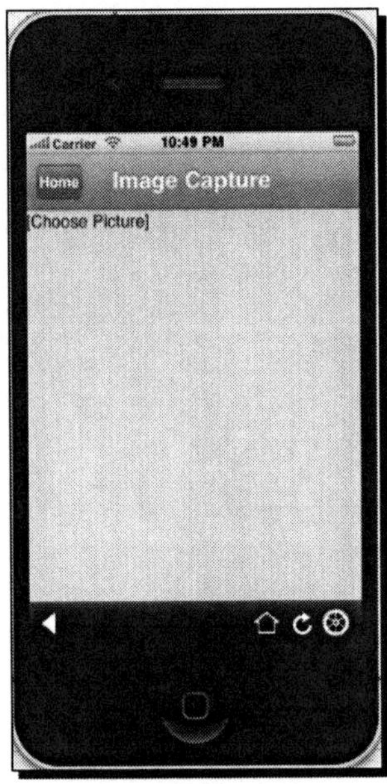

7. Since there is no camera in the simulator it will ask to choose an image from the gallery:

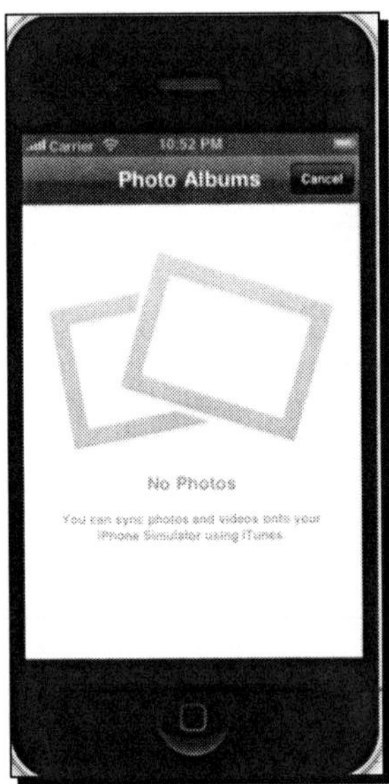

From this screenshot we can see that Photo Album has been opened and we can choose any image from it.

What just happened?

We have just created a link in our application to capture an image from the device's camera and also uploaded it.

Geolocation

Rhodes provides Geolocation capabilities to get the latitude and longitude of your current location.

The new Rhodes version can use both GPS location provider and network-based location determination. Network-based location is not as precise as GPS but in most cases it consumes less power and returns results faster than GPS. Rhodes will update the location using network data until GPS has started, after which only GPS will be used to get more precise data.

Geolocation information is available in two ways:

- As an asynchronous service through AJAX calls to a predefined local URL
- In a controller using Ruby calls to the `GeoLocation` class

GeoLocation Ruby class

Rhodes provides `GeoLocation` class for accessing the device location.

We can get the current latitude by:

```
GeoLocation.latitude
```

We can get the current longitude by:

```
GeoLocation.longitude
```

Test if the location system is up and has acquired the position:

```
GeoLocation.known_position?
```

Time for action – Adding Geolocation

We will now create a page in our application that will give the current location of the device.

Follow these steps:

1. Create a folder called `GeoLocation` in the `app` folder.

```
Create a file called controller.erb and write the following code:
require 'rho/rhocontroller'

class GeoLocationController < Rho::RhoController

  def index
    set_geoview_notification( url_for(:action => :geo_
viewcallback), "", 2)  if System::get_property('platform') ==
'Blackberry'
    render :back => '/app'
  end

  def geo_viewcallback
    WebView.refresh if @params['known_position'].to_i != 0 && @
params['status'] =='ok'
  end

  def showmap

     region = [@params['latitude'], @params['longitude'], 0.2,
0.2]
     map_params = {
          :provider => @params['provider'],
          :settings => {:map_type => "roadmap", :region => region,
                         :zoom_enabled => true, :scroll_enabled =>
true, :shows_user_location => true},
          :annotations => [{:latitude => @params['latitude'], :
longitude => @params['longitude'], :title => "Current location", :
subtitle => "test", :url => "/app/GeoLocation/show?city=Current
Location"}
                             ]
     }
     MapView.create map_params
     redirect :action => :index
  end

end
```

As we have seen, there is a `showmap` action. `MapView` class provides an embeddable map interface, similar to the ones provided by the Map applications. The above code would go into your controller and the map appears on the whole page. There are two providers supported now—Google and ESRI. Google supports iPhone, Android, and BB. ESRI supports iPhone, Android, BB, and WM.

2. Create a file `index.erb` and divide this page into the following three parts:

    - `pageTitle`: It contains the title of the page and in this case it is GeoLocation:

```
<div class = "pageTitle">
   <h1> Geo Location</h1>
   </div>
toolbar: It is the toolbar of the page and contains a Home button:
<div class="toolbar">
     <div class="leftItem regularButton">
       <a href="<%= Rho::RhoConfig.start_path %>">Home</a>
     </div>

   </div>
```

    - `content`: This is the main body of the page:

```
<div class = "contact">
   <ul>
<li>
Your location:
<br/>
// Checking the platform for WINDOWS. This will display the
current location on map view
<% if System::get_property('platform') != 'WINDOWS' %>
   <a href="/system/map?q=<%= GeoLocation.latitude.to_
s+','+GeoLocation.longitude.to_s %>"><%= GeoLocation.latitude.abs.
to_s + " " + (GeoLocation.latitude < 0 ? "South" : "North") + ", "
+
   GeoLocation.longitude.abs.to_s + " " + (GeoLocation.longitude <
0 ? "West" : "East") %></a>
<% else %>
   <a href="<%= url_for :controller => :Settings, :action => :
not_supported, :query => {:feature => 'Native Map'} %>" ><%=
GeoLocation.latitude.abs.to_s + " " + (GeoLocation.latitude < 0 ?
"South" : "North") + ", " +
   GeoLocation.longitude.abs.to_s + " " + (GeoLocation.longitude <
0 ? "West" : "East") %></a>
<% end %>
```

```
    //Displaying the latitude and longitude using GeoLocation API
    Latitude: <%= GeoLocation.latitude.to_s %><br/>
    Longitude: <%= GeoLocation.longitude.to_s %>
</li>
<li>

   Geo-location information available asynchronously,
    so you may have to <a href="/app/GeoLocation" target="_
self">refresh page</a>
    to see results of Ruby calls
    // Checking the platform for WINDOWS. This will display a link
and on clicking on it will show current location on Google Map

<% if System::get_property('platform') != 'WINDOWS' %>
        <p><a href="/app/GeoLocation/showmap?latitude=<%=
GeoLocation.latitude.to_s%>&longitude=<%= GeoLocation.longitude.
to_s%>&provider=Google"
            target="_self">[show Google map at location <%=
GeoLocation.latitude.to_s%>,longitude=<%= GeoLocation.longitude.
to_s%> ]</a></p>
<% else %>
        <p><a href="<%= url_for :controller => :Settings, :action =>
:not_supported, :query => {:feature => 'Google Map'} %>"
            target="_self">[show Google map at location <%=
GeoLocation.latitude.to_s%>,longitude=<%= GeoLocation.longitude.
to_s%> ]</a></p>
<% end %>

<br>
        <p><a href="/app/GeoLocation/showmap?latitude=<%=
GeoLocation.latitude.to_s%>&longitude=<%= GeoLocation.longitude.
to_s%>&provider=ESRI"
            target="_self">[show ESRI map at location <%=
GeoLocation.latitude.to_s%>,longitude=<%= GeoLocation.longitude.
to_s%> ]</a></p>
</li>
</ul>
</div>
```

3. Add a link for `GeoLocation` in `index.erb` in the app folder:

```
<li><a href="GeoLocation"><span class="title"> Geo Location</
span><span class="disclosure_indicator"/></a></li>
```

4 Start the simulator:

```
Rake run:iphone
```

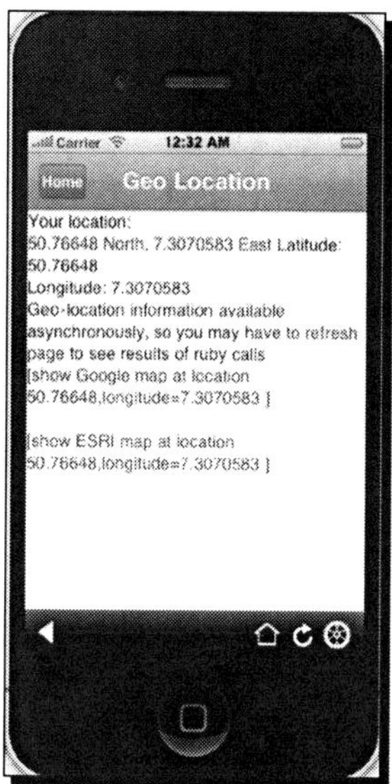

We can see that your location latitude and longitude is displayed on the screen.

5 Clicking on the **Show Google map** link will open the Google map marking your current location on the map. We can see the map in the following image with the current location marked in it with red:

6 Clicking on your location opens the MapView marking your current location:

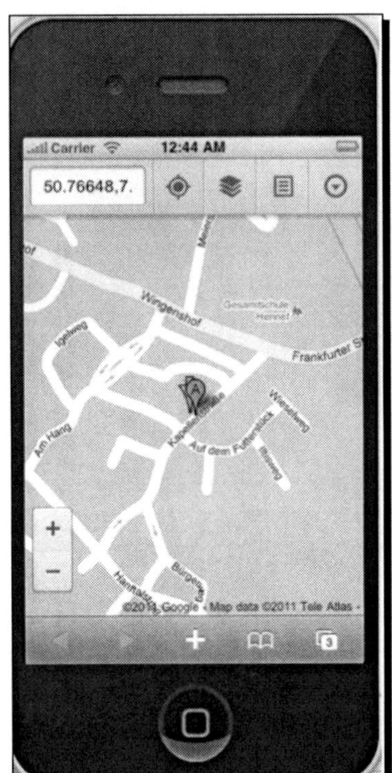

What just happened?

We have created a page that is displaying the location of your device. It also forms a link to open it in Google Maps.

Alerts

Rhodes provides System Alert methods, which helps to show a custom popup. You may call on system alert methods to show popup, vibrate, or play audio files from your controller.

The most used method is `show_popup`, which brings the app upfront and shows the specified message. The simple syntax of showing a popup looks like:

```
Alert.show_popup "Some message"
```

This will show an alert with the message **Some message**.

We can customize the popup title, icon, buttons, and specify callback to be called on any button click. This is the basic syntax:

```
Alert.show_popup( {
     :message => 'Some message',
     :title => 'Custom title',
     :icon => '/public/images/icon.png',
     :buttons => ["Yes", "No",
         {:id => 'cancel', :title => 'Cancel all'}],
     :callback => url_for(:action => :on_dissmiss_popup) } )
```

This command will show a popup with the message **Some message**, title as **Custom title**, an icon, and two buttons, and will call a callback `on_dissmiss_popup`. The popup window always closes after clicking on any button.

With `Alert.show_popup`, the following arguments are available:

- `:message` – This is the text to be displayed in the popup window.
- `:title` – This is the title of the popup window.
- `:icon` – This is the image to be displayed in the popup window. Its value can be one of the predefined values or the path to the image file.
- `:alert` – This shows an alert icon('!').
- `:question` – This shows a question icon('?').
- `:info` – This shows an informational icon.
- `:buttons` – This is an array of buttons for the popup window. Each button is defined by its ID and title. A button can be specified by a hash with `:id` and `:title` keys or just String—in this case, both ID and title will be set to this value.
- `:callback` – It is the URL to be called on the click of any button. This callback will be called with `@params` hash containing three keys: `:button_id`, `:button_title`, and `:button_index`.

There are also other options available in the `Alert` class:

- `hide_popup` – It closes the current opened popup:

  `Alert.hide_popup`

- `vibrate` – It vibrates for the specified number of milliseconds, up to 25500; if 0 or no duration is specified, it will vibrate for 2500 milliseconds:

  `Alert.vibrate(duration_in_milliseconds)`

- `play_file` – It plays a specified file if the media type is supported by the phone. The file should be included in the application. For example, if the file is in the `public` folder, the file name will be `/apps/public/file_name.mp3`. The media type should be either specified explicitly or may be recognized from the file extension. Known file extensions are: `.mp3` – audio/mpeg; `.wav` – audio/x-wav.

  `Alert.play_file(file_name.ext, media_type)`

- `show_status` – It shows the status messages:

  `Alert.show_status(title, status_text, hide_button_label)`

The status window will close after clicking on the hide button.

- `status_text` – The text to be displayed in the status window.
- `hide_button_label` – The label of the hide button.

Time for action – Creating alerts

We will now create a page in our application and show various popups on that page.

Follow these steps:

1. Create a folder `Alert` in `app` folder.
2. Create a file `controller.rb` in the `Alert` folder and add the following code:

```
require 'rho/rhocontroller'
class AlertController < Rho::RhoController
  // index is page which will show all the link for popup
  def index
    @flash = "Alerts Example"
    render :back => '/app'
  end

// This action will create simple popup
 def simple_popup
    @flash = "A Simple popup"
    Alert.show_popup "A simple message "
    render :action => :index, :back => '/app'
  end
//This action will create a popup which has title
  def popup_with_title_button
    @flash = "Show popup with Title and Button"

    Alert.show_popup(
        :message=>"Some message with button\n",
```

```
        :title=>"Some Title",
        :buttons => ["Ok"]
      )
    render :action => :index, :back => '/app'
  end
//This action will create a popup with buttons
  def popup_button
    @flash = "Button with callback"

    Alert.show_popup(
        :message=>"The new password can't be empty.\n",
        :title=>"MyTest",
        :buttons => ["Ok", "Cancel"],
        :callback => url_for(:action => :popup_callback)
      )
    render :action => :index, :back => '/app'
  end
  //This action will create a popup with a lot of options
  def show_popup_complex
    @flash = "Show popup page"

    Alert.show_popup :title => "This is popup", :message => "Some
message!", :icon => :info,
      :buttons => ["Yes", "No", {:id => 'cancel', :title =>
"Cancel"}],
      :callback => url_for(:action => :popup_callback)

    render :action => :index, :back => '/app'
  end
//This action will create a popup with wait screen
  def show_wait_popup
    @flash = "Show popup page"
    Alert.show_popup :title => "Wait...", :message => "Wait ..."
    sleep 3
    Alert.hide_popup
    render :action => :index, :back => '/app'
  end
//This action is popup callback
  def popup_callback
    puts "popup_callback: #{@params}"
    WebView.navigate url_for(:action => :index)
  end
 //This action will vibrate the device
  def vibrate
```

```
      @flash = "Vibrate page"
      Alert.vibrate
      render :action => :index, :back => '/app'
    end
    // This action will cause the device to vibrate for 10 sec
    def vibrate_for_10sec
      @flash = "Vibrate for 10 sec page"
      Alert.vibrate 10000
      render :action => :index, :back => '/app'
    end
    // This action will play a file
    def play_file
      @flash = "Play file page"
      Alert.play_file @params['file_name'], @params['media_type']
      render :action => :index, :back => '/app'
    end
    // This action will play a file
    def play_file_1
      @flash = "Play file page"
      Alert.play_file @params['file_name']
      render :action => :index, :back => '/app'
    end
  // This will stop playing the ringtone
    def stop_playing
      Rho::RingtoneManager.stop
      render :action => :index, :back => '/app'
    end

  end
```

3. Now, create a file `index.erb` in the `Alert` folder and add the following code:

```
//Title of the page
<div class="pageTitle">
  <h1><%= @flash %></h1>
</div>
//Toolbar of the page
<div class="toolbar">
  <div class="leftItem regularButton">
    <a href="<%= Rho::RhoConfig.start_path %>">Home</a>
```

```
    </div>
  </div>
  // Main content of the page
  <div class = "content">
      <%= link_to 'Simple Popup', { :action => :simple_popup
}%><br/>
      <%= link_to 'Popup with Title and button', { :action => :
popup_with_title_button }%><br/>
      <%= link_to 'Button with Callback', { :action => :popup_button
}%><br/>
      <%= link_to 'Complex popup', { :action => :show_popup_complex
}%><br/>
      <%= link_to 'Show wait dialog', { :action => :show_wait_popup
}%><br/>
      <%= link_to 'Play 20 Flip Strings.mp3', { :action => :play_
file_1, :query => {:file_name => '/public/alerts/20 Flip Strings.
mp3'} }%><br/>
      <%= link_to 'Play information_bar.wav', { :action => :play_
file_1, :query => {:file_name => '/public/alerts/information_bar.
wav'} }%><br/>
      <%= link_to 'Vibrate', { :action => :vibrate }%><br/>
      <%= link_to 'Vibrate for 10 sec', { :action => :vibrate_for_
10sec }%><br/>
      <%= link_to 'Stop playing', { :action => :stop_playing
}%><br/>
  </div>
```

This will list all the alert option links. And when we click on these links, the popup will be shown.

4. Add link in the `index.erb`.

```
<li><a href="Alert"><span class="title"> Alert Example</span><span
class="disclosure_indicator"/></a></li>
```

5. Start the simulator:

```
rake run:iphone
```

When you click on **Alerts Example** you will get the following screen:

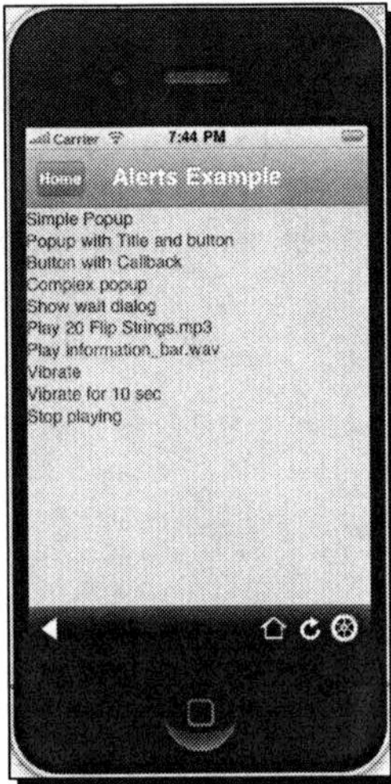

We will discuss a few of these popups:

- **Simple popup**: When you click on simple message:

  ```
  Alert.show_popup "A simple message "
  ```

  This will be shown as follows:

- **Popup with Title and button**: It will show a popup with a message, title, and an `OK` button:

  ```
  Alert.show_popup(
          :message=>"Some message with button\n",
          :title=>"Some Title",
          :buttons => ["Ok"]
      )
  ```

This popup will look like:

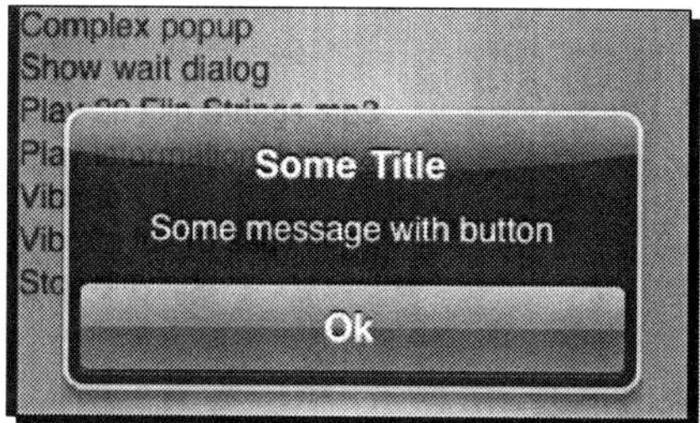

- **Complex popup**: Complex popup code will display three buttons and has a callback, which will be called when a button is clicked:

```
Alert.show_popup :title => "This is popup", :message => "Some
message!", :icon => :info,
      :buttons => ["Yes", "No", {:id => 'cancel', :title =>
"Cancel"}],
      :callback => url_for(:action => :popup_callback)
```

This popup will look as follows:

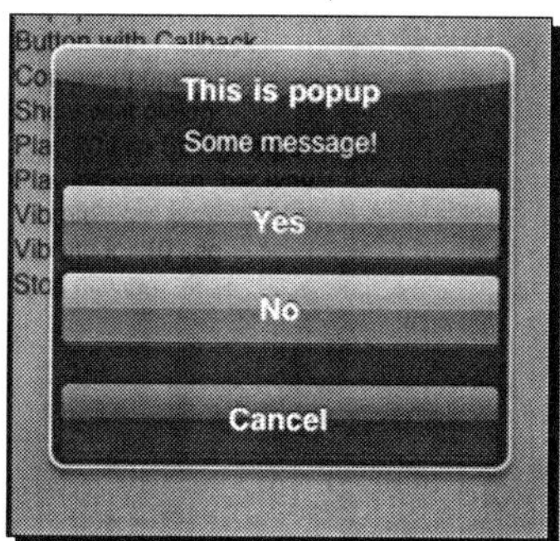

- **Wait screen**: The wait screen will be displayed for 3 secs and then it will disappear:

```
Alert.show_popup :title => "Wait...", :message => "Wait ..."

    sleep 3

    Alert.hide_popup
```

The wait screen popup looks as follows:

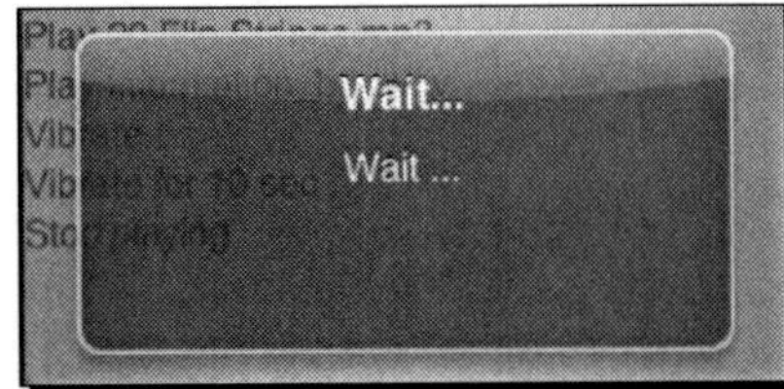

What Just happend?

We have created all the basic popups that can be created using the Alert class. We have also played music files and ringtones.

Other device capabilities

We will now discuss the various other device capabilities supported by Rhodes.

Barcode

Rhodes supports use of barcode from the device using Barcode API. It tries to recognize a barcode on an image:

The basic syntax looks like:

```
Barcode.barcode_recognize(image_file_full_path)
```

Barcode recognition functionality is realized as Rhode Native extension. You should add `Barcode` to extension list in `build.yml` located in your application folder. `Barcode.barcode_recognize(image_file_full_path)` returns a string with recognized code or an empty string if not any recognized barcodes on the image. To process barcode data we can get a picture from a camera which will use barcode recognition.

For barcode recognition, Rhodes uses:

- Zbar library for iPhone, Android, and Windows Mobile platforms
- ZXing library for the BlackBerry platform

Ringtone manager

Rhodes also provides ringtone access and playback using `RingtoneManager`. We can do the following operations:

- To get all the available ringtones, use the following command:

```
@ringtones = RingtoneManager::get_all_ringtones
```

- The variable returned by `get_all_ringtones` will be a hash where key is a user friendly name of the ringtone and the value is the full file name.
- To play a given ringtone:

```
RingtoneManager::play @ringtones['My Ringtone']
```

- Halt playing of a ringtone:

```
RingtoneManager::stop
```

Currently implemented for Android, Blackberry, and Windows mobile. On Blackberry, only the user installed ringtones are accessible. System preinstalled ringtones are not accessible due to Blackberry limitations.

Bluetooth

Rhodes application provides access to Bluetooth serial port connection using Bluetooth API. We can connect between:

- A phone and another phone
- A phone and a PC
- A phone and an external Bluetooth device.

For doing this, there are two classes available:

- `BluetoothManager`
- `BluetoothSession`

BluetoothManager

There are various methods available with `BluetoothManager` Bluetooth API:

- We can check the availability of the Bluetooth on the device using the `BluetoothManager` by using the following command:

```
Rho::BluetoothManager.is_bluetooth_available
```

- It returns true if Bluetooth is available otherwise it returns false.
- We can switch off Bluetooth by by using the following command:

```
Rho::BluetoothManager.off_bluetooth
```

- We can change the local device name:

  `Rho::BluetoothManager.set_device_name(name)`

- We can get the local device name for the current device:

  `Rho::BluetoothManager.get_device_name`

- We can get the last error:

  `Rho::BluetoothManager.get_last_error`

  It will return `OK/ERROR/CANCEL`.

- We can create a Bluetooth session by:

  `Rho::BluetoothManager.create_session(role, callback_url)`

- Here, we need to pass the following parameters:
  - `role` – It may be `ROLE_SERVER` or `ROLE_CLIENT`
  - `callback_url` – This url will be called after a session was created or canceled.

  These are Parameters are received in the callback:
  - `status` – `OK / ERROR / CANCEL`
  - `connected_device_name` – name of the connected device

BluetoothSession

The following method is available with `BluetoothSession`:

- We can disconnect from the device using the following command:

  `Rho::BluetoothSession.disconnect(connected_device_name)`

- We need to pass the parameter `connected_device_name`, which is the name of the connected device. It will return `OK/ERROR`.
- It will get the session status:

  `Rho::BluetoothSession.get_status(connected_device_name)`

  It will return received but not read data size. It will return -1 if error, 0 if empty.

- We can get read data with the following command:

  `Rho::BluetoothSession.read(connected_device_name)`

- We have to pass a parameter `connected_device_name`, which is the name of the connected device, and it will return an array of bytes.
- We can write data with the following command:

  `Rho::BluetoothSession.write(connected_device_name, data)`

- Here we have to pass `connected_device_name` and `data` as parameter. `connected_device_name` is the name of the connected device and data must be an array of byte/fixnum.
- We can read string using the following command:

  ```
  Rho::BluetoothSession.read_string(connected_device_name)
  ```

- Here, `connected_device_name` is the name of the connected device and it returns string.
- We can write string with the following command:

  ```
  Rho::BluetoothSession.write_string(connected_device_name, data)
  ```

- Here, we have to pass `connected_device_name` and data as parameter. `connected_device_name` is the name of the connected device and data must be string. And, it returns OK/ERROR.

Timer

Rhodes provides the RhoTimer class to use the timer in your application:

In your controller, you may start the timer using `Rho::RhoTimer` class using the following command:

- `start_timer` – start timer and call callback after an interval.

  ```
  Rho::RhoTimer.start_timer(interval_milliseconds, callback_url,
  callback_data)
  ```

  Example:

  ```
  Rho::RhoTimer.start_timer(1000, (url_for :action => :timer_
  callback), "test")
  ```

  Here, `timer_callback` will be called after the timer is started.

- `stop_timer` – stop timer by callback.

  ```
  Rho::RhoTimer.stop_timer(callback_url)
  ```

Summary

In this chapter, we learnt:

- How System classes can be used to access System properties
- How to perform PIM contact CRUD operations
- How to get the location using GPS
- How to create Alert messages
- How to use the Ringtone Manager to access the ringtone of the device
- How to use the Bluetooth of the device
- How to use the Timer

Index

Symbols

:action option 159
:alert argument 229
:all argument 72
:buttons argument 229
:callback 108
:callback_param 108
:callback argument 229
:children label 123
:conditions argument 72
:disabled option 159
:first argument 72
:icon argument 229
:icon option 159
:info argument 229
:label option 159
:max_value option 136
:message argument 229
:min_len option 135
:min_value option 136
:offset argument 72
:order argument 72
:orderdir argument 72
:per_page argument 72
:question argument 229
:regexp option 135
:reload option 159
:repeatable label 123
:search_parms 108
:select argument 72
:selected_color option 159
:source_names 108
:title argument 229
:type label 123
:use_current_view_for_tab option 159
:validation label 123
:validators option 135
:web_bkg_color option 159
.backButton style button 152
.blueButton style button 152
.deleteButton style button 152
.regularButton style button 151
@default_menu 155
@employees instance variable 42
@params["source_id"] 108
@params["sync_type"] 108
@params["status"] 108
@tabs array 160

A

alerts
  about 228-230
  creating, steps 230-233
Android
  about 151
  push for 138
Android SDK installation
  about 23
  operating system 23
  steps 24, 25
  URL 23
application, Rhogen
  building 33
  building, for smart phones 33-37

application directory 179
application menu
about 154
default menu 154, 155
architecture, Rhomobile
backend application 12
Rhodes application 10
Rhosync application 11, 12
arguments, Rhom
:all 72
:conditions 72
:first 72
:offset 72
:order 72
:orderdir 72
:perpage 72
:select 72
create 73
new 73
paginate 73
save 73
update_attributes(attributes) 73
association
@companies object 71
company_id 70
creating, between employee and company 70, 71
employee.rb file 70
find command 70
authentication
about 115
in Rhodes 116

B

backend application 12
Backend service
connecting to 96-101
Barcode 236
BlackBerry
MDS Simulator, setting up 139
push for 138
Blackberry SDK installation
about 20
operating systems 20
steps 21-23
URL 20
bluetooth 237
BluetoothManager 237
BluetoothSession 238
build.yml 37, 59

C

camera
about 219
images, capturing 219-223
picture, clicking 219
picture, selecting from album 219
code
about 130
digging, for edit page 134
digging, for new page 130
digging, for show page 132, 133
configuration, Git 183-186
content div 153
controller 39, 53, 55
controller action menu
creating 156, 157
country property 204
create_errors 176
create argument 73
create functionality
testing 104, 105
create method 218
Create operation 101
CRUD operation
for calendar 218
for events 218
on contacts 212- 218
CRUD operation, RhoSync used
about 101, 104
create functionality, testing 104
delete functionality, testing 106, 107
update functionality, testing 105

D

data
filtering, with search functionality 109-114
datasets
filtering, with search functionality 108, 109
delete_all method 72
delete_errors 176

delete functionality
testing 106, 107
delete operation 101
destroy method 72, 218
device-specific style
about 143-145
adding 145-147
layout behavior, customizing 147
device_id property 204
device_name property 204
device capabilities, Rhodes
about 236
Barcode 236
bluetooth 237
BluetoothManager 237
BluetoothSession 238, 239
ringtone manager 236
timer 239, 240
device SDK installation
about 20
Android SDK installation 23
Blackberry SDK installation 20
iPhone SDK installation 25
directory structure, Rhodes
app 37
build.yml 37
icon 38
navigating 37
public 37
Rakefile 37
rhoconfig.txt 37

E

edit page
code 134
title section 135
toolbar section 134
employee-application-rhodes directory 189
employee application, Rhodes
creating 32
new page, creating 62-66
employee application, RhodesRhogen command, exploring 33
employee object 177
error value 109
exit application, system class 206, 207

F

FAQs 12, 13
find(*args) Advanced proposal 78
find command 70
find method 72
first view
creating, metadata used 122, 123
index page, creating 123-125
fixed schema model 80, 81
full_browser property 204

G

geolocation
about 223
adding, steps 224,-228
GeoLocation Ruby class 223
GeoLocation class 223
Get(find) method 218
get_api_token 116
get_license_info 116
Git
about 186
git add command 186
git commit command 186
git diff command 186
git init command 186
git add command 186
git commit command 186
git diff command 186
git init command 186

H

has_calendar property 204
has_camera property 203
has_network property 204
home page
employee view, linking 40-50
home pageurl_for, exploring 51, 52
home pageviews, linking to 39

I

IDEs
installing 29

in_progress value 108
input style
changing 59-62
installation, Git 183-186
installing, Rhomobile
about 15, 16
on Linux 19
on Mac 19, 20
on Windows 16-19
iOS
push for 137
iPhone
about 150
transaction animation, adding 162, 163
transition styles, adding 161
iPhone SDK installation
configuration, steps 28, 29
operating system 25
steps 26, 28
URL 25, 26
is_emulator property 204

J

job system
asynchronous job system 83

L

layout.erb 145
Linux
Rhomobile, installing 19
locale property 204
logs
about 178
configuring, for Rhodes application 178, 179
finding 179
logs, finding
for Android 179
for BlackBerry 180
for iPhone 179
lower_name method 170

M

Mac
Rhomobile, installing 19, 20
md 176
metadata
index page, creating 123
Rhodes translator gem, installing 122
starting with 121, 122
used, for creating first View 122-126
validation 135
view, getting for company 127-130
methods, Rhom
about 72
delete_all 72
destroy 72
find 72
model
about 39, 53
creating 38

N

new argument 73
new page
code 130
content section 130, 131
title section 132
toolbar section 131
new page, employee application
creating 62-66

O

Object-Relational Mapping. *See* **ORM**
ok value 109
ORM 67

P

pageTitle di 149
paginate argument 73
phone_number property 204
phone sleep, system class
disabling 207
enabling 207
PIM contacts
about 210
creating 210, 211
CRUD operation 212-218
CRUD operations, for calendar 218, 219
CRUD operations, for events 218, 219
destroying 211

reading 211
updating 211
ping 117
platform property 203
ppi_x property 204
product_spec.rb file 174
products, Rhomobile
Rhodes 6, 7
RhoGallery 7
RhoHub 7
RhoSync 7
property option 79
push
for, Android 138
for, BlackBerry 138
for, iOS 137
for phone 136
Rhodes application, setting up 136, 137
testing, in web console 139, 140

R

Rakefile 37
Read operation 101
record
filtering, by company 73-76
filtering, by gender 73-76
reset 117
rhoconfig.txt 37, 57, 58
RhoContact class
methods 218
Rhodes
about 6, 7
application, building 31, 33
application, building for smart phones 33-37
data, storing in phone 79
directory structure, navigating 37, 38
employee application, creating 32
model, creating 38, 39
Rhogen command, exploring 33
Rhodes application
about 10
cloning 189
code, committing 191
committing 190, 191
components 11
connecting, to RhoSync 91, 92
data, transferring from RhoSync server 92-96
setting up, for push 136, 137
testing 165-167
Rhodes data, storing in phone
fixed schema model option 80, 81
property bag option 79
Rhodes Unit Test
writing 169-171
RhoError class 181
RhoGallery
about 7, 197
creating, steps 198-200
features 197
Rhogen command
exploring 33
rhogen command 148, 166
rhogen generator 165
RhoHub
about 7, 183
builds for different phones, creating 194
functionalities 7
Git, configuring 183-186
Git, installing 183-186
Rhodes code, steps for creating 195, 196
RhoSync application, deploying 196
RhoSync application, deploying steps 196, 197
RhoHub online editor
about 193
features 193, 194
RhoHub project
about 186
creating 186, 188
Rhom
company model, creating 68, 69
exploring 68
index.bb.erb file 68
Rhomobile
about 5
architecture 10
family 5
FAQs 12, 13
features 9
installations 15, 16
installing, on Linux 19
installing, on Mac 19
installing, on Windows 16-19

platforms 9, 10
products 6
RhoSync
about 7
components 83
RhoSync, components
administration console 83
asynchronous job system 83
REST API 83
synchronization framework 83
RhoSync application
about 11
code, committing 191, 193
create 177
creating 84
creating, rhosync command used 84
default test, running 171-174
delete 178
deploying 191
deploying, to RhoHub 196
query 176, 177
RhoSync application 87
RhoSync rake task, running 86
rhosync utility 84
test, creating for company model 178
testing 171
unit test, creating for source adapter 174-176
unit test application, creating 174
update 177, 178
web interface, disabling 88
RhoSync REST API
about 116
create_client 118
create_user 117
delete_client 118
delete_user 118
get_api_token 116
get_license_info 116
list_clients 118
list_users 117
ping 117
reset 117
RhoSync source adapters
about 89
creating 89, 91
rhosync utility 84
ringtone manager 236

S

save argument 73
screen
loading 160
loading image, setting 161
screen_height property 203
screen_orientation property 203
screen_width property 203
search functionality
data, filtering with 109-114
datasets, filtering with 108, 109
search method
:callback 108
:callback_param 108
:search_parms 108
:source_names 108
syntax 108
setup_test_for(Employee,'testuser') 176
show_popup method 228
show page
code 132
content section 132, 133
title section 133
toolbar section 133
Smart phone CSS/HTML architecture
Content (<div id="content">) 152
pageTitle (<div id="pageTitle">) 149
toolbar (<div id="toolbar">) 149
toolbar button styles 151, 152
SpecRunner controller 166
splash_screen option 160
SSH-Keygen 184
SSH key
setting 183
system class
about 203, 204
country property 204
device_id property 204
device_name property 204
exit application 207
full_browser property 204
has_calendar property 204
has_camera property 203
has_network property 204
is_emulator property 204
locale property 204

other applications, managing 207
other applications, starting 208-210
phone_number property 204
phone sleep, disabling 207
phone sleep, enabling 207
platform property 203
ppi_x property 204
screen_height property 203
screen_orientation property 203
screen_width property 203
using 204, 206

T

tab bar
about 157
tabs, creating 157-160
test_create(record) 176
test_delete(record) 176
test_query 176
test_update(record) 176
timer 239, 240
transition styles, iPhone
adding 161

U

unit testing
about 165
Rhodes application, testing 165-169
update_attributes 50
update_attributes(attributes) 73
update_errors 176
update functionality
testing 105
Update operation 101
url_for
exploring 51, 52
use_layout_on_ajax argument 147

V

validation options, metadata
:max_value 136
:min_len 135
:min_value 136
:regexp 135
:validators 135
about 135, 136
view
about 39-56
editing 59-62
employee view, linking to homepage 40-50
linking, to home page 39

W

web console
push, testing in 139-141
Windows
Rhomobile, installing 16-19

About Packt Publishing

Packt, pronounced 'packed', published its first book "Mastering phpMyAdmin for Effective MySQL Management" in April 2004 and subsequently continued to specialize in publishing highly focused books on specific technologies and solutions.

Our books and publications share the experiences of your fellow IT professionals in adapting and customizing today's systems, applications, and frameworks. Our solution-based books give you the knowledge and power to customize the software and technologies you're using to get the job done. Packt books are more specific and less general than the IT books you have seen in the past. Our unique business model allows us to bring you more focused information, giving you more of what you need to know, and less of what you don't.

Packt is a modern, yet unique publishing company, which focuses on producing quality, cutting-edge books for communities of developers, administrators, and newbies alike. For more information, please visit our website: `www.PacktPub.com`.

Writing for Packt

We welcome all inquiries from people who are interested in authoring. Book proposals should be sent to `author@packtpub.com`. If your book idea is still at an early stage and you would like to discuss it first before writing a formal book proposal, contact us; one of our commissioning editors will get in touch with you.

We're not just looking for published authors; if you have strong technical skills but no writing experience, our experienced editors can help you develop a writing career, or simply get some additional reward for your expertise.

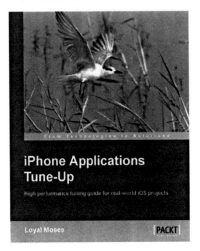

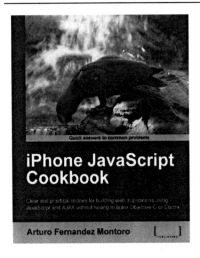

jQuery Mobile First Look

ISBN: 978-1-84951-590-0 Paperback:216 pages

Discover the endless possibilities offered by jQuery Mobile for rapid Mobile Web Development

1. Easily create your mobile web applications from scratch with jQuery Mobile
2. Learn the important elements of the framework and mobile web development best practices
3. Customize elements and widgets to match your desired style
4. Step-by-step instructions on how to use jQuery Mobile

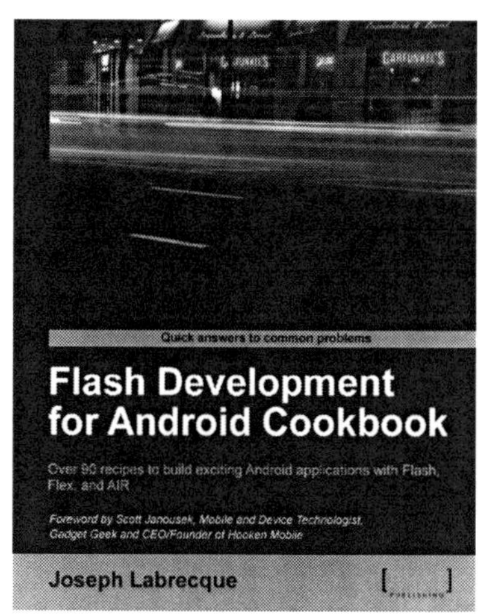

Flash Development for Android Cookbook

ISBN: 978-1-84969-142-0 Paperback: 372 pages

Over 90 recipes to build exciting Android applications with Flash, Flex, and AIR

1. The quickest way to solve your problems with building Flash applications for Android
2. Contains a variety of recipes to demonstrate mobile Android concepts and provide a solid foundation for your ideas to grow
3. Learn from a practical set of examples how to take advantage of multitouch, geolocation, the accelerometer, and more

Please check **www.PacktPub.com** for information on our titles

CPSIA information can be obtained at www.ICGtesting.com
Printed in the USA
238981LV00004B/47/P

9 781849 515160